Made in France

Manchester University Press

★ ★ ★
★
★ **European**
★ **Politics**
★
★ ★ ★

Series Editors: Professor Dimitris Papadimitriou (University of Manchester), Dr Kathryn Simpson (Manchester Metropolitan University) and Dr Paul Tobin (University of Manchester).

The *European Politics* series seeks to tackle the biggest issues facing Europe in the twenty-first century.

Previously published under the *European Policy Research Unit (EPRU)* name, this long-established and highly respected series combines an important scholarly legacy with an ambitious outlook on European Studies at a time of rapid change for the discipline. Its geographical coverage encompasses the European Union, its existing and aspiring members, and 'wider Europe', including Russia and Turkey, and the series actively promotes disciplinary, theoretical and methodological diversity.

The editors particularly welcome critical scholarship on the politics and policy making of the European Union, on comparative European politics, and on contemporary issues and debates affecting the future of Europe's socio-political and security outlook. Key areas of interest include Brexit, the environment, migration, identity politics and the ever-changing face of European integration.

Previously published:

Regulating lobbying: A global comparison, 2nd edition
Raj Chari, John Hogan, Gary Murphy and Michele Crepaz

Towards a just Europe: A theory of distributive justice for the European Union
João Labareda

Made in France

Societal structures and political work

Andy Smith

MANCHESTER UNIVERSITY PRESS

Published by Manchester University Press
Oxford Road, Manchester M13 9PL

www.manchesteruniversitypress.co.uk

British Library Cataloguing-in-Publication Data
A catalogue record for this book is available from the British Library

ISBN 978 1 5261 5423 1 hardback
ISBN 978 1 5261 7202 0 hardback

First published 2021
Paperback published 2023

Typeset
by Sunrise Setting Ltd

For Marnie

Contents

Tables

Acknowledgements

An analogy with how many independent builders operate helps to capture how this book was made: whilst doing work on other projects, they build a house of their own using material and skills gleaned whilst otherwise engaged. In many ways, this is what I have been doing for the last thirty years or so, and in particular since early 2018 when I first began to put to paper a wide range of thoughts about France, the French, how they are structured and why. Whilst conducting research on the arms, agriculture and digital industries, I steadily put together the architecture for this book and its requisite materials. Along the way, the following colleagues and friends have kindly given detailed comments on draft chapters: Cyril Benoît, Nathalie Berny, Nicolas Charles, Olivier Cousin, Marina Honta, Gilles Pinson and Vincent Tiberj. Many others have contributed ideas and suggestions. Last but certainly not least, my wife Caitríona Carter, herself also a political scientist, has provided numerous comments and a great deal of general encouragement.

Before bringing to a close these brief comments on 'the making of', one final point needs underlining about the book as a whole. To quote John Lydon (aka Johnny Rotten), 'This is not a love song'. Nevertheless, in a way it is a letter to France and the French – not a love letter, though; more one addressed to an old friend I think I know quite well, rather like and am comfortable with. But also one I, along with the social science drawn on below, consider to be complex and deeply troubled.

Abbreviations

AOC	*Appellation d'origine contrôlée*
Bac	*Baccalauréat* (the highest French high school diploma)
BTS	*Brevet de technicien supérieur*
CDC	*Caisse des Dépôts et de Consignations*
CEO	Chief Executive Officer
CFDT	*Confédération française démocratique de travail*
CFTC	*Confédération française de travailleurs catholiques*
CGC	*Confédération française de l'encadrement*
CGT	*Confédération générale du travail*
CIVB	*Conseil interprofessionnel du vin de Bordeaux*
CTF	*Conseiller technique sportif*
DGA	*Direction générale de l'armement*
DRAC	*Direction régionale des affaires culturelles*
DUT	*Diplôme universitaire de technologie*
EC	European Community
ENA	*Ecole nationale d'administration*
EU	European Union
FNSEA	*Fédération nationale des syndicats d'exploitants agricoles*
FO	*Force Ouvrière*
GATT	General Agreement of Tariffs and Trade
INAO	*Institut national des appellations d'origine*
IUT	*Institut universitaire de technologie*
LRM	*La République En Marche*
MDC	*Maison de la culture*
MEDEF	*Mouvement des Entreprises de France*
MODEM	*Mouvement Démocrate*
NGO	Non-governmental organization
OECD	Organisation for Economic Co-operation and Development
PACS	*Pacte civil de solidarité*
PCF	*Parti communiste français*
PIRLS	Progress in International Reading Literacy Study

PS	*Parti Socialiste*
RPR	*Rassemblement pour la République*
SME	Small or medium-sized enterprise
UDF	*Union pour la démocratie française*
WTO	World Trade Organization
WWF	World Wildlife Fund
ZEP	*Zone d'éducation prioritaire*

Introduction: Societal structuring and political work

In today's world where, from country to country, so much now seems so similar, how can one begin to account for the big differences which lurk just below the surface? As tackling the crisis sparked by the 2020 COVID-19 virus has shown so starkly, these differences distinguish but also often distance people and peoples from each other. Is the key to understanding societal variation to be found in culture, history, geography, economics, power or ideology? Using these terms separately or in combination, since the late nineteenth century social science has striven towards explanation of inter-country differences, but with rare and often fleeting success. Today, faced with the apparent homogenization of social practices across the globe, the task of explaining diversity seems to have become even tougher. This book is an attempt to tackle this challenge directly but from an angle which is rarely used for explaining societal difference: a monograph on one particular nation state. Rather than engage solely in comparative analysis with other countries, that method will instead be drawn upon in order to tease out the singularity of contemporary French society, explain it, and in so doing propose some generic claims about inter-societal difference.

More specifically, this book is centred upon what societal structures – asymmetric power relations and institutions (i.e. stabilized norms, rules and conventions) – have been made in France, by whom and why? But it is also concerned with what these parameters *have made* in terms of the people living in that country. In a word, 'Made in France' encompasses here both what structures French society and how it in turn has structured the human beings who grow up, work, play, age and die within it. Crucially, however, although deeply ingrained, these societal structures are never entirely static and impervious to change. On the contrary, they are constantly being worked upon politically, either in order to change them or to shore them up. Indeed, this is precisely why the chapters in this book take the reader 'from the cradle to the grave', the first aim being to show progressively how France's societal structures fit together, sometimes with difficulty but often seamlessly. The second aim is to explain why these structures affect virtually all the ways people live and behave in this country.

Despite the apparent straightforwardness of these aims and claims, they obviously require explanation and justification, particularly as they would not be automatically accepted by many other specialists of France or of comparative analysis. Indeed, the societal structuring presented and analysed in this book stems from a structuralist and constructivist theoretical perspective that is often misunderstood by many such social scientists, and criticized by a significant number of them. Consequently, this introductory chapter defines and promotes the concepts and line of argument which make up the analytical framework upon which *Made in France* is based. Without wishing to hammer home its overarching message in a tearing rush at this stage, what I seek to show is that in France, as in many other countries, societal structures are made, replaced or remade by identifiable actors whose thought and actions can and should be rigorously studied. This 'political work', however, does not merely entail 'ideas', nor does it take place in a power vacuum where asymmetries of resources can simply be overcome by 'the right views' being voiced at 'the right time'. On the contrary, precisely because societal structures are key components of the governing of any polity, work to gain power is part and parcel of sustained and contested efforts to impose visions of social life upon others. In so doing, the actors engaged in this work seek to affect the very structures which configure the spaces within which they operate. In short, in contrast to the 2016 bestseller – *How the French Think* – which romps through the history of this country by describing the writings of Paris-based philosophers and public intellectuals (Hazareesingh, 2016), this book sets out to explain how thinking and acting, throughout France and over the life cycles of its population, is structured by power relations, institutions and political work.

Before proceeding to define my key terms and arguments, however, I must first justify, and even come clean on, why France has been chosen as the subject of analysis. Answering this question is inseparable from revealing how I personally have both come to know this country and develop my viewpoint on societal difference. Having been brought up in three ex-British colonies (Nigeria, New Zealand and Fiji) then England, I arrived in France in December 1988 at the age of 25. Travelling lightly with a BA in politics from the University of Exeter, and some time after scraping through with a C in 'A'-level French, the only thing I initially managed to do for a living was to teach English in a variety of Parisian language schools. Having stumbled upon a liking for teaching in this way, I then went back to university in Grenoble to study for an MA, then a PhD in political science. After six years in that part of France, I then somewhat miraculously got my first tenured academic job at the University of Bordeaux, where I have worked ever since.

Not wishing to bore the reader with any more autobiographical detail, it is nevertheless important to declare from the outset that this book is very much the fruit of an ongoing personal and scientific journey. From the first of these angles I have obviously spent the last thirty years living in France and being affected by its societal structures and politics. During the same period, I have progressively discovered the richness of social science in general, and that of France in particular. All these experiences have obviously come to permeate my thinking, research and, consequently, the content of this book. Indeed, one of my principal reasons for writing it is to bring together, and draw deeply upon, a wealth of excellent research tools and results that are too often published only in French, thereby rendering them inaccessible to a broader readership. This material, original research of my own and a range of statistics and other quantitative data has generated the knowledge upon which the following chapters are based.[1]

A second, more analytical, reason for choosing France as the subject matter of this book is quite simply that the changes and resistance to change it has experienced over the last three or four decades are particularly fascinating and, I consider, apt to generate insights into similar, yet significantly different, processes that have taken place in many other countries. In a word, although this book seeks to identify the singularity of this country and its societal structures, it does not defend the idea that France is somehow 'exceptional'. Indeed, developed more fully in the third section of this introduction, the book tackles instead three broad sets of issues which have affected much of the world since the 1970s. Nevertheless, these have each taken on particular guises in contemporary France.

The first is the impact of neo-liberal thinking, political doctrine and policy recipes. Although in France the years 1944 to the mid-1970s were marked by the introduction of national planning and, more pervasively, the development of a strong, *dirigiste* (interventionist) state, since then much has changed. Indeed, in the face of what is often seen as the worldwide neo-liberal onslaught that has taken place since the 1980s, many specialists of France label the succeeding period a 'retreat from *dirigisme*' (Gualmini and Schmidt 2013: 347). However, too often research has tended to both overstate the mutations in societal structures and modalities of political work that have actually taken place and, moreover, attribute this change directly to the rise of neo-liberalism (Culpepper *et al.*, 2006). In reality, much that was made in France during *les trente glorieuses* (1945–75) still remains intact, thereby providing an example of the reproduction of societal structures that also needs explaining. Studying contemporary France thus provides a means of analysing the actual societal impact of neo-liberal thought and action, i.e. how it has been translated and implemented in that country (Waquant, 2012).

A second broad theme which studying France enlightens is a process of internationalization generally labelled as 'globalization'. Frequently linked directly to neo-liberalism, globalization is often used to encompass the effects of reductions of national barriers to, and increased volume of, international trade through tariffs and taxes, the rise of multinational ownership of large corporations and the emergence of the World Trade Organization (WTO) as global capitalism's key regulator. Moreover, it is often lumped together with a range of disparate phenomena such as standardization within the fashion and cinema industries, or the cosmopolitan character of contemporary social and business elites. Globalization is also said to explain the rise of the tourist industry, intense use of air transport and, of course, the spreading of viruses such as COVID-19. All the above are general trends that have indeed impacted upon virtually all the countries in the world since the late 1980s. Moreover, be it in the domains of culture or economic activity, France is rightly or wrongly often seen as being one of the homes of resistance to an intensification of the overarching internationalization of socio-economic life and governance that globalization is said to encapsulate. However, the accuracy of causal claims made for globalization, and its impact upon French societal structures and politics in particular, have yet to be convincingly shown. One of the aims of this book is thus to take the measure of the effects of different strands of what has been synthesized by this term. Specifically, it seeks to reach generalizable conclusions about globalization's causal impacts upon change or its absence in different domains of life as it is currently lived in France.

Finally, this book also seeks to tackle a third cross-cutting and more deeply sociological theme: the social mobility of its population and how it has affected institutions, power relations and governing practices. Defined initially as the ability of individuals or groups to move up or down the 'social ladder', and thus 'vertically' (Sorokin, 1927), today the term social mobility generally also encompasses 'horizontal' shifts, notably those that concern beliefs and values (Bréchon *et al.*, 2019a). Over the past four decades, displacements have clearly taken place in the revenue and status of France's population, as well as its values. First, as Thomas Piketty (2014) in particular has demonstrated, the rich in France have got much richer, whilst the revenues of large swathes of the population have stagnated in real terms. Secondly, whereas in the period 1950–80, a generalized shift towards post-materialism could clearly be discerned as in other relatively affluent countries (Inglehart, 1971, 1977), since then this trend has transpired to be less clear-cut and more complex. Indeed, for some groupings of these inhabitants, notably the most and least educated, much has changed for better or worse, whereas for others continuity has predominated (Peugny, 2013). How can one make sense of these patterns and how do they relate to societal structures? A great deal of research has, of course, been devoted, directly or indirectly, to social mobility (see Mayer and Tiberj, 2016). Amongst the claims made, the best-documented is that far from becoming 'a middle-class society' dominated by 'post-materialist values', differences in revenue, status and values have become even more patently linked to combinations of the generational cohort into which one is born and the socio-economic conditions of one's family (Tiberj, 2017). I will return to this claim below, but it is important to also flag at this stage two, more radical, extensions of it. The first is Norris and Inglehart's thesis that, like many other Western democracies, in recent years France has experienced the rise of 'authoritarian populism' (2019). The latter is manifested in particular by increased support for the extreme right *Front National* party (now called *Le Rassemblement National: RN*), 'anti-system' voting more generally and sustained public demonstrations (notably those of *les gilets jaunes* in 2018–19). However, these authors also highlight that beyond its mistrust of elites, this populism is also authoritarian because, through a process of 'cultural backlash' against post-materialist values and practices, it has repoliticized latent social conservatives who, socio-economically, are members of both the working and middle classes.

A second, rather different and perhaps complementary, thesis regarding social mobility is that, since the 1970s, significant parts of France's population have experienced a new form of '*embourgeoisement*' which, moreover, has deepened a cleavage which separates them from those who have not participated in this trend. Specifically, having documented the spreading throughout society of practices initially associated with the bourgeoisie (notably property ownership, holidaymaking and leisure activities), the claim made – notably by Gilles Laferté (2018) – is that this *embourgeoisement* has reshaped the contours of French society by inciting its population as a whole to prioritize not just the acquisition of property, but has also entailed a growing preoccupation for goods and services which, supposedly, 'enrich' (Boltanski and Esquerre, 2017) the lives of individuals and their families.

Without necessarily buying into this claim, or that of authoritarian populism, this book will repeatedly examine the contradictions which have arisen from how individuals, groups and public actors have sought to conciliate modes of *embourgeoisement* and populism with the rest of their respective social practices and value hierarchies. More fundamentally still, the question addressed in the chapters that follow targets less social mobility *per se*. Instead, its possible relationship to societal structures and their change or continuity will successively be identified and explained.

In summary, this book will engage repeatedly in general debates about the specific forms taken on by, and the impacts of, neo-liberalism, globalization and social mobility in France, but also elsewhere. Before providing a longer presentation of these three themes, explanation of the analytical framework used throughout the volume must now be provided.

Societal structures as institutions and asymmetrical power relations

As I mentioned briefly earlier, the foundations for my approach to societal singularity and comparability are built around a structuralist and constructivist political sociology of institutions and asymmetries of power. Both these terms will now be defined as pervasive and interdependent societal structures.

Institutions: stabilized rules, norms, conventions and expectations

Since the late 1980s, much of social science has reinstated institutions as key elements which structure societies (March and Olsen, 1986; Steinmo *et al.*, 1992). Defined not as organizations (e.g. the French Ministry of Education) but instead as stabilized sets of norms, rules, conventions and expectations (Hall and Taylor, 2009), institutions shape thought and practices in many ways. Before expanding upon this definition, however, it is important to explain briefly how, in my own research, I have come to give such importance to institutions, then the way this concept will be used throughout this book.

In line with a range of leading political scientists (Abdelal *et al.*, 2010; Mangenot and Rowell, 2010; Parsons, 2015; Hay, 2016) and sociologists (Fligstein, 2001; François, 2011), constructivism first guided my research to closely examine the role of 'social representations' within the structuring of societies, i.e. to produce data on representations of reality and how individuals and groups seek to 'naturalize' them within and between social units such as families, professions, firms, interest groups and public authorities. Crucially, however, the perceptions, preferences and positions developed during and through such a process do not take place in a social or political vacuum where the possible framings of societal challenges and antidotes are limitless. On the contrary, at individual, intra- and inter-organizational, and societal scales, these perceptions, preferences and positions are all heavily structured by institutions. Put succinctly, envisaging institutions as key social structures meshes inextricably with an epistemology which enables research to take culture seriously, but without using it as a blunt explanatory variable. Instead, by considering that institutions are both key building blocks of cultures and are themselves shaped by what is considered 'normal' and 'to be expected', the task of analysis is to enlighten the two sides of what is ultimately the same coin.

This point can be illustrated and expanded upon by highlighting how and why most societal domains have been institutionalized for decades (e.g. schooling), if not centuries (e.g. defence). Indeed, because the history of such institutionalizations has so often become invisible, it is easy to forget that the actual existence of such domains stems from each possessing their own durable set of institutions. Indeed, this will book will argue that the very categorization of a domain of socio-economic activity as a distinct societal entity only stabilizes when it becomes ordered institutionally, i.e. when it possesses a configured set of interlocking and interdependent institutions (Jullien and Smith, 2014). In the case of schooling, for instance, its rules concerning funding intermingle with others regarding the content of curricula as regards religion, or the expectations of teachers, parents, bureaucrats and politicians as regards the 'performance' of schools and education policies.

The second key contribution of allying constructivist epistemology to compatible institutionalist theory (Hay, 2016) is to stress that institutions not only constrain what individuals and groups are able to do, they provide the very conditions under which this activity can occur durably and with a relatively high degree of predictability. An edifying example here is property rights. In any society, the latter determine who owns what and the rights this gives them. Moreover, property as an institution enables individuals, groups and organizations to set goals for the future and move towards them on a daily basis, for example by improving and increasing the value of their housing. It follows that institutions provide durable parameters on how people within a society usually think, express their thoughts and act. Durability does not however mean permanency, since these guidelines are never fixed in stone then applied inexorably. Instead, institutions must be seen as contingent: they will survive as long as sufficiently powerful actors manage to maintain and reproduce them. Indeed, if one views society from a constructivist *and* institutionalist viewpoint, a basic assumption is that, as contingent societal structures, institutions always need studying as the products of sustained agency, deliberation and choice.

Unequal power relations as societal structures

Crucially, however, people within any society do not take part in public debates and social choices on an equal basis. Because of asymmetries in resources ranging from wealth and social standing to access to information, such interactions take place within highly structured power struggles. For this reason, throughout this book I will consider asymmetric power relations to be a key dimension of what structures French society and, moreover, one which is constantly linked to institutions as defined above. To do so, I will draw upon Field Theory in particular, because it is the approach best equipped to describe and unpack inequalities of power within any given societal domain. That said, for many of the components of France's society and polity analysed in the chapters that follow, a lack of sufficient data will preclude full-blown, statistically backed field analysis. Instead, this theory of power relations will be used more generally as a 'rudder' for guiding analysis to focus upon powering and domination when explaining institutional change or reproduction.

So what exactly is Field Theory and what is its added value? Developed initially by Pierre Bourdieu (1992), a field denotes a social space within which actors possessing varying types and amounts of resources ('capital') struggle to determine, then assert their relative value. For example, this concept guided Bourdieu's own research on the bureaucracy of the French state to discern the configuration of 'forces and struggles' which constitute its underlying structure of actor positions – a field of forces, which also explains why so often actors from the same field nevertheless unite in order to autonomize themselves from non-field members (e.g. senior state civil servants v. 'outsider' politicians: Bourdieu, 1989). The empirical description of each field is achieved first by studying the objective distribution of different 'capitals' which position each actor as regards others. This can be done in terms of organizations and inter-organizational interdependence. For example, in the case of European defence, Mérand and Barrette (2013) painstakingly set out the material, relational and symbolic capital of a wide range of administrations, armed forces and companies in order to discern their respective positions within the field. Moreover, as Didier Georgakakis has shown in the case of the European Commission and Parliament, field analysis can also be conducted at the level of individual actors, their respective careers and trajectories. Data on these points enabled him to distinguish between the different amounts of 'capital' developed by actors who have invested in the EU scale of government for many years and those who, by contrast, have engaged in it only relatively briefly (Georgakakis, 2013).

But mapping a field cannot and should not be reduced to the mere identification of quantifiable social and political capital. Instead it must also entail the reconstitution of how the actors concerned have worked cognitively and symbolically in order to protect or enhance their respective field positions. Often corresponding more or less to a profession, each field possesses a specific set of recurrent issues, 'rules of the game' and 'common sense', which also participate strongly in determining and reproducing its internal hierarchy (Mérand, 2015). For example, as our study of the European wine industry showed when tracing institutional change to struggles within the economic, bureaucratic and scientific fields (Itçaina *et al.*, 2016), competition within each field is often ferocious. However, it remains channelled within and by institutionalized parameters such as rules on the definition of what constitutes wine, what a wine produced in certain regions (e.g. Bordeaux or Rioja) can or cannot contain, and how area-specific wine guilds are led, run and represented at local, national and EU scales.

Institutions therefore participate in the structuration, internal dynamic and external dealings of fields, just as the latter's hierarchy and dynamics affect institutional change or reproduction. When moving towards empirical examinations of this key relationship, however, one must constantly address the question of their respective 'reach'. For example, if many of the institutions that now structure economic competition in France have been set at the scale of the EU, the field in which it operates is simultaneously and heavily shaped by nationally established and reproduced rules, norms and conventions, but also those that exist at the global scale around the WTO. Consequently, the multi-scalar character of institutions, institutional orders and fields needs taking into account when describing, then analysing the structuring of power relations in any social domain. Indeed, as will be repeatedly highlighted throughout this book, this multi-scalarity is frequently a source of contingency, not only because of conflict over the content of institutions (e.g. trade tariffs), but because of the intra- and inter-field frictions it simultaneously generates (e.g. within and between the economic and bureaucratic fields).

Political work as agency to affect societal structures

Thus far societal structures have been defined, but their contingency – i.e. the possibility of their change – has only been alluded to. It is therefore time to be more specific on this point by underlining why, although they are generally relatively stable, both institutions and asymmetrical power relations are always susceptible to modification and sometimes even deep change. The claim made here is that all degrees of change to both types of societal structure, including significant continuity, are the result of what I call 'political work'. Indeed, the very object of this work, and what makes it political, is to change or to reproduce institutions and power relations. Carried out, successfully or not, by a wide range of actors, political work is not however random or simply another word for 'mobilization' or indeed 'politics' itself. Rather the agency this concept enables us to systematically identify and unpack consistently takes place through and around three recurrent and overlapping processes: problem definition, policy instrumentation and legitimation (Smith, 2016, 2019).

Problematization

A first way actors in any polity seek to change or reproduce institutions and the state of power relations is by redefining the 'problems' which both these types of societal structuring ostensibly address. Here it is vital to immediately reject the functionalist and positivist acceptations of such problems as self-evident issues that simply arise from social malfunctioning. For example, as chapter 3 will explain in full, at least in countries like France, in the late nineteenth century 'poverty' did not become a social problem because all concerned recognized that for a section of the population a lack of revenue engenders poor quality of life. For a start, the protagonists who were most active in this issue area at the time had long disagreed profoundly about life quality, what constituted adequate revenue and, above all, the causal linkage between these two notions. The analytical consequence of this observation is to take on board the constructivist postulate that problems only become social when actors in key positions in the society concerned reach compromises on how what is at issue should be defined. More precisely, as Joseph Gusfield showed so clearly in a seminal book using the example of 'drunk driving' (1981), initially at least, several alternative framings of any problem invariably exist. For example, accidents linked to drivers under the influence of alcohol can be defined as an individualized problem caused by the driver's lack of responsibility for their own action. But it could also be attributed to inadequate licensing laws, or even the excessive freedom given to alcohol producers to market their product 'irresponsibly'. From the point of view of analysis, what this means is that research must always examine clearly how any problem became 'social' and how, in turn, this process has affected its mutation into a 'public problem', i.e. one meriting public intervention (Rochefort and Cobb, 1994).

Empirically, studying problematization thus entails going back in time in order to establish how the definition of 'the problem' concerned first stabilized, then tracing its subsequent developments. Indeed, in many instances a 'public problem' can itself be considered to be an institution in that it encapsulates, stabilizes and tends strongly to reproduce a specific set of not only norms, conventions and expectations, but also value hierarchies, e.g. 'social protection'. Moreover, through institutionalizing in this way, a 'public problem' also heavily impacts upon the sets of actors deemed to be eligible to discuss and update its definition. French agriculture since the 1950s provides a case in point. As of that decade, 'the problem' of agriculture in France changed radically from being essentially one of maintaining a large peasantry on the land, to 'modernizing' production so as to increase national output, lower prices and foster urbanization (Jobert and Muller, 1987). But this redefinition did not simply occur spontaneously. Rather it was worked for over several years by a new coalition formed by a distinct set of farmers and state bureaucrats, both of whom had initially been marginalized within their respective fields. Indeed, not only did these actors come to power alongside the institutionalization of the 'public problem' they had espoused. Ever since, their hegemonic control over French agriculture has largely been maintained through a constant stream of political work centred upon problem definition.

Here is not the place for delving deeper into this example, nor for discussing refinements of the theory of public problems that have developed since the 1980s (see Gilbert and Henry, 2012). At this stage, instead it is important just to reiterate that within the political work analysed in this book, examining the transformation of 'issues' into public problems will provide a key means of understanding societal structures in France, their change or their stasis.

Policy instrumentation

Struggles over institutions and power relations obviously frequently also, and often simultaneously, take place over initiatives to modify or replace the policy instruments which ostensibly tackle the problems defined in each field. Such instruments are technologies of government which can take a variety of shapes. Some are 'regulatory' in the sense that they seek to define what is either compulsory or considered socially desirable. In the first instance, rules enshrined in law are the preferred option, such as obligations to insulate new housing to a certain standard. Meanwhile, regulating to encourage certain outcomes is often implemented through softer norms which governments or trade associations would like economic actors to adopt, such as the type of nutritional information they print upon the labels of foodstuffs. A second type of policy instrument is distributive because here the aim is to modify behaviours and induce certain social outcomes using the incentives of subsidies (e.g. to instal solar panels in car parks) or tax credits (e.g. to encourage investment in new housing). Finally, and perhaps more pervasively, policy instruments can also take the form of the very categories through which public policies are implemented, such as the eligibility criteria for receiving child benefits or being defined as 'a farmer'. Indeed, ultimately there is no end to what precise measures a policy instrument can encompass. For this reason, constructing typologies of instruments is of limited analytical value. Instead, research in recent years has rightly concentrated instead upon two overlapping dimensions of these key aspects of public policy.

The first starts purely and simply from considering that policy instruments are never ideologically or socially neutral (Lascoumes and Le Galès, 2007).

Although often presented by their implementers as concerning only 'technical detail', and therefore as being non-political, such instruments always bear the imprint of certain value hierarchies (e.g. the freedom to use electricity v. the societal need to save it) and causal narratives (e.g. instruments to increase demand for solar panels by artificially reducing their price) as opposed to others. Moreover, the output and outcomes of each instrument will favour certain actors and publics, whilst neglecting or omitting other potential beneficiaries (e.g. nuclear power plants v. small, localized energy producers).

This first aspect of research on policy instrumentation dovetails with a second concerning the political work engaged in by actors to propose and institutionalize each instrument. Indeed, rather than focus solely upon what certain researchers call 'the career' of a policy instrument (Halpern *et al.*, 2014), it is crucial to concentrate analysis upon who mobilizes in favour of it, and the resources they possess, develop and deploy in order to do so. From this angle, for example, Penissat and Rowell (2015) convincingly showed that the European Socio-economic Classification adopted by the European Commission in the early 2010s resulted directly from the choice of experts on labour issues made by the hierarchy of that organization. Indeed, this choice of experts stemmed from the very definition of the public problem of work that the senior Commission officials involved shared amongst themselves and, moreover, sought to propagate within the rest of their organization, but also within the EU's member states.

Legitimation

Indeed, this example also serves as a timely reminder that the political work conducted to define problems and to set policy instruments is inseparable from that conducted to bolster the social and political legitimacy of the actors involved in either of these processes. Indeed, the arguments developed within such work are not purely of a cognitive nature. On the contrary, they invariably mobilize symbols which seek to seduce the target audience concerned by appealing to their emotions. For example, politicians and public administrations often couch their propositions in terms that are sensitive to the 'national impacts' of their respective policies (e.g. reassuring French car workers that 'traditional' producing regions will be preserved). Some of this political communication is, of course, pure rhetoric that is empty of social meaning and without significant consequences. But other such discourse has considerable causes and effects which need studying as a vital dimension of institution creation, maintenance or change. Known as 'legitimation' since the pioneering work of Max Weber, it entails 'a variety of processes that renders the very existence of coercive power tolerable and even desirable, i.e. that makes the conducting of this power appear to be socially necessary, or even as a social good' (Lagroye, 1985: 402; Foret, 2008). It follows that research simply must analyse carefully the work done by actors to render 'normal' and 'natural' the problem definitions and policy instruments they advocate and defend. Crucially, this work is not only cognitive and symbolic, it is also deeply relational in the sense that it constantly involves efforts to construct and maintain groupings and alliances of actors within organizations themselves, between such entities (e.g. administrations, private companies, non-governmental organizations: NGOs) and, in many instances, across national borders (e.g. at the scale of the EU or in and around the WTO). Indeed, it is precisely by analysing legitimation's impact upon the constant interplay between institutions and power relations that research can best reveal how the societal structures of any polity have been built, reproduced over time and, at times, significantly changed.

In summary, by defining societal structures in terms of institutions and power relations, a solid theoretical basis has been built from which to define this book's dependent variable and thus what it seeks to explain: the change or reproduction of what has structured French society since the 1980s – i.e. what has been made or remade in France in terms of institutions and inequalities of power. I have also set out the concept of political work as the independent variable that enables research to identify and explain the causes of this change or its absence. What now needs to be done is tying these key elements of my analytical framework more firmly to the three causal claims which, by providing the book's underlying themes, will progressively be put to the test of empirical demonstration in the seven chapters that follow.

Causal claims and the overarching narrative of this book

When contemplating how to structure this volume I was confronted with the following dilemma: how could societal structures and political work in France be described and analysed relatively extensively, but without falling back upon tired, static and limiting separations between 'the social', 'the economic' and 'the political'? The best solution I eventually found was to divide up my material in chapters that differ in terms of the slices of French life they each relate and unpack. For this reason, France's institutions and power relations are set out below in seven chapters which take the reader 'from the cradle to the grave'. This is done around topics that successively encompass early childhood, education, work, business, entertainment, political mobilization and, finally, growing old and passing on. Inevitably this outline has generated a number of gaps. For example, no chapter covers policing or the judicial system. Nevertheless, what proceeding in this way has enabled me to do is to emphasize that the political work analysed in this book is a pervasive part of societal structuring, and vice versa. For instance, as will be underlined in chapter 7, inheritance rights in France take the shape they do because of the political work done upon them (or not), work which itself can only be understood by simultaneously explaining institutional durability and power asymmetries. In addition – and just as importantly – not being shackled by a-sociological definitions of the social, economic and political has also meant that I have been able to address the three themes flagged earlier (regarding neo-liberalization, globalization and social mobility) across a relatively wide range of issue areas. Indeed, this is why these introductory pages will now come to a close by revisiting those three themes. The aim here is to turn each theme into a causal claim to be tested over the course of the empirical chapters.

From neo-liberalization to a partial return to liberalism

As I began to indicate in the opening pages of this book, many academic specialists of France consider that since the 1980s the societal structures and governing of this country have changed radically because neo-liberalism has taken root, then flourished within its borders. By this they mean that a brand of liberalism which not only advocates 'free markets', but also the refounding of the state in order to bring them about and regulate them, has come to permeate the thought and action of virtually all the most powerful actors of French society, and those of its economy and government in particular. In short, they claim that a transformation to freer markets backed by a stronger state committed to 'market fundamentalism' has taken place (Wacquant, 2012). Consequently, 'neoliberalism has not been about less government, but about shifting the techniques, focus and priorities of government' (Isin, 1998: 173). In particular, this has been achieved by emphasizing that all members of the population should consider themselves as individually responsible for their respective lives, rather than as members of groups or classes (Larner, 2000). Moreover – and crucially for this book – many such analyses underline that the bedding in of neo-liberalism is especially visible in France because they consider that its doctrine and policies have replaced a set of beliefs and governmental interventions which, over the period 1945–85, had favoured instead public involvement in the economy and redistributive, Keynesian technologies of government. In this sense, the advent of neo-liberalism in France has often been characterized as a 'watershed' (Jobert and Théret, 1994; Schmidt and Thatcher, 2013).

When the evolution of this polity since the 1980s is examined as a whole, at first glance the neo-liberalization thesis seems compelling. In France as elsewhere, there is much evidence to suggest that the definition of public problems and the content of policy instruments has changed considerably, and this often in a direction neo-liberal ideologists would applaud. However, establishing such a correlation does not actually demonstrate causal linkages between change in societal structures and the ideology of neo-liberalism (Pinson and Morel Journel, 2017).[2] Indeed, when one examines both political work and its societal outcomes in contemporary France, one soon discovers that the impact of neo-liberalism *per se* has rarely played a key causal role. Instead, it is more heuristic to consider first that policy recipes formalized within neo-liberal doctrine have provided some inspiration for many actors seeking to introduce deep change in institutions and power relations. Nevertheless, the full content of their proposals has almost always been shaped as much, if not more, by the strength of other influences, notably commitments to a state wedded, in thought *and* practice, to principles of 'meritocracy', the governmental shaping of markets and the safeguarding of national 'prestige'. In addition, in the French case, too many academic commentators seem to have forgotten that until 1945 the governing of France, and of its economy and social policies in particular, was dominated by traditions of liberalism which actually gave the state only a minor role to play (Kuisel, 1984). Crucially, seen from today, in this book I will go so far as to consider that the *dirigiste* period 1945–85 is actually best described as: 1) an exception rather than as typical of French history as a whole; but also, 2) an exceptional period during which the state developed resources and power which it retains to this day.

More precisely, the claim I seek to deepen and substantiate across the following seven chapters is that although the legacy of *dirigisme* remains strong and manifests itself in the societal structures of today's France, that of classical liberalism is even stronger. In a word, the first paradox this volume will seek to elucidate is how and why France is both liberal and *dirigiste*. In so doing, I will demonstrate that the combination of both these traits does not simply add up to neo-liberalism.

Globalization: from a cause to a weapon

As mentioned above, 'globalization' is another transnational phenomenon that a variety of commentators have evoked in order to explain recent change in French societal structures. From the outsourcing of Renault's car production to Romania, to reductions in governmental spending, globalization has been deployed as an explanation of both socio-economic strategies and public policies. There is no denying that in both the car industry and the inner workings of France's Ministry of Finance, many of the previously dominant practices in France have indeed changed over the last three to four decades. However, as a body of research conducted elsewhere shows (Hay, 2006), it is deeply misleading to identify globalization as being their cause. High levels of international trade and the opportunistic practices of multinational companies existed well before the 1980s. Moreover, if the advent of the WTO has undoubtedly further freed up cross-border trade, for France the completion of the European single market has had far deeper impacts. For this reason, there is little evidence to suggest that globalization itself has actually caused significant modification of France's societal structures. Rather, the very term 'globalization' has instead played the role of a rhetorical and symbolic weapon with which actors within France itself have striven to change both their own economy and society (Goyer and Glatzer, 2016) and that of the EU more generally. Indeed, given the importance of the latter for the governing of France, together with the role played by French actors within the EU's own governing (Jullien and Smith, 2014), it is crucially important not to conflate globalization with the European integration, its government and its effects at the national scale. Moreover, over the last half-century what has been made in France has also been made in Europe and, indeed, has participated strongly in 'making Europe'. For all these reasons, the second claim this book as a whole will progressively seek to discuss, sharpen and test is that, at least in France, over the last three decades 'globalization' has played the role of a rallying totem – one that has repeatedly galvanized both those who seek to radically change the country's societal structures, as well as those committed, on the contrary, to protecting what they see as its vital national *acquis*.

From 'populism' and embourgeoisement *to the hardening of individualization and materialism*

As with globalization and neo-liberalism, at least on the surface, the terms 'populism' and '*embourgeoisement*' appear to encapsulate trends in social (and political) mobility that have accelerated in France over the last forty years. This said, particularly because, like neo-liberalism and globalization, they are often used normatively, it is important first to define the terms more carefully than I did at the beginning of this introduction, discuss them briefly in the light of French societal structures and recurrent practices as I perceive them, then formulate sharper and better justified causal claims.

As indicated earlier, Norris and Inglehart's thesis is that, like other Western democracies, since the 1980s France has witnessed a rise of what they call 'authoritarian populism' (2019), i.e. the emergence then consolidation of a broad set of social and political thought which not only mistrusts elites 'in the name of the people', but which also proposes the reintroduction of authoritarian methods of government in the name of 'public order', 'traditional values' and 'national identity'. Seen by many as one of the movements which exemplify this trend, *les gilets jaunes* will be analysed directly in chapter 6. But the book as a whole will provide many other occasions to assess the extent to which populism of the type defined by Norris and Inglehart has affected change or continuity in France's societal structures. Specifically, particularly within chapters on childhood, education and political engagement, I will revisit the claim that the value hierarchies and political behaviour of authoritarian populists have impacted upon how France's 'public problems' have been defined, instrumented and legitimated.

Turning now to *embourgeoisement*, as Gilles Laferté explicitly recognizes, deploying the term supposes that a restratification of society has taken place. More precisely, this term describes the advent of a certain type of social mobility, one that entails 'the accumulation of economic capital (revenue and property) and the respect of the established social order, i.e. a recognition of the legitimacy of bourgeois domination' (Laferté, 2018: 11). It should be reiterated that Laferté uses the term to make precise claims about change in the socio-economic practices and status of cereal farmers in a specific French region; he does not analyse social mobility in France as a whole. Nevertheless, his analysis has a wider interest because it concludes that the mobility that he has observed in great detail has been generated by economic rather than educational success. In so doing, the farmers he studied have strongly tended to adopt the values traditionally equated with the political right – the enterprise spirit, independence, individual merit, materialist consumption – and all this more than giving priority to cultural or educational achievement (Laferté, 2018: 20). Moreover, to supplement that finding, he also uses indicators related to actual social practices, for example the importance such farmers and their families now attach to housing and its physical appearance (307), its separation from the farm as a place of work (267), holiday-making and leisure (in particular the taking up of golf and skiing: 323). This said, when transposed to the scale of France as a whole, does all the above add up to a socially significant shift that can accurately be qualified as *embourgeoisement*? Rather than rejecting that radical claim outright at this stage, I prefer to consider provisionally that this term, either fortuitously or for sound reasons, actually encompasses two sets of phenomena that are important to analyse more carefully, but not necessarily together.

First, Laferté's analysis chimes with data from other, survey-based, research which shows that a form of individualization has increased in France over the last few decades. Specifically, not only do a greater proportion of the population now live on their own than hitherto, and this even when they are 'in a couple' (Astor, 2019: 39). More fundamentally, 'the experiences of life are more individualized', as can be seen today, for example, in dominant attitudes to work as inextricably linked to 'personal investments' and quests for 'self-esteem' (Bréchon *et al.*, 2019b: 365–367). However, this does not necessarily mean that the French have become more individualistic, nor that individualization in this country is simply the result of the 'success' of neo-liberalism. Instead, the claim this book will test is that in different domains, and during phases of life ranging from infancy to old age, in France 'the individual' has (re)become an institutionalized category of social and political thought and action. Consequently, 'the individual' has frequently been a key component of problem definitions, policy instruments and legitimation. Indeed, as Camille Peugny underlines (2013: 12), the 'success' of 'the individual' as a category has in turn engendered 'the growing invisibility of the social', a sharp decline in analyses in terms of social classes and, I would add, a corresponding neglect of asymmetric power relations.

The second issue about which the concept of *embourgeoisement* invites re-examination concerns materialism. In contrast to the much-cited thesis that, since the 1950s, the Western world as a whole has become increasingly orientated by 'post-materialist' values centred upon civil liberties, self-expression and hedonism (Inglehart, 1971, 1977), there is now a great deal of evidence that this claim was not only overstated at the time, but that this overstatement stems from at least two theory-fuelled flaws. The first of these shortcomings concerns what Vincent Tiberj calls the latent 'developmentalism' of Inglehart's analysis (Tiberj, 2017: 23–24), i.e. its a-historicism. By considering that once income and educational levels had risen beyond a point, then post-materialist values would inexorably spread throughout each society, Inglehart failed to envisage that the rapid rise of such values could have been the result of conditions specific to a particular period in time. Indeed, what we now know is that as of the late 1970s (i.e. the ending of continuous economic growth and a certain social redistribution of income and life chances), the spreading of post-materialism slowed dramatically. This evidence spills over into the second criticism of Inglehart's thesis: its neglect of socio-economics. As Tiberj also underlines, by opposing 'economic values' to ones of 'social liberalism', then concentrating upon the latter, post-materialist theory ended up becoming 'unidimensional'. For this reason, even in its most recent iterations which, as outlined above, hypothesize the rise of 'authoritarian populism' and 'cultural backlash' (Norris and Inglehart, 2019),[3] post-materialism fails to fully take into account the return of concerns about 'economic fears' which, since the 1990s, have become highly prominent in the thinking of a large proportion of the French population (Tiberj, 2017: 170–190). Consequently, whilst continuing to take seriously the effects of 'post-materialism' upon French private and public life, it is vital to simultaneously grant at least an equal amount of research effort to how people in France think about, and act around, issues of economic security. Indeed, the claim made here is that since the 1990s the country's population as a whole has actually become *more* materialist in two contrasting ways.

On the one hand, for the poorer segments of this society, existential security has come to consistently trump other considerations not only during their individual practices, but also when they seek to influence collective and public decision-making. On the other, for much of the rest of the population, a renewal of materialism has also increasingly come to manifest itself, but here through the acquisition of ostentatious material goods (e.g. large cars), together with the defence of their right to do so through collective and public action.

At this stage it would be foolhardy to jump to any hasty conclusions over the claims set out above regarding authoritarian populism, the rise of individuation and the rediscovery of materialism. Indeed, given the massive uncertainty linked to the aftermath of the COVID-19 crisis, all these claims will need re-examining. More fundamentally still, this introduction is no place to conclude as regards the extent of the impact of either this theme, or that of neo-liberalism or globalization, upon French societal structures. Nor is this the moment to conclude upon how and why this impact has or has not been achieved. Instead it is high time to discover now the empirical realities these claims do or do not fit with. In a word, let's now allow the following chapters to identify what has actually been made in France over the last four decades, how, by whom and why?

Notes

1 All translations into English taken from French sources are, of course, my own.
2 As these authors conclude, instead 'we need analytical frameworks that guide research to analysing processes of neoliberalization alongside other transformative processes, that can articulate the logics of neoliberalization with other logics, whose effects might reinforce, neutralize or contradict the effects of neoliberalization' (Pinson and Morel Journel, 2017: 212).
3 These authors do now consider that economic concerns have participated in the 'political mistrust' dimension of populism. However, they consider that it has not been a cause of the revival of 'authoritarianism', a trait which for them constitutes populism's second key dimension (Norris and Inglehart, 2019: 166).

1

Childhood, families and initial schooling: Conservative primary socialization

Introduction

If nearly 12% of France's residents were born elsewhere, the vast majority came into this world in a French hospital or home. Their first months and years would have been spent in a family situation of varying types involving different modes of childcare before, at the age of 3, or even as early as 2 years 6 months, beginning their respective school lives. Put bluntly, the question to be answered here is not so much *what is it like being a child in France?* but *why is it so?*

Of course, on one level everyone's childhood is different. Parents and families are diverse, as are parenting styles, locations and individual schools (Lahire, 2019). However, recurrent patterns of thought, norms and behaviour can nevertheless be discerned. Indeed, in keeping with the thesis of this book as a whole, this chapter shows that societal structures – i.e. institutions and power relations – together with the political work that changes or reproduces them, are key. As sets of stabilized rules, norms and conventions, institutions set parameters upon the lives of French children by strongly guiding parenting and schooling practices. Moreover, they also shape the very fields of family support and education within which these practices take place, and therefore affect asymmetries of power between pupils, parents, teachers and administrators in particular. More fundamentally still, these institutions and power relations only came into being, and have since been reproduced or changed over time, as a function of how political work has been undertaken to structure social and public action around children and childhood.

Put differently, the subject matter of this chapter is both how initial socialization takes place in France and how this very process is structured by institutions, power relations and work that is political. Socialization is, of course, a fundamental concept of the social sciences which, over the last 150 years, has given rise to a plethora of studies and intense theoretical debate (Dubar, 2010). If virtually all the specialists of socialization concur that

parenting and schooling are crucial processes during which children incul-
cate societal dispositions and 'rules of the game', explanation of how and why
this takes place has generated three distinct approaches, each inspired by
major social theorists. At the risk of caricaturing each of them, the first
emphasizes the top-down imposition of societal institutions upon relatively
passive children (e.g. Durkheim, Parsons), whilst the second highlights the
reproduction of societal norms via social classes and the 'symbolic violence'
they generate (Marx, Bourdieu). Meanwhile, a third approach envisages
socialization instead as an interactive process during which each child recre-
ates for themselves what they learn from their family members, peers and
teachers. In short, it is envisaged as a more creative process, constantly generating compromises between the taught and the learnt (Weber, Mead).
Given that the subject matter of this chapter is less the description of socialization as a process and more what steers it societally, structuralist elements
from institutionalist and field theories will play an important role in the
interpretation of research results that follow. Nevertheless, because of the
importance I give to political work, together with the distinctly plural character of contemporary French society (Beaud, 2018), room will be also left
for analysing the scope for contingency that has nevertheless remained
around French family and schooling institutions.

Indeed, as will be shown throughout, in France these institutions and
fields have been the object of numerous attempts by collective or public
actors to train children, parents, childminders and teachers to act in certain
ways and not others. As the specialist literature has documented in detail,
contemporary French life has been particularly marked by a succession of
state-led attempts to influence the thinking and behaviour of the nation's
children, as well as by the resistance this has repeatedly inspired. Indeed,
precisely because the introduction of compulsory, non-clerical schooling in
the period 1890–1905 was crucial to the development of the primary school
as a major vehicle for realizing the republican ideal, it has been 'sacralized'
ever since (Déloye, 1994). Just as importantly, the Vichy governments of
1940–44 both enabled supporters of private Catholic schools to gain back
some of the ground lost to anti-clericalism and also paved the way for
extending public education to children beyond the age of 14 (Paxton, 2001).
More recently, since 1989 a controversy over the right of Muslim children
to wear veils at school has durably reinserted the issue of religion within
education back upon the French political agenda (see chapter 2). Indeed,
governmental responses to this and other issues related to the diversification
of ethnic groups, and thus the values of parents, feature highly upon what
today is often presented as a deep challenge to the institutions of French
family life and schooling. At the same time, however, other challenges have
also been defined and brought to the fore, notably by holders of the belief

that France's economy is insufficiently 'competitive' – a trait they blame in part upon the schooling of its pupils. In this way, for example, powerful economic and political actors have used neo-liberal recipes and the mantra of globalization to construct France as being 'behind'. From this definition of 'the public problem', they have then called for deep change in how the nation trains its young to think and behave. Meanwhile, certain trends in social mobility, notably increased individualization and materialism, have fuelled and mediated all these examples of political work.

Against this backdrop, and by focusing upon the period since 1985 in particular, the central argument developed in this chapter is that although some institutional change has undoubtedly occurred in response to the tensions outlined above, for the most part the rules, norms and conventions which structure French family life and primary schooling, together with the fields in which they are set and reset, have remained very much intact. As will be shown, whereas in the 1970s many French commentators predicted 'the end of the family', and some change in patterns of living has actually occurred, its institutions remain largely in place (Segalen, 2005: 5). More profoundly still, the values which generated these institutions in the first place continue to heavily influence their reproduction by being defined and hierarchized in remarkably similar ways. Indeed, in most instances, reproduction, and indeed 'social conservatism' (Norris and Inglehart, 2019), has largely prevailed over calls for change. Specifically, the positioning of the adult rather than the child at the centre of the family and educational institutions has been preserved. Indeed, in many instances, this trait has even been enhanced.

To outside observers in particular, this claim may seem strange. Foreign tourists frequently remark that France is both 'children friendly' in terms of their acceptance in restaurants and other public places, as well as being a country where children are relatively 'well-behaved'. However, as the first part of what follows will explain, the apparent gap between these anecdotal but recurrent observations and my central claim of adult-centred conservatism can be explained as follows: from life at home to playing in a crèche, French infants are expected to not only respect formal rules, but to conform to a relatively rigid set of norms and conventions. Moreover, and not surprisingly, this approach is codified and intensified once they go to school. As the second part of this chapter will highlight, schooling from the age of 3 is highly advantageous to parents, providing them as it does with free day care. However, this institution not only gives great power to the state, but also to teachers as a corporation that dominates the educational field, to determine schooling policies and, in so doing, to keep parents, as well as research-informed specialists of education, firmly at a distance.

Getting born,[1] being an infant and fitting in with adults

Conformity begins at home, but it also takes place within the hospitals and other forms of medical and child care which heavily structure the first three years of the life of any child living in France. By progressively examining the diversity of what now constitutes a home and a family in this country, it will quickly become evident that this entity is by no means purely a 'private' matter. Quite the contrary: virtually from the moment a pregnancy is detected, a set of adult-centred institutions, power relations and value hierarchies begin to impinge upon and orientate the way a child will come into the world, then be brought up in the home and beyond. Resistance to these vectors of socialization, of course, remains possible and often takes place. However, the social forces they unleash generally prove too strong and, consequently, largely shape how most children in France are brought up, think, feel and act.

The cradle months

In the French case, 'the cradle' very much begins during pregnancy due to the combined effects of social norms and public policies which largely support the having of children. Specifically, although the figures since 2015 are down on preceding years, Tables 1.1 and 1.2 show that France has a higher birth rate than many other developed countries. This rate is lower than that of Ireland, roughly the same as in the UK and significantly higher than that of other large European countries such as Germany, Italy, Spain and Poland.

France's relatively high birth rate, together with the 'natalist' public policies that support it, have deep historical roots which go back to an initial

Table 1.1 French births and birth rates (per 1,000 inhabitants)

	Number of births	*Birth rates*
2018	758 000	11.3
2017	767 000	11.4
2016	783 640	11.7
2015	798 948	12.0
2014	818 565	12.4
2013	811 510	12.3
2012	821 047	12.6
2011	823 394	12.7
2010	832 799	12.9
2009	824 641	12.8

Source: INSEE, www.insee.fr/fr/statistiques/3676604?sommaire=3696937, consulted 10th May 2020.

Table 1.2 Birth rates in Europe compared, 2017

Country	Birth rate (births/1,000 population)
Ireland	14
UK	12
France	11.4
Poland	10
Germany	9
Spain	9
Italy	9

Source: Eurostat, https://ec.europa.eu/eurostat/statistics-explained/index.php/Fertility_
statistics, consulted 10th May 2020.

definition of this nation possessing a demographic 'problem'. This social construct emerged in the late nineteenth century, then took on significantly higher social meaning following the decimation of its male population during the First World War. As Claude Martin in particular has underlined (2017: 33), since laws in 1938–39, then the creation in 1946 of a family branch within the new national social security system, 'family' sectorial policies have directly encouraged the having of children. Policy instruments have included tax credits, family benefits, their reinforcement as of the third child and subsidized price reductions for *familles nombreuses* (ones with three or more children). Indeed, at its high point in the mid-1950s, family policy accounted for no less than half of the nation's social security budget! Moreover, a high birth rate has also been encouraged indirectly by support for organizations and companies willing to offer part-time employment, in particular by giving employees Wednesdays off (the day of the week when *maternelle* and primary schools have been shut since the early 1970s). The ambitions of family policy have certainly been curtailed since then, as unemployment began to preoccupy much of the social security system. Moreover, this trend has deepened since 1997 when family benefits became linked to income levels – particularly for *familles nombreuses*. More generally, the trend over time has been towards a more 'selective' family policy (Martin, 2017: 38–39), together with a certain 'dualization' as regards support for child-minding which distinguishes between those in and out of work. Nevertheless, when compared to many other countries, policies in favour of raising children remain relatively strong in today's France.

Moreover, in order to fully understand French approaches to the having of children, one next needs to grasp the linkages between the fields of family support and health which overlap strongly in this country. Although patients today increasingly have to contribute more to the costs of their healthcare than they did in the late twentieth century, the vast majority of an individual's health expenditure in France is covered by the social security system (funded through employment-linked national insurance contributions or the state), topped up by forms of relatively inexpensive *mutualist*[2] or private insurance schemes. Moreover, beyond providing further encouragement for mothers to have babies, the relative generosity and high reputation of the French health system also goes some way to explaining the considerable medicalization not only of birthing in France, but of the way the health of infants is tracked. Indeed, this in turn dovetails with the importance of doctors not only within French healthcare and science, but also French society as a whole.

This high level of medicalization can first be appreciated when one realizes that today only 0.5% of mothers in France give birth at home, compared to 2.3% in the UK and nearly a third in the Netherlands. This represents a sharp change since 1950, when 45% of births in France still occurred at home. In the French case, a general international trend towards hospitalized birthing has been consistently reinforced by a national social security system that does not reimburse the costs of home birthing (unlike in the Netherlands, the UK or Germany, for example). More generally, in France it is doctors, not midwives or specialized nurses, who strongly tend to dominate decisions over care of the child and advice to parents during the time spent in hospital around birthing (Jacques, 2007).

This dominant position held by doctors is largely extended during the relatively intense medical support given to children and their parents in France during infancy. Although general practitioners often still take on this role, since the 1970s specialist paediatricians have increasingly been turned to, particularly by middle- and upper-class parents. Indeed, organized essentially as individualized socio-economic operators known as *la médecine libérale*, the vast majority of non-hospital doctors in France see themselves as independent of the national health system, and this despite the fact that they are structurally dependent upon it for their high levels of revenue and autonomy. This perceived independence manifests itself in many ways, ranging from generally conservative, often non-research-based modes of patient advice (e.g. on breastfeeding), to high levels of involvements in local and national politics. Indeed, through both individual engagement and the work of their powerful interest groups, notably *l'Ordre des médecins*, throughout French history, doctors have consistently, and usually successfully, worked to either resist state intervention in healthcare or bend it to fit with their own problems definitions, preferred policy instruments and value hierarchies (Hassenteufel, 1997). In a word, doctors are clearly positioned at the centre of the French health field.

Finally, in addition to the impact of family-support and health policies, it is impossible to fully understand how childhood is structured in France without taking into account the vast and crucial issue of gender relations, and of the role of women in particular. Although since the 1960s a certain number of modifications regarding the place of women in French society have taken place, as Eric Macé (2015) has cogently argued, many of the institutions, power relations and value hierarchies central to patriarchy in France, and in particular those that concern childhood, remain largely in place (Théry, 1998; Maruani, 2005).

Taken only at face value, a certain number of statistics tend to obscure and even contradict this claim. If one examines the number of marriages in France, for example, in 2017 only 228,000 occurred, reflecting a ratio of 3.5 marriages per 1,000 persons – a rate that has fallen sharply from one of 7.8 in 1970. Indeed, today's French marriage rate compares with one of 4.9 in Germany, 4.5 in the UK and 3.2 in Italy. However, in order to fully grasp the extent to which hetero and homosexual adults in France are currently in long-term relationships with a partner, one needs to factor in all the couples who live together outside marriage, and this either within a relationship recognized by the state (via a *Pacte civil de solidarité* – PACS – of which there were no fewer than 190,000 registered in 2016) or without such legal recognition. More interestingly, although there is little evidence that long-term relationships have less social significance than hitherto, their meaning has nevertheless changed over the last five decades (de Singly, 2000). An initial indicator here is the age at which people marry for the first time: higher than before but with continuing differences between men and women (see Table 1.3).

More revealingly still, in particular for our analysis of childhood in France, is the durability of long-term relationships. The most reliable statistics here concern formal divorces,[3] of which there are around 130,000 per year, a ratio of 1.8 marriages for every one divorce (compared to 2 in Germany, 1.9 in the UK and 1.4 in Italy). Forty-five per cent of French marriages end in divorce, which is the cumulative effective of ten married couples out of a thousand divorcing each year. In addition, around 80,000 *PACS* are now dissolved each year.

One of the major consequences of divorce has naturally been its impact upon the very notion of the nuclear family which, in France and widely

Table 1.3 Age of first marriage

	Women	Men
1950	23	26
1970	23	25
1990	26	28
2016	31	33

Source: INSEE, www.insee.fr/fr/statistiques/1892240?sommaire=1912926, consulted 10th May 2020.

elsewhere, prior to the 1970s and particularly from 1945 to 1975, had so deeply structured childhood and its institutions, power relations and value hierarchies. Although this trend is by no means entirely new,[4] today more than 1.6 million under-18s in France (out of 13.5 million), i.e. 12% of them, live in 'blended' families (8% of all families),[5] and no fewer than 16% live with single mothers or, to a lesser extent, single fathers.[6] The irony of this situation is that this trend has frequently increased the dependence of many children upon their mothers at a time when a significant proportion of fathers of other children have begun to play a larger role in bringing them up. This divergence, or even 'dualization', not only reflects differences in socio-economic resources, notably the levels of income and education of the parents in question (after separating, lower-resourced fathers are much less likely to share childcare than wealthier or more educated ones).[7] More generally, greater differentiation of family life and internal power relations has developed since the 1960s. De Singly (2017), for example, distinguishes between several 'types' of family: the traditional father-dominated but domestically matriarchal, the shared work but father-dominated, the single mother, etc. Moreover, opinion surveys on what makes a 'successful couple' conclude that today having children is given less importance than forty years ago: 65% saw this as very important in 1981 and 1990, a figure that had fallen to 54% by 2018 (Astor, 2019: 154).

Of course, one of the key factors to be taken into account when seeking to explain what causes each family type is the rate and mode of employment of women in general, and of mothers in particular. In 2011, 67% of French women between the ages of 20 and 64 had a job (as opposed to 76% of men), but one-third of these women only worked part-time,[8] often in order to be able to look after their children (see chapter 3). Moreover, of the nearly 400,000 workers who stop work every year to take care of pre-school children, virtually all are women (Pailhé and Solaz, 2009). Superficially, these figures appear to show that French family policy is child-centred. However, a closer look at who takes parental leave or works part-time, under what conditions and why, reveals that this public policy largely conserves age-old childcare patterns. In so doing, it provides further evidence for the claim of adult-centredness developed throughout this chapter.

First steps: interactions with the outside world

Not surprisingly, the number of mothers working, either full-time or part-time, has an impact upon the ways children are cared for, when and by whom. Indeed, answers to these questions provide a way into the deeper issue of what structures the initial interactions of infants in France with the wider world beyond their respective immediate families. The minding of pre-school children then raises two further questions, one regarding the content of the playing they experience at this stage of their lives, the other concerning where this takes place in terms of space, place and housing.

As a study conducted every seven years since 2002 has shown,[9] when mothers in a couple work, they tend to pay child-minders or crèches to mind their children, whereas when single mothers work, they rely more on their family and friends to do so. In all, 30% of these children are cared for uniquely by their mothers, 48%[10] by paid child-minders (32%) or crèches (16%), and the rest by grandparents or friends (18%) and only 4% by fathers (see also Francou *et al.*, 2017). Indeed, studies have shown that in France grandparents are involved in child-minding on a regular or occasional basis for no fewer than two-thirds of pre-school children (Kitzmann, 2016).

Of course, the difference between 'regular' and 'occasional' can be vast, thus rendering 'care by grandparents' an extremely vague category. Nevertheless, the key point to retain here is that prior to their going to school, four out of five children in France are cared for most of the time by adults who have no, or very little, training in this field. This is most obviously the case for the parents themselves and their own parents, who all rely chiefly upon experience and 'on the job' learning. But the same can also be said for the huge contingent of paid child-minders who look after a third of pre-school children in France. There is, of course, much to be said for this mode of care, particularly in terms of its strongly affective dimension. Moreover, it should be recalled that many of the adults concerned – parents, grandparents, other relations – consider that they 'have no choice' but to act as they do, notably because the cost of paid childcare would be prohibitive. For these reasons, it is not my intention to belittle this social practice or to criticize it as such. Nevertheless, analytically one needs to take the lowly professionalized character of pre-school child-minding into account if one wants to grasp many of the continuities in the socialization of children in this country. Institutionalized practices concerning matters such as the respect of other people, or accepted modes of disciplining, do not change or reproduce themselves. They only mutate when actors armed with reflexivity and new knowledge work politically to modify what behaviour is considered appropriate and indeed legitimate.

The issue of smacking children deemed to have misbehaved provides a case in point. Although a plethora of studies conducted in many countries since the 1960s have shown the negative short- and long-term effects of smacking (Gershoff and Grogan-Kaylor, 2016), and despite legislation adopted by the *Assemblée nationale* to outlaw it in late 2016, this form of parental violence is still common in French homes and public spaces. A comparative study in 2007 highlights that 50% of parents surveyed in France smack their children, and up to 85% use violence of some kind as punishment (Bussmann *et al.*,

2012). Indeed, the content of public debate in 2016–17 around this legislation highlights just how many adults in France consider that those caring for children should be authorized to hit them 'when necessary'.[11] At the time of writing, no systematic evaluation of the impact of the legislation introduced has been published;[12] however, my own anecdotal but frequent observation of parenting and childcare practices reveals that smacking is still a prevalent mode of discipline in France. Indeed, this is a clear reminder that changing the law does not necessarily change either institutions or actual behaviour.

The more general argument I wish to make here is that, just as in many other comparable countries, childcare in France is predominately conservative because it is structured by institutions, power relations and value hierarchies that have largely been inherited from the past. These have repeatedly been legitimated with arguments that stress the cardinal virtue of 'common sense' and that because 'parents know best', they should be left free to determine how they care for their children.

There are obviously many exceptions to this trend, given that a significant proportion of children in France are cared for in ways that draw upon different visions of what 'makes sense' and sources of knowledge about what constitutes best practice. Indeed, a good means of observing considerable change introduced in this way concerns children's play. To begin such analysis, let us first recall that well into the 1950s, children in France were expected to play carefully so as not to damage their toys, their clothing or themselves. Indeed, Wylie's anthropology of French rural life, *Village in the Vaucluse*, stresses how different accepted play was to that he and his children had experienced in their native United States (1957: 47–49). His astute observations on this point contrast sharply with how children in France play today, together with the limits set on this activity by a combination of parental authority and social norms. To begin with, play itself has become widely recognized as what pre-school children should be doing and encouraged to do. As we will see in the following section, any remotely formalized learning is now largely reserved for when a child starts school around the age of 3. Meanwhile, play has come to be seen not just as fun or, alternatively, as a means of learning language and a range of socially accepted 'facts', but also as a way of discovering how to relate to other children and to adults. This development has, of course, occurred in parallel with the expansion and diversification of what constitutes play in general and of the objects with which it can take place. Although in France formalized sports, games and arts are rarely proposed to infants, they are generally encouraged to exercise (or at least expend their energy: *se dépenser*), if possible outside and probably in one of the thousands of playgrounds found throughout French cities, towns and villages. And one scarcely needs to mention the number of toys put on the market and advertised extensively by an industry that has literally taken off since the 1960s: today around 240 million toys are bought in France each year, a country within which toy sellers boast an annual turnover of 3.4 billion euros.[13] None of this materialism would surprise a reader used to similar phenomena that occur in most countries of the global North, nor would they find unfamiliar the emergence in recent years of concerns that many infants are now getting too much exposure to a range of television, computer and telephone screens. Similarly, in France as elsewhere, many public concerns are voiced about the low levels of exercise many French children now get every day, a phenomenon many experts link to rises in infantile obesity and even diabetes.[14]

This in turn, however, raises the question of where children in France live, both in terms of types of physical environment and of housing. As is relatively well known, divided up into around 36,000 communes, France is the country in the world that has the most administrative units. Given that the population of a commune can range from as little as one person (Rochefourchat in Le Drôme) to 2.2 million (Paris), this figure means little. But needless to say, the vast majority of these units are thinly populated. It is thus more relevant to grasp that 83% of people in France live in large urban areas, 12% in communes close to those areas, and only 5% in entirely rural settings (Brutel and Levy, 2011). Indeed, 19% of the total population live in the Paris region alone (Île-de-France), 10% in Rhône-Alpes and nearly 8% in the region around and to the east of Marseille (Provence-Alpes-Côte d'Azur). From this perspective, therefore, France is very similar to many other developed countries in that for most of its children, life is essentially urban and most frequently takes place in or around large cities.

This trait in turn also goes some way to explaining that of the 29 million main residencies in France, 44% are flats and only 56% are houses. Thirty-five per cent of all these habitations have five rooms or more, but 20% have only two or one room.[15] Indeed, other indications of housing inequalities are that 58% of all homes are owner-occupied, whilst the remainder are rented from either private owners or belong to the category of 'social housing' (now just under 20% of the total housing stock). Moreover, no less than 45% of this stock was built before 1945. All these traits, of course, impact strongly upon the immediate environment of children, where they play and with whom they interact during their infancy.

A different point related to housing concerns mobility from two angles. The first is the amount of time people have lived in their current home. In this respect, 50% of the population have been there for more than ten years, which gives some idea of the social meaning accorded in France to property and geographical immobility, together with the relatively low importance given to moving house in order to 'rise up' what is known elsewhere, and particularly in the UK, as 'the housing ladder'. For most children in France, this trait not only provides a form of stability, but also often means that they are more likely to live in close proximity to their grandparents than their peers in, say, the United States.

A second angle related to housing and mobility concerns car ownership: there are currently around 29 million cars in France, and 81% of households have at least one car.[16] These figures, of course, tell us something about the importance attached to car ownership in general, and thus materialism in this country. But for much of the population, owning a car has also become an essential part of getting and keeping a job (Jullien and Lung, 2011; Marchal, 2014). Indeed, particularly in the majority of households – i.e. those which feature two persons in work or seeking employment – driving to work, often over considerable distances and despite structural congestion, is an integral part of the organization of lives, transport and the damage to health and the environment caused by both. All these impacts affect, indirectly but surely, how young children grow up in France.

More generally, without claiming to be comprehensive, this section has laid out a number of recurrent features of French living patterns which reveal key institutions and power relations that shape how infants in France enter the world, then begin to discover their place within it. Be it within the home or outside it, these societal structures that impact upon pre-school childcare and the immediate environments of infants – notably the social security and health fields – contribute strongly to what they learn to consider to be familiar, 'normal' and even 'right'. More fundamentally still, adult-centred concerns and interests lie at the heart of these institutionalized parameters. As such, the range of aspects related above plays a vital role in initial socialization – one that dovetails with what subsequently occurs in the more formalized, and ostensibly standardized, settings of school.

Initial schooling: happy days, but for who?

Schooling has, of course, been at the very centre of studies of socialization since at least the late nineteenth century, a period during which, moreover, the foundations of the contemporary French education system were largely laid. Following the Enlightenment then the French Revolution, education came to be seen as a primary means of cultivating 'good citizens' and, increasingly, good workers. Key historical events include the Education Act (1806) and Decree, an 1833 act that forced each commune to establish at least one primary school, another education act in 1866 establishing the secularization of teaching and curricula and the official separation of church and state in 1905. Most fundamentally of all, the introduction of compulsory schooling between the ages of 7 and 13 by the Minister of Education,

Jules Ferry in 1881–82, together with the standardization of curricula which accompanied this move, is widely seen as having played a key part in 'turning peasants into Frenchmen' [sic] (Weber, 1976). More precisely, ever since, education has been defined as a means of infusing children in France with a national identity strongly intertwined with 'Republican values'. Indeed, this commitment was remade by the state in 1958 within the constitution of the Fifth Republic, backed strongly by its first President, Charles de Gaulle, then implemented through the Debré Act of 1959.

Today schooling in France is compulsory between the ages of 6 of 16, and in practice takes place within four types of school: *maternelle* (for children aged 3–6), primary (6–11), intermediate *collèges* (11–15) and higher *lycées* (16–18). The impact of the latter two upon the socialization of French children will be analysed in the following chapter. Here we shall be concerned instead by how the two former types of school participate in transitions from infancy to childhood. In so doing, the following two themes will be developed. From one angle, we will revisit the image widely held outside France that in this country all schooling is centralized around a national curriculum so rigid that at any time the Minister for Education knows what is going on in each classroom from Brittany to the Côte d'Azur. Although today such an image is wholly inaccurate, the degree of national control of education nevertheless remains a key feature and source of tension within the educational field. The other recurring question to be addressed is the power of teachers as a key driver of the reproduction of educational goals and methods within this field. Beyond what they do in the classroom, teachers are not only a well-resourced corporation. As national civil servants they are formally part of the state and thus of its internal frictions.

L'école maternelle: elementary school *à la française*

Along with Belgium, France is exceptional in that nearly all its children between the ages of 3 and 6 go to a school that is free and funded by the state. In 2017–18, 2.5 million children attended one of these pre-primary schools (*écoles maternelles*), of which there were around 14,000, virtually all public.[17] These figures translate into approximately 800,000 children per year, 86,000 teachers in total, an average school size of six classes and an average class size of 25.3 pupils.[18]

The first thing to note here is that the *école maternelle* is a form of schooling that has only developed strongly since 1945 as part of the welfare state and family policy in particular. Partly because it in effect constitutes a form of childcare that for parents is entirely free, virtually all children attend. Indeed, many parents seek to get their children into school from as early as 2 years 6 months: in September 2017, no fewer than 92,000 became pupils before their third birthday. Given the young age at which schooling thus begins, it is perhaps not surprising that it is labelled *maternelle* even today and, moreover, that this adjective is rarely remarked upon, even by committed feminists and/or fathers who are highly active in the care of their children. Of course, at the time schooling from the age of 3 became universal, feminism and active fathers were decidedly rare. Indeed, the schools themselves have become dominated by women to the extent that today 82% of teachers in this type of school are of this sex. In addition, virtually all the relatively large numbers of support staff in each *maternelle* are also women (known by the acronym of their job title – ATSEM (*Assistants territoriaux spécialisés des écoles maternelles*), of which at the time of writing there are almost one per class and 60,000 in total). Indeed, given that so few other professional environments are so women-dominated, an outside observer is struck by the extent to which these establishments usually have an atmosphere that is quite different from that of the rest of French education, and indeed socio-economic life in general.

So what is actually taught and informally transmitted to children in France between the ages of 3 and 6? In the first year in particular, relatively little formal teaching takes place. Instead, each class is above all geared to managing the transition into social beings of most children. Since so few of them have attended crèches or nurseries, much of the curriculum is devoted to learning to interact with others, respecting their personal space and obeying the teacher. In so doing, a great deal of time is spent on artistic activities of various sorts and, quite simply, play. Indeed, breaks in the morning, at lunch and mid-afternoon are all important moments for parameter-laden 'disorder' that also play their part in socialization (Wylie, 1957: 65–66). Here the school canteen plays a major role. Although a minority of parents still collect their children for lunch at home, most *maternelle* pupils have to learn to eat in a group, respect precise rules (about seating, being served, how to eat) and consume food they may have never come across before. Indeed, many parents see the canteen as a key vector for getting their child to vary their diet and improve their table manners – often in vain!

Back in the classroom, more formal teaching of subjects unsurprisingly increases in year two and, especially, in year three. Children are progressively introduced to letters and numbers with the goal of their being able to begin to read and master very basic arithmetic before they go on to primary school. A certain uniformization of subject matter and teaching supports is introduced at this stage, thereby partly nourishing the myth of the centralization of French education. Indeed, certain specialists of learning criticize the 'primarization' of the *école maternelle* and what they see as its ever-increasing focus on academic subjects rather than other, more broadly educational, matters. Such critics consider that this trend also leads to an excessive focus on 'performance', one that in particular discriminates against children from less-favoured homes (Garnier and Brougère, 2017). Others are alarmed by what they see as relatively large class sizes (sometimes more than thirty children, even if the average is closer to twenty-five) and regret that most teaching assistants have had little formalized training. More generally, such critics underline that the rupture in childhood constituted by beginning school at 3 years old simply does not exist in many other comparable countries. They then conclude that there is a need to rethink the whole 1–6 age range in order to develop a more global, holistic approach to learning during childhood (France Stratégie, 2018).

Despite the relatively gentle character of such criticisms, they have yet to have had much effect upon parents, teachers or policymakers. Quite the contrary: the vast majority of parents see *l'école maternelle* as a huge success and even as a prime example of 'the state getting it right'. Most children are depicted by their parents as enjoying this level of schooling and the environment in which it takes place. Accordingly, most parents consider that this is 'not where the problem is'. Consequently, they either do not involve themselves in the school at all, or perhaps just help out on the occasional trip or to organize the end-of-year *fête de l'école*.

By contrast, teachers, of course, are constantly on the front line and therefore directly involved in either reproducing what goes on within this level of schooling or, in the case of a minority, working for relatively small changes. To understand the role they play from either angle, it is first important to grasp that in France they are virtually all now highly qualified, with each teacher possessing the equivalent of a two-year Masters degree. Those who take a specialized Masters in education and training, as well as 'external candidates', must pass an exam (*concours*) at the end of the first year. During the second year, experience of teaching in actual schools is progressively introduced. However – and crucially – all concerned generally undergo relatively little specialized training. Instead, teachers in *écoles maternelles* and primary schools alike tend strongly to learn on the job. This is one of the reasons most consider themselves first and foremost to be part of a profession with a strong *esprit de corps*. Indeed, over the last two decades, this feeling of belonging has been an important prop at a time when their salaries have declined in real terms, whilst popular and political expectations as regards what schools should be achieving has never been higher. However, such professional solidarity and unity can also be a cause or accelerator of resistance to reflexivity, let alone change. The two examples which follow illustrate the thin line that separates *esprit de corps* from a logic of corporatism, particular when neither is counterbalanced within the educational field by a strong, consistent and positive role being played by either parents or more generalist representatives of the state.

The first example concerns the injection into the curriculum of an introduction to the English language. Fed by policy elite concerns about the 'backwardness' of French secondary school pupils as regards learning English, and thus fears over 'globalization', in 2002 the Ministry of Education decided that as of the following school year, all children in *écoles maternelles* were to spend several moments a week learning some of the basics of a foreign language (not necessarily English), in particular via games and songs. However, this goal was to be achieved by the teachers already in post, regardless of their knowledge of a language other than French or of their aptitude to teach it. If many teachers have positively embraced this challenge by drawing upon their own personal knowledge of and interest in languages, the overall result has been haphazard and largely improvised within each school. Although there are many exceptions to this 'rule', the teaching profession as a whole has not committed to this pedagogical innovation. Given that neither parent representatives nor, more importantly still, bureaucrats from the Ministry of Education have got behind it, the impact of national policy in this domain has been decidedly limited.

My second example of corporatism in French early education concerns how the vast majority of teachers successfully mobilized in 2016–17 to return to a four-day week, i.e. with Wednesday as a day off for all *maternelle* and primary school pupils. This episode is particularly interesting because the question of 'school rhythms' has long been a subject of public debate in France. In a compromise between church and state typical of the Third Republic, Thursdays were traditionally given up to the former for catechism or its equivalent. This was traded off against pupils having to go to school every Saturday morning. In 1972, Thursdays were swapped for Wednesdays and, during the 1990s, in most regions the Saturday morning was dropped, in large part because upper- and middle-class parents wanted to be able to go away for the weekend. Around these changes, reflection and debate has rumbled on ever since over the length of the school week and indeed day (currently usually from 8.45 a.m. to 4.45 p.m.). Increasingly this debate has been fuelled by evocations of the 'rhythms' of schools in other countries and research data on each system's effects upon the tiredness and optimal learning times of children in general. Indeed, using this data and examples of foreign 'success', during the presidency of François Hollande, the government introduced legislation to shorten each school day and to reintroduce compulsory schooling on Wednesday mornings. More precisely, this arrangement freed up time within each day for non-scholarly activities not run by teachers (such as arts and crafts or physical exercise). In so doing, however, it forced teachers 'to give up their Wednesday'.

Most non-residents of France would be astonished at the outcry which ensued over the introduction of a policy designed to improve the well-being of children and their chances of learning at school. The teachers themselves were the most vociferous opponents of the reform, denouncing a change they claimed would make the children 'even more tired' (because they could no longer sleep in and 'rest' each Wednesday). This unsubstantiated claim was largely taken as objective reality, and this despite evidence from other countries that pupil tiredness can be dealt with in other ways. Moreover, the fact that working parents have to get their children up at the same time every day, regardless of whether there is school or not, went largely unheard. Local municipalities often also complained because they had to foot most of the bill for the running of non-scholarly activities during the school day. However, what ultimately killed this policy change is that most parents sided with the teachers, first because they too believe dogmatically in the mantra of 'tiredness' and, secondly, because at the level of elementary and primary schooling their belief that 'teacher knows best' is still unshakeable. Indeed, here again is an example of how the 'pragmatism' of the practitioner's knowledge has trumped a move to shift social practices on the basis of systematic data and peer-reviewed research (Frandji and Morel, 2017). Little wonder then that in 2017 the Macron presidency quickly bent with the wind made by teachers, local politicians and parents so as to abandon the four-day week without any evaluation of the policy instrument at issue or, indeed, reflexivity-informed public debate.

In summary, whilst it is true that *l'école maternelle* remains one of France's most consensual institutions, the examples of language teaching and the school week just presented reveal the strength of teachers within the educational field, underlying fault-lines in French society, and, above all, the power of conservatism to paper over these cracks using dogma and the register of 'tradition'.

Primary school: the beginning of the end for consensus over schooling

Indeed, from the moment children move on to primary school at the age of 6, they and their parents start to realize that they have begun direct engagement within a long process of highly structured schooling which is frequently controversial. When one actually experiences this transition through and with one's child or children, much is, of course, obscured by the force of the rituals that strive to normalize it in so many ways. First and foremost, each child continues to 'live' school through their respective teacher and class. Superficially, this relationship is much like it was in the *école maternelle*: one teacher continues to monopolize all the subjects taught and to retain strong hierarchic control over any teaching assistants who may also be present in the classroom. However, right from their first year in primary school, pupils soon realize that their *maîtresse* or *maître* is much stricter in controlling discipline than before and that the learning of certain skills (notably reading and arithmetic) now has clear priority. Of course, in many ways this is no different to primary schooling in many other countries. Nevertheless, what is stronger in the French system is the emphasis placed upon the omniscience and autonomy of the teacher, together with the distance most of them maintain as regards the parents of their pupils.

The primacy of the teacher's role is shaped in part by the structures of each primary school and of primary schooling itself. Spread over five years, the latter begins with a class of *Cours préparatoire* (commonly known as CP), two years of *Cours élémentaires* (CE1 and 2), then two more of *Cours moyens* (CM1 and 2). There are currently 37,000 primary schools in France with around 4.3 million pupils in total and an average class size of twenty-three. Although this size may vary considerably from school to school (and region to region), what is constant throughout the country is that the director continues to teach a class and, therefore, has little time or indeed authority to impact upon the teaching of their immediate colleagues. Consequently, each teacher has considerable autonomy to apply the 'programme' developed within the Ministry of Education. Indeed, this autonomy is jealously guarded by the teaching trade unions and, more generally, teachers as a corporation.

Nevertheless, a national programme (or curriculum) does exist and even constitutes the policy instrument around which much of the relationship is forged between the government and senior civil servants located in Paris and its 'street level bureaucrats' – i.e. the teachers, who constitute the interface with pupils and, most often indirectly, their parents. Indeed, as a highly visible reflection of the social role attributed to schooling in France, the programme itself is regularly the subject of intense and emotion-filled debates between politicians, administrators and teacher representatives. Formally revised by a national committee (*le Conseil supérieur des programmes*), in reality each Minister for Education and their staff tend strongly to seek to modify the programme in a top-down manner (Sawicki, 2012a: 16). For example, in April 2018 the Minister for Education, Jean-Michel Blanquer, went so far as to publish a series of guides for primary school teachers on how to teach reading and writing and, more generally, 'to reinforce the mastering of the fundamentals'.[19]

As regards the implementation of such instructions on the ground, state administrators organized in each region in powerful *Rectorats* are ostensibly in charge of this task. Teachers themselves then translate them in ways that more or less respect the letter of the law, thereby avoiding theoretical reprobation from national inspectors who, in practice, tend to be remarkably lenient. In this way, a lot of rhetoric and ink is spent upon each revision of the national programme, but actual change in teaching practice is incremental and slow. Moreover, what is clearly absent from all processes

mentioned here is any sustained involvement with either academic specialists of education or parents. Despite the level of education of French teachers or their administrators, their distance from academic research created by
professional competition and the championing of 'practitioner knowledge'
has been well documented (Van Zanten, 2006: 242; Dubet and Duru-Bellat,
2015). What French researchers themselves have yet to really highlight,
however, is how parent associations have been so deeply marginalized, and
even trivialized, within their country's primary education system. Both these
absences have been particularly prominent within two key aspects of contemporary primary schooling: how reading is taught and, more generally,
the evaluation of educative 'performance'.

The capacity of primary school pupils to read has been reprioritized in
France partly because a regularly published international study (Progress in
International Reading Literacy Study: PIRLS) has found that although the
level in France is higher than in the rest of the world as a whole, it is lower
than that of Europe and the Organisation for Economic Co-operation and
Development (OECD). Moreover, this level has progressively fallen since the
first such study in 2001, and this despite the fact that more time is spent in
French schools on learning language (i.e. in this case French) than in nearly
any other country. Indeed, in France, PIRLS's findings have taken on particular significance for two reasons. First, its 2016 edition in particular has
highlighted how little French primary teachers consent to undergo on-the-
job training about reading compared to their counterparts in other nations
(38% of French pupils are taught by teachers who have never benefited from
such training, compared to an average of 22% elsewhere). Secondly, the
apparent rise in literacy difficulties has occurred at a time when French
schools have largely stopped *le redoublement* – a practice dating back to the
early nineteenth century which, by decoupling the age of the pupil from what
class they are in, meant that pupils who did not reach a certain level would
redo the year in question. Indeed, in 1970 as many as 22%, and in 1980
12%, of French primary school pupils still repeated their first year of primary
school. Partly because research has shown that such repetition often has negative, reinforcing impacts upon pupil self-esteem and approaches to learning,
but above all because it is expensive for the state (each extra year costs the
state 5,500 euros per child at primary level), *le redoublement* at this level is
gradually being phased out. However, as of 2018, Minister Blanquer began
to challenge this trend, taking backing from many teachers, parents and even
pupils who have publicly come out in favour of this long-standing practice.

More deeply, however, a key point often missed by proponents of 'the fundamentals' and *le redoublement* is that pupils from different family and social
backgrounds frequently come at learning language itself from different trajectories. As Bernard Lahire has stressed in painstaking and ground-breaking

research on this point, primary school pupils tend to fall into one of two categories: those who are readily familiar with a 'scriptural social form' and those who instead are more at ease with an 'oral-practical' one (Lahire, 2000: 52–59). Pupils from middle-class backgrounds, where reading at home and discussion with adults is encouraged, tend to dominate the former category, whereas pupils from working-class backgrounds generally find themselves in the latter. According to Lahire, however, French primary schooling consistently favours the scriptural social form whilst denigrating the oral-practical one. This leads to an institutionalized forgetting of the constraints inherent in the written word. These greatly hinder the learning of reading and writing by pupils raised in predominately oral-practical language 'configurations'. Such pupils find it very difficult to study the French language for itself, as most teaching incites them to do. Lahire concludes that more egalitarian results at school can only be achieved if teaching in France shifts radically away from focusing upon the technologies behind linguistic practices (and thus thinking in terms of codified results) and towards 'the concrete appropriation' of what language condenses and transmits. More generally, he has urged that pupils who hail from 'oral-practical' backgrounds no longer be seen as 'handicapped' or unwilling to learn, but instead be framed as children who need to be accompanied and encouraged to getting the most out of their schooling (Lahire, 2000: 295).

More generally, be it as regards the sort of statistics-based studies conducted by PIRLS or the ethnographies conducted by academics like Lahire, those who dominate education in France, and at the primary and *maternelle* stages in particular, are particularly reticent to engage with the results of research, other than when its findings immediately suit their respective purposes (Dubet and Duru-Bellet, 2015).

Overall, clearly the French primary school, along with the elementary schooling which it 'follows', has changed radically since the 1950s. As Guy Vincent describes in fascinating detail (1980), teachers who began their careers in the decade after the Second World War underline themselves how much this form of education had shifted from one based purely upon passively listening to an omniscient *maître* or *maîtresse* and learning by rote, to another which, by the early 1970s, had incorporated considerable pupil participation and learning through structured play. Nevertheless, certain key elements of the initial 'Republican' model clearly remain, notably an emphasis upon the importance of written French, the strict correction of errors and the all-powerful status of the teacher. Indeed, it is far less clear that much has changed in this regard since 1975. Not surprisingly, as we will see in the following chapters, France's elementary and primary schools are definitely more convivial and homely entities than the *collèges* then *lycées* which their pupils move on to. Indeed, as in many other countries, most people in France fondly recall their early days at school. But that period also contains features that can often have effects that are far from positive. Moreover, these effects tend only to deepen once pupils leave these environments for the bigger establishments which await them as they move into pre-adolescence.

Conclusion

Much more could and should be said about how children in France are initially brought up and educated. This chapter has nevertheless laid out some of the main features which shape these two key dimensions of socialization. In so doing, it has also stressed the extent to which they, and the institutions and power relations that underpin them, are driven by adult-centred definitions of social problems and legitimate public action to 'solve' them. Just as childcare and schooling at the *maternelle* stage transpires to be dominated by what suits adult carers, doctors and teachers, schooling from then onwards becomes even more adult rather than child-centred. Indeed, neither the child nor the people who usually know them best (their parents) are genuinely consulted about the content or procedures of education. In this way, fundamental conservatism predominates, thus largely fuelling the reproduction of institutions and power relations over the period studied. In addition, actors who have worked politically to modify these key societal structures have seldom equipped themselves with problem definitions, policy proposals and modes of legitimation that have proved up to the task. This in part explains why neo-liberal and globalization-type arguments have gained little purchase. But nor have more 'progressive', child-centred arguments initially developed in other countries. Indeed, other than via increased individualization and materialism, the social mobility since the 1980s that has touched other parts of life in France has, at least to date, had virtually no impact upon what structures the schooling of young children in this country. Instead, the weak challenges to the status quo that have emerged have been relatively easily brushed off by powerful actors who are mostly content to reproduce the status quo. To do so, these actors have drawn instead upon the strength of institutionalized rules, norms and expectations regarding infancy and initial schooling, as well as their own dominant positions within the health, educational and bureaucratic fields.

Notes

1 A line from one of Bob Dylan's earliest songs, 'Subterranean Homesick Blues' (1965).
2 *Mutualist* insurance operates through non-profit organizations whose board members are elected by those who take out insurance with them. In practice,

most people in France pay a fixed sum every month to a *mutualist* insurance organisation to which they 'belong', either directly or via a scheme operated by their respective employer.

3 It is important to recall that in France the touchstone for a rapid rise in divorces was a law passed in 1975 that no longer required proof of 'wrongdoing' by one or both partners to justify the annulment of a marriage – a law which, of course, reflected much deeper changes in dominant social beliefs and practices as regards conjugality wrought since the early 1960s.

4 As Segalen underlines (2005: 123), until the 1950s death used to break up many more marriages. This also made remarriage common (except for widows over 40), along with the phenomenon of what we now call 'blended families'. Indeed, it is actually the period 1945–75 that is the exception. Other than during this short but so-frequently referenced period, blended families have always been common in France, as in numerous other countries.

5 www.jurifiable.com/conseil-juridique/droit-de-la-famille/divorce-france-statistiques, consulted 25th June 2018.

6 www.insee.fr/fr/statistiques/1280687, consulted 30th July 2018.

7 Indeed, it is vital to recall that in 2016 no less than 13.6% (i.e. more than 1 in 8) of France's population were living below the poverty line (defined as 60% of the median income level after social transfers). Of these people, 35% belonged to mono-parental families (source *Le Monde*, 5th September 2018, drawing upon a combination of figures generated by INSEE and Eurostat).

8 www.insee.fr/fr/statistiques/1281064, consulted 30th July 2018.

9 Data and report published in 2016 and accessible via http://drees.solidarites-sante.gouv.fr/etudes-et-statistiques/open-data/famille-enfance-jeunesse/article/l-enquete-modes-de-garde-et-d-accueil-des-jeunes-enfants, consulted 5th July 2019.

10 http://drees.solidarites-sante.gouv.fr/etudes-et-statistiques/publications/etudes-et-resultats/article/le-choix-de-la-creche-comme-mode-d-accueil-entre-benefices-pour-l-enfant-et, consulted 30th August 2019. By comparison, the average figure for all OECD countries was 32%, whilst in Germany it is as low as 23%.

11 See, for example, www.liberation.fr/france/2016/12/30/a-partir-de-2017-on-ne-fesse-plus_1538187, consulted 1st August 2018.

12 Olivier Maurel, founder of the anti-corporal punishment organization Oveo, told *The Local*, a newspaper created for foreigners living in France: 'Without that law in place there will always be parents who take advantage and hit children harder and more often than the current law permits ... After they banned smacking in Sweden [in 1979] the rate of child deaths caused by abuse has dropped to 0.6 percent per 100,000. In France it remains at 1.4 per 100,000.' www.thelocal.fr/20150304/france-violates-treaty-on-smacking-children, consulted 1st August 2018.

13 Indeed, 37% of sales occur in December and the average budget per child for Christmas presents is a startling 350 euros. www.entreprises.gouv.fr/politique-et-enjeux/qualite/securite/secteur-economique-jouet, consulted 1st August 2018.

14 See on this point the analysis and recommendations published by the *Haute autorité de la santé* in 2011. www.has-sante.fr/portail/jcms/c_964941/fr/surpoids-et-obesite-de-l-enfant-et-de-l-adolescent-actualisation-des-recommandations-2003, consulted 30th August 2019.

15 In *La France des Belhoumis*, Stéphane Beaud describes in detail the lives of eight children raised by their Algerian parents in a three-room flat. In so doing he identifies with finesse how the impact of this physical environment on these children, combined with other social and economic features of their lives, rendered their childhoods particularly challenging (2018).

16 www.insee.fr/fr/statistiques/3569225?sommaire=3569247&geo=FE-1#LOG_T2, consulted 1st August 2018.

17 In 2018 only 137 of these schools were private.

18 www.education.gouv.fr/cid128334/assisesecolematernelle.html#Les_objectifs_des_assises_de_l_ecole_maternelle, consulted 3rd September 2019.

19 www.education.gouv.fr/un-guide-reference-et-quatre-recommandations-au-service-de-la-maitrise-des-savoirs-fondamentaux-l-6959, consulted 3rd September 2019.

2

Secondary, professional and higher education: When 'merit' reproduces inequalities

Introduction

The paths of socialization we began to explore in the previous chapter, of course, continue as each child approaches adolescence, goes through this complex stage of their personal development, then comes out of it 'the other side', after leaving school in a variety of ways. During this period of ten to fifteen years, a great deal of time is spent in establishments of secondary, professional or higher education. As in many other countries, in France these forms of education are frequently, even constantly, the subject of intense public debate. If every adult does not have a child, they have all been to school themselves and work with, or employ, young adults who are going through, or who have just left, formal education. As the reform of France's higher secondary school system (the *lycées*) of 2017–19 has again recently testified, virtually everyone has an opinion on it. Indeed, as the report commissioned by the government to launch this process underlined (Mathiot, 2018), the central issue involved is one of educational justice, and indeed quite simply societal justice: how can France as a country reform the institutions that underpin its school system in order to provide all its 16- to 18-year-olds with a chance to not only obtain meaningful diplomas, but also the foundations for fulfilling lives? Moreover, can and should such reform also encompass neo-liberal policy recipes, responding to 'globalization' or the effects of recent social mobility?

Explaining the depth of the controversies that mark the French variant of secondary and higher education can only be done by examining the contemporary effects of the institutions and power relations bequeathed by history which heavily structure this domain. As will be highlighted, part of this history is chronologically distant. Nevertheless it still heavily shapes the very existence of what constitutes both its basic organizational units – 'the *collège*', 'the *lycée*', 'university', '*les grandes écoles*' – and blurry distinctions between 'public' and 'private' education. However, what has happened in the last forty years is just as important: during this period, not only have governments

firmly committed to upgrading education – beginning with the first Mitterrand government's goal-setting of 80% of children obtaining *le baccalauréat*
(known as '*le bac*') at the age of 18 or 19. They have also sought to confront
the rise of unemployment through schooling and higher education. More
deeply still, in terms of political work a central challenge has been to reform
the institutions and power relations that structure schooling and higher
education. Indeed, rising to this challenge has proved particularly difficult,
in part because it has been paralleled by a shift from a 'Fordist' mode of
capitalism – one which employed large numbers of young people without
either lengthy schooling or diplomas – to a more 'financialized' economy
that has reduced the employment of such workers in France itself.

Sociologists stress that schools and higher education establishments cannot hope to neutralize societal inequalities which have much deeper roots.
Moreover, they highlight the dangers of governmental policies which have
transformed the right to succeed through one's education into success at
school being an individualized duty (Dubet, 2014: 10). Many French pupils
and students do, of course, 'succeed', but as many as 80,000 a year leave the
educational system without any diploma (out of 800,000 in total who leave
annually).[1] To take up the thread developed in chapter 1, this point underlines the extent to which secondary and higher education in France is also
adult-centred. If one can often be fooled by appearances, teenagers and even
post-teenagers are still in many ways children in the sense that their minds
have yet to be fully formed and, in particular, they often have difficulty in
taking responsibility for themselves. But in France, just as in many other
countries, this fundamental point is covered up beneath considerations about
what they must become as adults: productive workers and responsible, some
would say docile, citizens. In so doing their vulnerability, but also their
creativity, is all too often 'corrected' out of them.

What is therefore at issue, however, is not only about individuals and
their respective development and/or pathologies; it concerns fundamental
societal inequality. What has become glaringly obvious is that the goal of educational justice has not been achieved by the discourse and practices framed
in terms of 'equal opportunities' which have had more political resonance,
but not necessarily educational success, in other countries such as the UK
(Charles, 2015). Instead, the emphasis placed in France upon educational
organizations as inequality-correcting mechanisms needs unpacking and
revisiting, in particular because of the emphasis they continue to place upon
'merit'. This key term initially emerged around the French Revolution as a
means of delegitimizing the monarchy and, more generally, the aristocra-
cy-based *ancien régime*. Instead of inheriting social and economic rights at
birth, the underlying theory of action and justice was that through their own
competence and efforts, each French citizen could now obtain them through

proving their own merit (see article 6 of the Declaration of Human and Citizen Rights of 1789). This element of a new theory of the just society was subsequently translated into instruments of policy and government, notably during the Napoleonic era. Indeed, as this chapter's second section will underline, it was during the First Empire that merit became both a widely proclaimed social value and a principle for organizing recruitment to both the civil service (via competitions known as *concours*) and the most prestigious parts of French higher education. Ever since, more than equality, merit as a value and as a principle has continued to heavily structure what young people in France experience both after secondary school, but also during these school years. 'Meritocracy' is therefore not just the guiding principle of the national educational field. It lies at the very heart of French republicanism, producing in its wake many undoubted benefits, but also numerous and brutal 'Darwinian' effects for those who do not measure up to its yardsticks. Ultimately, the question the primacy of meritocracy in the structuring of French education poses to policymakers and citizens alike is what inequalities are deemed 'tolerable'?[2] To begin to examine how different parts of the population have responded to this question, secondary schooling is the place to start.

Secondary schooling: 'merit' v. social and educational structures

Given the elements outlined above, since the French Revolution, secondary schooling has been one of the main issues that fuel the division between citizens who locate themselves politically either on the right or the left. Initially, this divide was centred almost exclusively upon the issue of religion. Perhaps surprisingly seen from today, despite the secular driver behind much of the revolution itself, it was not until 1882 that religion was taken out of state schools with the banning of prayers and catechism. Ever since, schools have been seen as organizations for socializing children to understand and accept 'civic responsibility' on an individual basis and in the name of republican values (Déloye, 1994: 35).

Indeed, the 1940s was in many senses a watershed given that, during the Vichy regime, then after the Second World War, a massive increase of post-primary education took place. In so doing, a new form of intermediate school – *le collège* – emerged for children between the age of 11 and 15. Meanwhile, more children were progressively encouraged to stay on at school through successive reforms of *le lycée*. These slowly brought to an end its life as the sanctified preserve of the elite and the bourgeois. Throughout this process, the state's Ministry of Education and the teaching profession have monopolized the educational field. Consequently, they have been omnipresent in introducing and implementing reforms, whilst at times resisting change and protesting against its effects. In this respect, as Van Zanten has underlined (2006: 229), four dimensions of centralization have heavily affected the French ordering of secondary education: central government to school directives, the bureaucratic power of state rectors and inspectors, the national corporatism of teachers, and the near-total absence of users (pupils or parents) from decision-making. Indeed, both pupils and their parents are objects rather than subjects of the secondary school system (Van Zanten, 2006: 250). However, as will be shown below, her point regarding parents needs pushing a stage further in order to grasp their generalized acquiescence to, and thus legitimation of, the power relations and institutions which structure secondary education, and more generally the educational field, in France to this day. If the child in the teenager has so systematically been overlooked within this stage of schooling, this is also because parents, collectively and individually, have rarely sought to draw upon academic research, or indeed practical experiences in other countries, to push the state and teachers to modify their mindsets, procedures and practices.[3]

When 'intermediate' pushes up and pulls down: le *collège* as make-or-break point

Although the school leaving age was raised from 13 to 14 in 1936, then initial reforms to encourage more children to stay on longer at school were adopted during the Vichy regime (Paxton, 2001), le *collège* as an institutionalized form of intermediate school emerged from the Second World War and the period that immediately followed: *la libération*. Pushed strongly by the French Communist Party (*le PCF*), initial moves to standardize intermediate schooling throughout the country became the object of a national consensus to which nearly all political parties contributed (Van Zanten, 2006: 232). However, actually expanding the physical capacity of the state to provide this schooling took time, as schools had to be built and a raft of new teachers trained and employed. In line with this movement, the school leaving age was raised to 16 in 1959, whilst the *collège* as we know it today (with its four levels: *sixième, cinquième, quatrième* and *troisième*) was first established by law in 1963. The upshot of this long process of expansion has been that in 2018 there were around 7,000 such schools located throughout France, an average of twenty-five pupils per class, with each *collège* constituting an organization within which the destiny of the children, then teenagers, who pass through them can either be brightened or darkened by the way they undergo this experience.

Crucially, unlike in countries such as Germany or pre-1970s Britain, in France there is no exam at the end of primary school which determines whether a pupil is directed towards a more academic or a more 'profession'-oriented type of school. Instead, particularly since a reform introduced in 1975 in the name of egalitarianism, all *collégiens* formally begin this stage of their lives on an equal footing. Nevertheless, in the course of their years at *collège* a form of streaming is progressively introduced which, by the age of 13, designates (many would say relegates) a significant number of pupils to the 'technical' branch of each school. Although ostensibly based upon 'merit' evaluated in the form of marks obtained, this streaming is also heavily affected by the social capital of each child. Teacher perceptions of their aptitude also play a major role, perceptions that are frequently filtered in terms of their ethnic origins (Beaud, 2002, 2018). Indeed, as will be shown through the examples developed below, societal institutions and power relations usually depicted as being 'beyond' the education system combine with it to produce a form of schooling that is deeply unequal. In all cases, what happens in *collèges* is crucial in determining whether each young person gets encouraged to develop their knowledge and skills positively, or through systematic discouragement they instead become downgraded and declassified, both educationally and socially.

Moreover, in the French case this structural phenomenon, common to many other countries, is supplemented by profound uncertainties about whether the role of the *collège* is to unify all its pupils as citizens or, on the contrary, to encourage them to develop in diverse ways in preparation for higher education and the world of work. Indeed, as Dubet argues, the *collège* is the part of French education where 'its vocation and very function is still the most ambivalent and conflictual' (2016b: 109). More precisely, this ambivalence is amplified by the educative methods which continue to dominate French education as a whole. In general, these methods remain centred upon transmitting knowledge as 'truth' in a top-down way (as in Belgium, Poland and Germany), rather than accompanying pupils to discover things for themselves (a model more prevalent in the US and the UK) (Dubet *et al.*, 2010: 117). In practical terms, this leads to the transmission of discipline-centred[4] knowledge and conformity to norms, rather than the acquisition of skills. Although many teachers in France are driven by a vocation to educate through using the savoir-faire they have progressively acquired, disciplinary aims remain deeply institutionalized (Dubet and Duru-Bellat, 2015: 119).

One collège, *but very different schools: the impact of geographical and* public–privé *divides*

As we began to discover in chapter 1, despite the emphasis placed upon a national education system, where a pupil lives and whether their school is public or private has significant impact upon their educational experience. Inequalities kick in considerably before children reach the age of 11, but once they get to *collège* these tend strongly to be systematically reinforced, often in 'symbolically violent' ways (Bourdieu and Passeron, 1970).

Of course, throughout most of the world, where a pupil lives has a huge impact upon the socio-demographic character of their school. France is no exception to this 'rule', because the sociology of each *collège* in particular largely reflects that of the neighbourhood within which it is located. Just as the country's social elites tend to live either in the '*chic*' central parts of large cities or their select outer suburbs (e.g. those located to the west of Paris), their children tend strongly to attend *collèges* whose pupils are drawn only from those areas. Conversely, the poorest families in France live either in suburbs of cities characterized by high levels of social housing and high unemployment (areas often stigmatized by the term *les banlieues*), or in similarly marginalized parts of small towns (Beaud, 2018). Indeed, numerous studies have shown that whereas until 1990 a significant degree of 'social mixedness' (*mixité sociale*) could be found in many of these neighbourhoods – and this due to the continued existence of working-class solidarities and of local activists committed to leftist ideals – since then, socio-spatial segregation has hardened due in particular to the slowing of upward social mobility, deteriorating social conditions and increases in racism (Safi, 2013). Despite some recent attempts by municipalities to halt this trend using positive discrimination, an overall trend towards a phenomenon akin to segregation has clearly taken place.

What is probably singular about the French case, however, is that this trend has been accompanied, and sometimes even intensified, by the highly structured flight of experienced teachers from schools and neighbourhoods reputed to 'have problems'. Some explanation of this trend can be found in teachers seeking to leave schools where discipline is hard to maintain and where, partly as a consequence, it is difficult to encourage pupils to invest in their studies or, quite simply, to learn. But focusing uniquely on such decisions made by individual teachers leads to overlooking the impact of the human resources policy of their employer: the Ministry of Education. In contrast to schools in many other countries, French *collèges* are not free to recruit the teachers they feel they require through an open process of advertising, application and selection. Nor are they free to offer them higher wages to compensate for teaching under 'challenging' conditions (Mons, 2007). Instead, because teachers in France are national civil servants with one salary grid, schools which become eligible for a new teacher are required to select from a shortlist of applicants sent to them by their region's *Rectorat*. Established on the basis of the number of 'points' each teacher has accumulated over the course of their career,[5] such a list may be relatively long for

schools in favoured areas, such as the centres of cities. However, they tend
to be decidedly short for schools located in less prestigious areas, but also
stocked full of teachers with few 'points', and this precisely because they
have only just begun their teaching careers. Despite governmental policies to
palliate this situation implemented in different ways since 1982 (for example through targeting *Zones d'éducation prioritaire* (*ZEPs*): Van Zanten,
2009), the overall result strongly reinforces socio-spatial inequalities, first
because 'the best schools' get the most experienced teachers and, secondly,
because schools with relatively poor exam results and problems of discipline
are fobbed off with teachers lacking in classroom experience. Of course,
armed with youthful energy, creativity and a sense of vocation, many of the
latter manage to do their job effectively and successfully. In so doing, they
help pupils hindered by unfavourable home or neighbourhood environments
to surmount their respective social handicaps. However, many other young
teachers quickly become discouraged and often leave not only the school
but the profession, thereby participating further in the downward spiralling
of the ship from which they have just jumped.

Moreover, research focused upon how teaching in *collèges* actually operates provides a means of showing how the structural challenges to learning
created by spatial inequalities and the allocation of teachers combines neg-
atively with the mode through which knowledge is disseminated at this level
in France. The emphasis upon learning in terms of disciplines tends strongly
to reward only the most academically inclined pupils (*les intellos*, to use the
language of their classmates), whereas the remainder of pupils end up being
discouraged or even stigmatized. More fundamentally still, as Dubet puts it,
'what pupils learn is less important to most teachers than completing the
programmes which they are charged with teaching' (2016a: 20). This in turn
reinforces a reduction in thinking about pupils uniquely in terms of the marks
they obtain, rather than as growing children and adolescents.

Moreover, one of the causes and consequences of socio-spatial inequalities in *collège*-level schooling which, particularly within France itself, is too
often overlooked concerns the impact of private schools upon the system as
a whole. No less than 26% of *collèges* are private and account for 22% of
all pupils for the relevant age group. Additionally, 97% of these schools are
Catholic. The reason these schools exist at all goes back to compromises
struck between the church and the state in the nineteenth century which
were updated first by the Constitution of the Fifth Republic adopted in
1958, and then by 1959's Debré Act. Although this legislation reiterated
that public education in France was to be free and secular, it also stipulated
that the state must be neutral towards religion. Moreover, and astonishingly,
the Debré Act authorized the state to actually provide private schools with
funding and even pay the salaries of its teachers! Although a short-term aim

was to accelerate the provision of places in schools at a time of population expansion, the long-term consequence of this development has not only been to consolidate and legitimate private schooling (and in so doing the individ-ualization of schooling as a whole), it has also delegitimated and weakened schools belonging purely to the state. Particularly since the 1990s, this has been exacerbated by increasing numbers of parents taking their children out of state schools and sending them to private ones instead. Indeed, this trend has been encouraged by the fees of the latter remaining relatively low because of the high levels of state subsidy these establishments continue to receive. When one adds in the temptation for teachers to also transfer to private schools, the combined result is a strengthening of pupils who are already strong, or who at least have already benefited from a head start in life, together with a further weakening of teenagers who have always had the deck firmly stacked against them.[6]

(Mis)managing ethnic difference: the case of Islam seen through 'the veil'

Given the overtly Catholic orientation of nearly all private schools in France, their continued and healthy existence also serves to reinforce the unfavour-able position of state schools in areas with large immigrant, or second-generation immigrant, populations, and in particular those who practise Islam to varying degrees. Already handicapped by the economic situation and socio-demographics of their respective neighbourhoods, over the last three decades many pupils whose ethnic origins are not 'purely French' and/or are simply not Christians have found themselves criticized for bringing to school signs of their religious beliefs. Indeed, the wearing of headscarves by Muslim college pupils has prompted at least three highly politicized national contro-versies and even legislation banning the wearing of all 'conspicuous signs of religions affiliation' in public schools. Why has this issue taken on such proportions and what lasting impact has it had upon intermediate-level school-ing in particular?

To answer the first question, revisiting three isolated incidents in turn provides a good place to start. The first occurred in 1989 at a *collège* in Creil, a commune with *ZEP* status situated in an outer suburb of Paris, when three girls were expelled by the school principal for refusing to take off their headscarves in the name of respecting their Islamic faith. The prin-cipal claimed to be acting to enforce the norm of secularism (*laïcité*), a move widely supported by many politicians and commentators in the press. How-ever, as Joan Scott underlines (2007), the massive coverage given to this event can only be understood by recalling that it happened at a time when French national identity itself was under discussion (around the bicentenary celebrations of the Republic) and the place of Islam in the West was generating rising anxiety (notably following the *fatwa* placed upon the British-Indian writer Salman Rushdie, as well as the beginning of the Palestinian *intifada*). Indeed, in the press the headscarf immediately became depicted as 'the veil', an image which in turn conjured up others of how women were then having to dress in countries like Iran. Publicized marches took place in support of the girls whilst, on the other side, a range of philosophers, or 'public intellectuals', as well as teacher unions, dramatically linked the issue to the very future of the Republic: 'the veil became a screen onto which were projected images of strangeness and fantasies of danger' (Scott, 2007: 10, 24). In the end, this issue was temporarily resolved by a decision from the *Conseil d'Etat* stating that such religious artefacts could be worn as long as they were not used to proselytise, new guidelines from the Ministry of Education to local school boards, and the decision by two of the three girls involved to take off their headscarves during class.

Five years later, however, 'the veil' was put back on the agenda by the ex-principal of the same *collège* in Creil, Eugène Chenière. Now a right-wing (*Rassemblement pour la République*: RPR) MP, Chenière introduced a private members bill to ban 'the ostentatious wearing' of signs of religious affiliation. After a year of continuous and acrimonious debate, the minister for education himself issued new guidelines which effectively enacted Chenière's plan. Once again, the *Conseil d'Etat* intervened by declaring the ministerial decree to be unlawful, but this, of course, did not stop a range of actors making political capital out of the episode, particularly representatives of the *Front National*, a party which at that time was attracting increasing levels of popular support. Indeed, this trend, together with a linked shift to the right by the *RPR*, largely explains why a new attempt to legislate was made in 2003 and, above all, why this time it was successful. Once again, cases of girls in secondary schools wearing headscarves were injected into public debate. Crucially for the argument made in this chapter, once again, ethnic difference was depicted as being not only a problem for schools, but a problem for the very social fabric of the neighbourhoods concerned.

In summary, this example of how approaching ethnic diversity has been so deeply mismanaged in and around French *collèges* – to the detriment of the already underprivileged – highlights just how (white) adult-centred this level of schooling remains. As Scott has highlighted, the dominant terms of debate about managing ethnic difference oppose 'the host' and 'the guest' (2007: 74). Instead of promoting allegiance to the Republic, the rigid application of secularism in schools has led to 'intolerance and discrimination' (Scott, 2007: 93). Indeed, specialists of Islam have highlighted the irony of how the headscarf issue has enabled the diversity of Muslims in France to unite and 'objectify' as a group (Roy, 2004: 15). In the process, moreover, it has reinforced a dogmatic dimension prevalent not only within much of France's teaching profession, but also more generally amongst other arch-defenders of 'the Republic'.[7] Indeed, since the 1980s *le collège* has progressively become a prime example of how the republican 'unicity' it ostensibly protects has, in practice, become instead a smokescreen behind which this level of schooling's institutions and asymmetric power relations has encouraged the individualization of social mobility.

High schools at a low point: *le lycée* and its 'uncontrolled expansion'[8]

Once the jewel in the French education system's crown, since the 1980s the *lycée* has also become an institution that is increasingly criticized for failing to live up to the considerable societal expectations it continues to generate. Indeed, the paradox here is that whilst on the one hand *lycées* have undoubtedly been 'democratized' since the 1960s (when only 30% of each year's pupils became *lycéens*, compared to around 75% today), on the other it is also the level of schooling where selection really kicks in – what Stéphane Beaud calls both 'the great parting of the ways' ('*le grand partage*' – 2018: 148) and the source of a 'cascade of contempt' ('*la cascade du mépris*' – 2002: 17) that affects so many 16–18/19-year-olds. Indeed, Beaud goes so far as to label the French high-school system 'segregationist educational democracy' (2002: 14). As will be shown when unpacking the institutions and power relations which, within *lycées*, strongly reinforce the position of teenagers who are already well resourced but further handicap the structurally underprivileged, it is simply untrue to consider that the state, teachers and other actors have not worked politically to change what takes place within *lycées*, its outputs and its outcomes. As debate surrounding *le Rapport Mathiot* in 2017–18 (Mathiot, 2018) testified, this level of schooling is constantly the object of intense political work. Nevertheless, for reasons I will highlight below, little has so far changed, or even looks likely to in the near future.

Bolstering the already privileged

In addition to whether their school is private (1,046 schools in 2017, i.e. 39% of the total number) or public (1,608: 61%),[9] a teenager's experience of life in a *lycée* will differ around three variables. The first is whether they attend a 'general' (70% of pupils) or a 'professional' *lycée* (30%). For reasons explored below, the legitimacy of the latter is constantly questioned, whereas that of the former retains a level of prestige that means it is consistently preferred by most pupils and parents.

The second variable to take into account is the geographical location of the school in question. Just as for *collèges*, those *lycées* in the centre of large cities are invariably the best resourced and where most teachers would prefer to work. Indeed, it is important to grasp that although formally all *lycéens* are designated to the *lycée* closest to their home, dispensation from this rule can be obtained provided a pupil obtains sufficiently high marks at *collège* and/or they desire to study a subject, notably a language such as Latin or ancient Greek, that is not taught in their local high school. In practice, this means that a select number of students from *collèges* in less-favoured areas who have previously got good marks, or studied an exotic language for strategic reasons, manage to access the most prestigious *lycées*. Such strategies take on slightly different guises in central Paris, in particular when ambitious parents seek to get their child into *lycées* (e.g. 'Henri IV') which have a track record of, and are famous for, producing an extraordinarily high percentage of France's political and economic elites (Maclean *et al.*, 2006). But the overall result is similar.

Finally, the third variable to be looked at when one encounters any teenager at a *lycée général* is to discover which of the four main 'sections' – science (*S*), literature (*L*), economics and society (*ES*), sciences and technologies of management and administration (*STMG*) – they have been channelled into as of the second year of high school (*la première*). The key point to retain here is that these four categories are anything but equal in terms of prestige and signification. Moreover, they do not necessarily even reflect the taste a pupil may have for some subjects rather than others. Instead, being part of the science section means not only that one will sit the *bac S*, it also means that one will benefit from a social marker of 'intelligence' and aptitude to play a leading role in society. This is particularly so because the *bac S* opens a door to the top places in higher education. Being accepted in this section is therefore a key moment of social selection within which the mastery of maths, in particular, plays the role of a social litmus test. In hierarchical terms, the literature and economics and society sections find themselves considerably below that of science. Specifically, whereas historically pupils studying literature were once seen as relatively prestigious (Bourdieu, 1989), since the 1980s this standing has changed considerably as more social status has been attached to professions linked to business and finance. Indeed, today a *bac ES* is generally seen more favourably by employers than a *bac L*. This said, both are clearly placed by all concerned in a much higher category than a *bac STMG* – or *bac technologique*. Although often studied for in a *lycée général*, the latter is frequently dismissed as a 'cut-price' diploma (and this despite the fact that this *bac* accounts for 20% of all the pupils who pass the *baccalauréat* each year).

The consequence of all the above is that although there is no question that infinitely more young people pass their *bac* today (*c.* 77%) than was the case in 1808 when Napoleon created this exam (1%), or even than in the 1960s (*c.* 30%), the *lycée* as an institution remains distinctly inegalitarian. Moreover, as will be highlighted in the second part of the chapter, no sustained public reflection exists regarding how the *lycée général* as an institution has impacted upon young people as a whole, and this despite the fact that it has 'spread in an uncontrolled fashion' (Beaud, 2002: 20).

Schools, vocational trainers or teenager-minders?
The ambiguities of lycées professionels

Whereas until the mid-1980s young people who were not academically inclined, and/or had poor marks at college, simply left school at 16 to either enrol on a short vocational training course or seek work immediately, since the creation of a *baccalauréat professionnel* in 1985, and of the *lycées professionnels* in which most of the pupils concerned study, this situation has changed dramatically. Today, no less than 30% of all *lycéens* sit the '*bac pro*', thereby contributing strongly to the overall expansion of this level of high-schooling. To fully understand what a *bac pro* is and its educational and social effects, however, one first has to bear in mind that this qualification and mode of schooling was introduced for two sets of reasons which often do not fit together easily.

The first reason was that by the mid-1980s, France had experienced a decade of rising unemployment and, in particular, that of its youth (see chapter 3). Moreover, during these years, employers began to complain more vociferously that the school system was not training its pupils in a way that made them employable. The more enlightened employers also recognized that unlike in West Germany in particular, employers in France were generally reluctant to take on apprentices and train them within their respective firms.[10] They therefore concluded that a form of high-school education which mixed traditional teaching with more practical dimensions would encourage greater engagement by companies in local employment and training policies.

However, it is just as important to grasp that the *lycées professionnels* were also created in the name of social justice by a range of politicians, administrators and social activists who believed strongly that all teenagers, including those from deprived areas or family backgrounds, should have the opportunity to continue their studies, and thus to self-development, after the age of 16. Indeed, from this angle the *bac pro* was seen as a vast improvement upon previous school leaving certificates, particularly because it could open the door for more pupils to go on to higher education if they so wanted.

In terms of implementation, the core of the *bac pro* model has thus always been to combine a curriculum of standard high-school subjects (tackled more through their practical dimension, e.g. within maths) with engagement with the economy through internships and courses taught by businessmen and women. Moreover, smaller class sizes are the norm (18.4 per class in 2017). Increasingly, however, the *bac pro* has diversified in order to fit with the economic sectors privileged either by the *lycée* in question and/or by the local economy. Indeed, there is not one '*bac pro*' but a plethora of '*bac pros*' (Vergnies, 2015); whereas there were five in 1985 (centred upon metalworking), today there are around 100. Indeed, in 2013 58% of *bac pro* students chose 'service sector' *bacs*, and only 42% 'industry' ones (Maillard, 2015: 175). Encouraged in part by the number of *lycées professionnels* that are private (no less than 43% in 2017), this diversification is generally seen as positive because it is intended to reflect a better 'fit' between the supply of teaching and demand from the economy. But the experience of more than thirty years now tells us that this demand is not always easy for the administrators of the *lycées professionnels* to decipher. In part, this confirms the intrinsic uncertainty of the world of business and work. But it also underlines that the French business world as a whole is still reluctant to invest heavily in this issue area (Buisson-Fenet and Rey, 2016: 8). This is reflected in the fact that the number of apprenticeships remains low: just 10% of all *bac pros* take this route. Moreover, it is important to grasp that the *bac pro* itself has increasingly been seen by the teenagers involved as a stepping stone to higher education. Revealingly, in a recent study Bernard and Troger (2015: 30) show that when they begin their *lycée*, no less than 59% of such pupils planned to go on to higher education once they had their *bac*, thus exacerbating 'dualization' within these schools (Palheta, 2012; Verdier, 2016: 21). As we will see below, this in turn has raised important questions about what pupils can actually get onto in terms of courses, and where such forms of higher education eventually lead them.

In conclusion, with around 75% of French teenagers now passing the *bac* each year, one could argue that over the last thirty years the 'democratization' of schooling in France has been a great success. However, it is important to underline not only the different types of diplomas and *lycées* this figure encompasses. More fundamentally still, although 87% of children of managers or equivalent get the *bac*, only 44% of children whose parents are skilled labourers do so.

Despite its numerous challenges and the changes, notably for those over 16, the French school system as a whole has not been transformed since the 1980s. Meanwhile, public opinion surveys show that support for the system has risen from 55% to 70% since 1981 (Zmerli, 2019: 273). Indeed, there is somewhat of a paradox here: although many different types of policy instruments have been introduced to improve the system both nationally and within schools, and although experts call stridently for deep change,[11] most of France's population seem to consider that schools feature amongst the institutions of which they are most satisfied and, in many cases, even proud. Not only does this statistic reflect the dominant position held by teachers within the educational field. Ultimately, this level of satisfaction, complacency or apathy partly explains why opponents of the current system find it so difficult to construct the very 'problem' of secondary schooling in new ways, and in so doing develop legitimacy for alternative framings and for themselves.

Post-secondary school: an 'invisibilized' machine of conservatism

Outsiders to France frequently have a positive image of French higher education, marked no doubt by images of 'left-bank' intellectuals such as Sartre and de Beauvoir, the aura of *La Sorbonne* or the presentation skills of politicians trained in one of *les grandes écoles*, for example Pascal Lamy or Emmanuel Macron. However, the reality of post-secondary education in France is much less glamorous, highly complex and deeply marked by social inequality. Indeed, if anything the 'cascade of contempt' so apparent at high school (Beaud, 2002: 17) intensifies in the even more competitive world of the *grandes écoles*, 'technical' schools and universities we will examine below. Throughout, what is important to retain is that social bias is not as flagrant as it is in countries such as the UK, where the public v. private school and Oxbridge v. the rest cleavages are more visible and consistently evoked in the public sphere and ordinary conversations. Nevertheless, equivalent forms of social partiality remain omnipresent. Indeed, it is only by carefully unpacking the institutions, power relations and political work which structure post-secondary education in France that their causes, effects and 'invisibilization' can be fully understood.

The best way to begin to understand French higher education and its internal diversity (see Table 2.1) is to immediately discard any idea that 'university' is its pinnacle. Currently no fewer than 1.6 million students are registered at one of France's sixty-seven universities and most eventually leave the system with a diploma that has some social and economic meaning. Moreover, the majority of academic staff working in universities are engaged in high-level research and publications in demanding national or international journals or publishing houses. Nevertheless, all this needs to be placed in a context where an elite group of specialized 'schools' – *les grandes écoles* – as well as a more diverse and less esteemed set of technical schools are proportionally accorded more resources and attract many students with the best secondary school results and, above all, highest levels of

Table 2.1 Shifts in French student numbers, 1960–2010 (thousands)

Year	University	BTS/IUT	Prépa	Grandes écoles and other[1]	Total
1960	215 (69%)	8 (3%)	21 (7%)	66 (21%)	310
1970	637 (75%)	51 (6%)	33 (4%)	130 (15%)	851
1980	805 (68%)	122 (16%)	40 (3%)	215 (18%)	1,181
1990	1,086 (63%)	274 (16%)	64 (4%)	293 (17%)	1,717
2000	1,278 (59%)	358 (17%)	70 (3%)	454 (21%)	2,160
2010	1,321 (57%)	359 (16%)	80 (3%)	560 (25%)	2,319
2017	1,330 (56%)	352 (15)	86 (4%)	590 (25%)	2,358

[1] This 'other' notably includes a rise in education in private centres of higher education, notably business schools. Charles (2014) calculates that this rose from 13 to 18% of all higher education places over the period 1990–2010.

Source: based on statistics published by the DEPP of the Ministry of Education, https://cache.media.education.gouv.fr/file/RERS_2018/28/7/depp-2018-RERS-web_1075287.pdf, and their analysis by Charles (2015: 25; 2019 personal exchange).

social capital. Dualism thus lies at the heart of the French higher educational field. This phenomenon will be analysed here first around its three strands – *grandes écoles*, technical schools, university – then through their combined effects upon France's education and society more generally.

The grandes écoles *as social not academic ambition*

If the first university in France was founded as long ago as the year 1200, most of the *grandes écoles* also have a long history, many dating back to the eighteenth century, then to a renaissance under Napoleon Bonaparte.[12] From the outset, each of these schools has been relatively specialized – for example, *Polytechnique* trains engineers whilst *Saint-Cyr* does the same for future army officers. The French word for training is the operative term here, because these schools are supposed to *former* (i.e. shape as much as actually train) their respective students. Indeed, such shaping is justified in law because most pupils have traditionally been expected to devote much of their subsequent careers working for the relevant branch of the state.[13] If this expectation and legal obligation is no longer as strong as it once was, the link between the *grandes écoles* and the state is still iron-clad.

Apart from the nebulous criteria used to judge that they are 'high-level' establishments, the *grandes écoles* set themselves apart from the rest of the higher education system by recruiting their students solely on the basis of the *concours* which each organizes annually. These entrance exams are highly selective both in terms of the written tests they feature, but also the socially biased character of their oral exams.[14] Indeed, this is why even today only 17%

of *grande école* students managed to gain access to their school immediately after their *baccalauréat*. For the remainder, a period of preparation for sitting the *concours* is undertaken that tends to take one of two forms.

The first is to enrol in a type of schooling formally called '*classes prépara-toires*' and known commonly as '*prépa*'. This singularly French institution, which accounts for only 7% of first-year higher education students, takes the form of an intense form of teaching that lasts two years and is aimed purely at the passing of entrance exams to one or more *grandes écoles*. Initially divided between science-centred *prépa* and literature-centred ones, Muriel Darmon (2013) has shown how and why a third branch centred upon eco-nomics and business has become at least equally important since the mid-1970s. However, these schools are by no means open to anyone who wants to attend them. Rather selection begins right here, a process reflected in 60% of *prépa* pupils coming from the upper or upper-middle class (i.e. from only 18% of the population) (Darmon, 2013: 16). Moreover, as Pierre Bourdieu in particular has underlined, in *prépa* one is very much a pupil, not a student (1989: 112). Indeed, according to his much-quoted analysis, given that within the *prépa* format working under urgency is 'an initiation-driven test' all about producing and rewarding 'docility', 'personal' research is discouraged in favour of syntheses of the lectures and reading set by one's '*maîtres*' [sic] (pp. 114, 123, 131). In any event, the results are clear: in 2016 no less than 38.5% of *grande école* students had studied in a *prépa*.

A second way of accessing an administrative or business-centred *grande école* is to begin one's higher education in a less prestigious *école* such as an *Institut d'études politiques*. Today known more often as *Sciences Po*,[15] these institutes offer five-year courses during which training for *concours* of either the *grandes écoles* or *corps* of the state is systematically an option. In reality, the careers now open to students who have been to a *Sciences Po* range widely from that of local civil servant, being an official in an international NGO or a manager of a large company. What is important to underline, however, is that *Sciences Po Paris* is clearly the best stepping stone for getting into the *Ecole nationale d'administration* (ENA), and thence the senior French civil service, via a fast-track system of recruitment and promotion.

As for the *prépas*, it is also crucial to stress that actually getting into a 'school' like a *Sciences Po* again entails passing a *concours*. Given the coded nature of how 'quality' and 'potential' is assessed by those marking these *concours*, once again social selection kicks in right from this stage, despite recent attempts made by some such 'schools' to attenuate this process. Indeed, just as in most *prépas*, at least until the fourth or fifth year, emphasis is placed upon learning how to synthesize and present orally, as well as regurgitating the content of set-piece lectures, rather than individual or group work that bears much relation to social science research. Consequently, at least during years 1 to 3, such schools tend strongly to train generalists better suited to working within public or private bureaucracies rather than science-informed research centres, NGOs or consultancies.

To sum up a subject that lies at the heart of how French social, economic and political elites are produced and consistently reproduced, it is vital to grasp that the institution of the *grande école* has had considerable influence both upstream and downstream of the years during which it trains a small, select tranche of France's youth.[16] As we have just seen, upstream of these schools lie the well-resourced *prépa* establishments and specialized schools, all of which are characterized by the *concours* that is their gatekeeper and the weight they place upon *formation* rather than academic learning *per se*. Moreover, to this list should be added the small number of prestigious *lycées* which, albeit public, are also selective due to the socio-spatial barriers they each possess. Meanwhile, downstream of the *grandes écoles* lies facilitated access into either the state's most prestigious ministries (e.g. Finance and Economic Affairs or the diplomatic corps), or a fast-tracked position within a large French company.[17] The principle of 'merit' may be omnipresent throughout, but this commitment is more procedural than one driven by a deep-seated desire to render France a more egalitarian country (Charles, 2015: 68, 81).

'Technical' higher education: selection of the fittest amongst 'the less fit'

Selectivity legitimated by procedural fairness is not, however, the monopoly of the *grandes écoles*, far from it. Indeed, and rather incongruously, this type of selection also lies at the heart of a broad band of technical higher education establishments within which many of France's skilled workers are trained between the ages of 18 and 20. Structured by two different types of diploma – the *Brevet de technicien supérieur* (*BTS*) and the *Diplôme universitaire de technologie* (*DUT*) – these schools are also only open to teenagers who are seen as 'suitable' by those who run them. Although none of these organizations actually hold *concours* to structure this selection process, they all proceed by analysis of results obtained at *lycée* and examination of 'letters of motivation'. Moreover, once again the emphasis is upon training to do specific tasks rather than upon learning in the broadest sense of the word. The latter point is perhaps unsurprising given the subject matter at the heart of either a *BTS* or a *DUT*. But what is startling is that the rapid rise in this form of higher education since the mid-1980s has had such durable effects upon the system as a whole, as well as more widely in French society.

If much has indeed changed over the past thirty years, it is also important to note that both the *BTS* and the *DUT* have longer histories which largely support the argument just made. In the case of the *BTS*, it was put in place in 1952 ostensibly to encourage the regeneration of skilled or semi-skilled work within numerous professions. In practice, this meant the creation of specialized technical schools initially attached to many *collèges*, then subsequently to certain *lycées*. As a two-year diploma, the *BTS* progressively became institutionalized within the educational system without attracting high take-up until the rise in unemployment that began to strike French youth as of the late 1970s. Indeed, as Orange underlines, it was really during the 1980s that the *BTS* began to take off, experiencing a growth of 194% in student numbers over this period (Orange, 2011: 174). Ever since, more stable growth patterns have taken root, thereby remodelling today's *BTS* system within which, each year, around 50% of its students hail from the *bac technologique*, a further 10–15% from the *bac pro* and the remainder from *bacs* obtained from generalist *lycées*. What is also important to retain is the type of teaching that predominates within *BTS* courses. Although a certain proportion of each two-year course is reserved for internships (twelve weeks in total), most teaching is lecture-based and very similar to that practised within *lycées*: students spend between twenty-five and thirty hours a week listening to lectures and taking notes. Indeed, this high level of continuity with the senior level of high school is regularly lauded by *BTS* teachers as being one of the assets of this form of higher education. From this angle, *BTS*s are presented to future students and their parents as being 'totally different from *la fac*' (university) – the latter being caricatured as 'unstructured' and abjectly lacking in student accompaniment.

In contrast to *BTS*s which are studied for in high schools, the *DUT* diploma is obtained in an *Institut universitaire de technologie* (*IUT*), i.e. actually within universities. Created in 1969 following the furore of May 1968 (Musselin, 2001: 59), the *IUT*s are therefore distinct parts of each university which possess two distinguishing features. First, their students still study for only two years (as for *BTS*s but unlike the rest of university courses). Secondly, their staff also have the right to select their students in order to fit the pre-set number of student slots allocated to them by the Ministry of Education and, since 2007, their respective university. As with many *BTS* courses, *IUT* ones recruit a great deal from the *bac technologique* and *pro* paths (around 30%). But many of their students possess instead a *bac général* in either *économie et société* or *sciences* (Orange, 2011: 174). Despite the often highly specialized nature of *IUT* teaching, many students now prefer to go to these institutes rather than 'take their chances' by choosing a more general course at university.

Indeed, despite concerns that the generalized shift in French higher education since the mid-2000s to the European standard rhythm of 3–2–3 years (a BA, an MA, a PhD) would sap the legitimacy and worth of both the *DUT* and the *BTS*, for the moment they have held up in student numbers and continue to receive strong political support from young people, educational administrators, employers and politicians alike. Notwithstanding this apparent success, the social impact of this type of higher education has nonetheless given rise to some controversy. On the one hand, specialists of the transition from education to employment have highlighted that *BTS* and *IUT* students benefit from having studied in an environment where paths to work, and how best to get on them, are constantly dealt with in the classroom (Delès, 2018: 50–52). Allied to the fact that each diploma is linked to a profession or vocation, this means that when students leave their respective course, the quest for a job has been normalized as something that does not need to be dramatized or even be a source of worry. Specialists of societal inequalities, on the other hand, are often strongly critical of these two types of diploma for two reasons. First, many criticize them for their 'utilitarianism', some even going so far as to conclude that they reflect a handing over of prioritizing educational content to the owners and managers of private companies (Orange, 2010).[18] Second, *BTS* and *IUT* courses are also criticized for their selective character, the argument here being that this not only reduces the recruitment chances of students from unfavourable social and family backgrounds, but also creates inequalities in terms of resources with the rest of the university system (Beaud and Mauger, 2017). Indeed, in order to grasp the meaning attached to the latter point in France, one must at last turn more directly to that attached to 'university' itself.

Universities: an option too often chosen by default

As Musselin has so clearly shown (2001, 2017), until the 1990s universities in France developed on the basis of faculties and therefore disciplines. Consequently, they rarely became independent and interdisciplinary organizations capable of and authorized to develop strategies and integrate into their respective local communities. This began to change when the Ministry of Education introduced a process of contractualization with each university in 1989, and has accelerated considerably since 2007 when much greater 'autonomy' has been granted to each of them. Partly encouraged by the EU's 'Lisbon' agenda and international higher education rankings, over the past ten to twenty years most French universities have been put under pressure to improve both their research and teaching outputs and outcomes. Given that our focus here is how students experience university, priority will be given to examining their points of entry into this form of education, what they experience within it and, finally, the impact of what they leave with upon their respective 'life chances'.

As regards getting into university in France, the basic principles are that anyone with a *bac* can do. Moreover, since fees are so low (between 150 and

600 euros per year; free for need-based grant-holders), money should not be an obstacle either. In practice, because for their first year certain courses in certain universities are oversubscribed, varying forms of selection at entry have in fact been deployed for many years. What the government under Macron's presidency has sought to do since 2017 has been to legally autho-rize this selection and to formalize it using a computerized application sys-tem aimed at all *lycéens* (Parcoursup: Frouillou *et al.*, 2019). Although many students, parents and academics have seen this policy change as positive in that it clarifies and systematizes a process that had, in their eyes, become chaotic and often arbitrary (for some courses, students' names were drawn out of a hat), others have seen it as an attack upon the very principle of 'university for all' (Bodin and Orange, 2019). This explains the intensity and venom which have marked debates over this issue, as well as the much-publicized student strikes and sit-ins which, in 2017–18, so frequently accompanied them.

One of the key arguments made by proponents of student selection at entry is that it ought to provide a means of responding to a key aspect of the actual experience of going to university that has been problematic since at least the 1990s: the high-level of drop-outs after the first year. At nearly 50%, this 'evaporation' rate is highlighted by those in favour of student selection, who claim that this not only reflects low student investment in their courses and high levels of absenteeism, but more fundamentally, it discredits univer-sity as an institution. Indeed, many claim that 'hypocrisy' over selection feeds a popular discourse of 'anything but *la fac*' and thence the rise of private education, notably in the form of business schools.[19] Opponents to such selection reply that although drop-out figures are high, this is only the case for certain subjects (notably law). Moreover, the first year at university should, in any case, be framed as a period during which students confirm whether or not they are on the right course. In addition, they argue that more resources should be devoted to first-year teaching in order to bring down class sizes from the heights they so often reach (lecture theatres of more than 500 are still common) and, above all, put in place practices that accompany students during their transition between *lycée* and university. More generally, as Beaud and Convert underline, 'university missed its rendez-vous with the working class during the period 1985–95, i.e. when it could have introduced a form of pedagogy designed to help children from this class to get through the crucial first year of their studies' (2010: 11).

Whether one sides with either the pro- or anti-selection cause, what is patently obvious is that for many subject areas, notably the social sciences and the humanities, French universities are drastically underfunded as com-pared to either their foreign equivalents or the *grandes écoles*. Apart from class sizes and therefore teaching methods, this underfunding is often reflected in the poor quality and upkeep of the buildings within which they take place, not to mention the workload and morale of university adminis-trators and academics. More fundamentally still, the very experience of going to university for many students is rendered much less pleasurable than in many other countries, in particular because any emphasis upon learning itself constantly runs the risk of being trumped by either the top-down and undiscussed transmission of knowledge favoured by much of the teaching staff, or simply fear of the next exam. Moreover – and crucially – such an experience of higher education is particularly prevalent for students from less-favoured social and family backgrounds. As we have seen earlier, rela-tively few such young people actually reach higher education, and those who do succeed are much more likely to do so via a university course than a *BTS, IUT* or, of course, a *grande école*. Given the way university is struc-tured and orientated, however, for such students the transition to higher education is frequently extremely difficult. Indeed, through in-depth ethno-graphical research, Stéphane Beaud has shown how the French university system has produced 'the deferred elimination' of working-class teenagers not only from the educational system, but ultimately from the world of ful-filling work itself. He therefore denounces an education system for leaving so many young people from challenging backgrounds in a 'no man's land' where they have neither succeeded nor totally failed (Beaud, 2002: 14, 16, 308).

In turn, one can only begin to understand how higher education is struc-tured in France, then structures much of its population, by realizing that so many of those who go to university in this country do so by default, i.e. because they have not managed to access a *grande école*, an *IUT*, a *BTS* course or, increasingly, an expensive private business school. Far from being caused simply by a highly visible public/private cleavage, as in so many countries, however, this situation is directly attributable to the state and its underlying republican doctrines and dogmas. Consequently, the higher edu-cation system as a whole actually makes different types of higher education establishments compete with each other, but on a playing field that is cer-tainly not level. Indeed, its 'slope' consistently helps certain types of estab-lishment and student, whilst penalizing others.

Conclusion

Taken together, the institutions, power relations and values which structure French intermediate, high-school then higher education have fundamental effects upon French society as a whole. The organizations concerned have deep and durable effects upon all the children, teenagers and post-adolescents who pass through them, i.e. virtually every person in the country (bar the migrants who, once arrived, nevertheless then have to interact with products of this system). As in most other nations, these effects include the confirmation or intensification of social inequalities and, therefore, life chances. What is more specific to France, however, is that this process, and the educational field more generally, is so centred upon the obtaining of diplomas and certificates. This concrete outcome of the philosophical and ideological commitment to 'merit', and the reduction of the latter to sets of procedures which ostensibly equalize the competition between young people (Charles, 2015: 68), para-doxically tends to intensify social inequalities rather than ameliorate them. Indeed, as Charles underlines, the overall result is profoundly dualistic: those who benefit from the French mode of selection are protected from arbitrary processes, often for life, whereas the non-selected lose everything, including hope (2016: 164). Ultimately, as Van Zanten underlines, this is why 'equal opportunities' in France fits closest to a 'liberal ideology centred upon the individual', rather than more egalitarian value hierarchies.[20]

Of course, as others have argued, school, and by extension higher education, cannot be held responsible for social inequalities that extend way beyond it. Like many other countries, France lacks a genuine policy for the young that is tuned in to the types of challenges which so deeply affect adolescents and post-adolescents (Dubet and Duru-Bellat, 2015: 100, 114). Moreover, with-out addressing fundamental social inequalities more directly than it does, the French state currently tends to expect too much from formalized educa-tion. It therefore constantly runs the risk of crushing teachers, lecturers and professors under a responsibility they simply cannot live up to. Indeed, in their comparative study of national approaches to education, Dubet *et al.* rightly recall that most of what we know we learn outside formalized edu-cation. Nevertheless, as they then conclude, at least in the case of France, schools and higher education organizations could still be better – particularly if the societal institutions and power relations which structure both them and education as a whole were recalibrated through political work to sys-tematically encourage each of these establishments to be 'the best they pos-sibly could be' (2010: 182–193).

Notes

1 www.cnesco.fr/wpcontent/uploads/2017/12/171208_Dossier_Synthese_Decro-chage_scolaire.pdf, consulted 7th October 2019.
2 As Dubet *et al.* underline, 'schooling systems do not just reflect social inequalities, they shape them in specific ways' (2010: 74). See also Charles (2014).
3 This is what Van Zanten has called an 'over-valuing of the experience' of teachers and undervaluing of education science and research (2006: 242).

4 Seven main disciplines are taught in this way: French, maths, history-geography, life sciences, physics-chemistry, languages and 'technology'. In addition, 'moral and civic education', physical education, art and music are also part of the standard curriculum.

5 These points relate in particular to the number of years worked, how many children each teacher themselves has, where they have worked previously and, above all, whether or not they entered the profession having passed a specialized exam in their discipline (*l'agrégation*).

6 On these points, see a recent issue of the journal *Formation-Emploi*: https://journals.openedition.org/formationemploi/6703, consulted 10th November 2019.

7 As Scott underlines, declaring wearers of headscarves to be 'enemies of the Republic' has 'rendered non-negotiable exactly that which has to be negotiated: the integration of different individuals and different kinds of individuality into a nation which had never been as homogeneous as its self-styled representatives claimed it to be' (2007: 150).

8 This expression translates a quote from Beaud (2002: 20).

9 It is important to underline that the generalized extension of the *lycée* system has largely been achieved through the creation of very large schools and high class sizes (the average public *lycée général* has 1,072 pupils, whilst the average for private schools is 439; their respective class sizes are 30.1 and 26.8).

10 This difference has been attributed, in particular by Maurice *et al.* (1982), to a deep 'societal effect'. Culpepper has subsequently analysed the French approach to the training of young people by seeking to explain the very low retention of French apprentices within firms compared to Germany. Indeed, this often results in the subsidized hiring of low-paid workers, then a discarding of them (2003: 87, 133 ff.). According to his analysis, this stems from a failure to convince companies to co-operate together, explained in turn by the weak aggregating capacity of employers' organizations, regional councils and unions. As he concludes, 'indiscriminate subsidies to companies for hiring trainees do not promote investment in general skills' (p. 192). See also more recent pleas for greater coproduction of training by companies alongside public bureaucracies (Bourdes *et al.*, 2014: 115).

11 According to Dubet, for example, it is above all meritocratic schooling that needs replacing by 'schools which seek to train individuals to be capable of behaving and mobilizing themselves whatever the level of their academic skills'. In so doing, he considers one would also remove the 'yoke' currently around the neck of teenagers and young adults by changing the conditions under which they enter the world of work (2014: 17).

12 Eight of today's *grandes écoles* stem from this era (*Polytechnique, Ponts et Chaussées, l'Ecole des Mines, Saint-Cyr, Navale, Normale supérieure, Agro, Vétérinaire*), two more were added in the nineteenth century (*Arts et métiers –* today's *CNAM*) and twentieth century (today's *Télécom Paris Tech*). To the list must be added the well-known *Ecole nationale d'administration* (ENA, founded in 1945) and *Hautes études commerciales* (HEC, founded in 1881, then reinvented in the early 1960s).

13 Indeed, this is the tenuous reason given for students at many of these schools actually being paid to go there. For example, in 2019 each *Polytechnicien* was paid 900 euros a month, whilst their opposite number at *ENA* received no less than 1342 euros. 'Grandes écoles: faut-il encore payer les élèves?', *Le Monde*, 20th July 1919.

14 As Allouch underlines, 'the concours is a radical form of selection that encourages social reproduction', generates 'a genuine market for the preparation' for them, and above all a pernicious form of 'social ranking' (Allouch, 2017: 10, 12, 26).

15 Of which, in addition to the largest and most prestigious (Paris), there are now nine: Bordeaux, Grenoble, Lyon, Toulouse, Rennes, Lille, Strasbourg, Aix-en-Provence and Saint-Germain-en-Laye.

16 Each year, only 2–3% of children from working-class backgrounds manage to access the *grandes écoles* (Beaud and Convert, 2010).

17 This said, the irony is that despite the financial and symbolic backing they constantly receive, many of the *grandes écoles* are no longer in sync with their initial objectives (e.g. today *Polytechnique* is as much about shaping business elites as it is about training civil servants specialized in industry and science; *ENA* has also increasingly been reorientated towards the world of finance and banking).

18 Indeed, some critics link what they see as a trend within education to a neo-liberal shift that has encouraged 'decollectivization', i.e. to firm-level bargaining as a means of undercutting labour market legislation or sectorial agreements (Baccaro and Howell, 2017: 89) (see chapter 3).

19 The number of students leaving these schools with a diploma has risen from 166,000 in 1990 to 484,000 in 2014.

20 Interview in *Le Monde*, 1st September 2018.

3

Going to work: Income, identity and collective action

Introduction

Just as in other countries, for most people in France working is first and foremost the activity through which they earn enough to live on and, wherever possible, make plans and investments for their future and that of their families. At the same time, because of the time one spends on it and especially the social meaning it possesses, work is also widely seen as defining who one is in society, whether one fits within it and self-perceptions of success or failure (Cousin, 2019). Indeed, through what Dubar calls 'the socialization of activity' (2010: 8), at work most individuals develop not only their skills, savoir faire and sense of self, but also collective identities. For these reasons, it is therefore impossible to understand either the French or the societal structures related to the labour market they have made without examining closely what work is in France, its meanings and effects.

In so doing, focusing upon work also enables this book to make its first in-depth exploration of the deep linkages between three key dimensions of socio-economic activity in contemporary France. First, work is deeply social, both in the sense that it involves collective action and is heavily structured by the modes of socialization set out in the previous two chapters. Secondly, and even more obviously, work is economic in the sense that most of it takes place either within organizations specifically designed to produce goods and services (i.e. companies of varying shapes and sizes) or within public entities whose vocation is to administer such productive activity (e.g. government ministries), or provide it with a variety of social services (ranging from schools to street lighting or cleaning). However, neither these social nor economic aspects of work are spontaneous emanations of supposedly natural 'markets'. Rather, work takes place within industries that are highly structured by institutions and asymmetric power relations within both the economic and bureaucratic fields. Alongside capital, workers, their skills and their costs are, and always have been, an integral part of any capitalism (Thelen, 2014). Indeed, this phenomenon has been rendered particularly salient in France by its much-publicized codification in labour law, notably between 1935 and 1970 (Didry, 2016). However, since the ending of regular growth in the mid-1970s, this centrality of labour, together with the institutions that shape it, is precisely why – often armed with 'globalization' scaremongering and neo-liberal policy recipes – representatives of capital in business and within the state have consistently sought to improve productivity rates and returns on investment by rendering work 'more flexible', less collective and more individualized (Castel, 2009: 24). Unsurprisingly, the representatives of labour have resisted such a trend, often but not always unsuccessfully. In all events, this renewal of the perennial tension between capital and labour provides this chapter with one of its central themes. Indeed, as has been convincingly shown by others (Méda and Vendramin, 2013), in France the historically antagonistic relationship between capital and labour has largely been replaced by another, more individualized, relationship opposing management and employees. Centred upon distinct organizations (companies, units of government, etc.) rather than social class, the emergence of increasingly individualized employment provides part of the following paradox: an unusually large proportion of the French population are deeply attached to work but are simultaneously unhappy with their respective workplace. To understand the first dimension of this paradox, this chapter will give considerable importance to the strong attachment to the sense of professional identity, and even of being an adult (Van de Velde, 2008), work so often provides in this country. Similarly, data will be presented to understand why French workplaces so often disappoint their personnel – a sense of disappointment that the sociologist Olivier Cousin likens to the bitter taste left by a failed love affair (2019).

A second theme tackled in this chapter concerns what is spontaneously defined as the opposite of work: unemployment. As the first section will underline, for the past forty-five years its continuously high level has had a lasting impact upon not only getting a job in France, but keeping it. This also links to the often 'precarious' conditions under which job retention takes place and the knock-on effects this has had upon self-esteem and identities. Moreover, unemployment has obviously placed France's social protection system under considerable strain. Indeed, work and social protection go hand in hand because when people are not in work, social protection can kick in or, alternatively, be used as a stick and carrot to 'get people back to work'. More revealingly still, work and social protection are integral parts of national approaches to economic policy in general and their underlying growth models in particular (Palier, 2018).

Beginning with an essentially structuralist depiction of work, non-work and their impact upon objective living conditions in France, this chapter then addresses its relationship to how a variety of workplaces are subjectively experienced. Having progressively revealed the institutions and power relations that structure work in France in this way, it goes on to analyse directly two sets of actors at the forefront of political work aimed at chang-ing or reproducing them: trade unions and business organizations. In so doing, the themes of 'flexibility' v. workers' rights' and 'social protection v. growth' will be discussed throughout. More generally, in the light of the information it generates on social mobility and how this has affected the value systems of individuals, the chapter will also begin to apply a generic social science question regarding 'moral economy' to France's contemporary population: what is 'their notion of economic justice and their working defi-nition of exploitation, i.e. their view of which claims on their product [are] tolerable or intolerable' (Thompson, 1968; Scott, 1976: 3–4). In short, by examining how and why the French work, I will attempt to shed light upon how, in the recent past, much of the population concerned have reacted to increased individualization at the workplace on the one hand and, on the other, shifts within materialism – shifts that go beyond the satisfaction of basic needs to include socially constructed desires of a quite different character.

The work–wealth–poverty relationship

Having first set out what people in France actually do in terms of work, one can then go on to examine its relationship to the highly uneven levels of income which this country features.

Where people work (or don't)

As Table 3.1 sets out, in 2014 around two-thirds of France's potential working population (between 16-year-olds and retirees) were in work, one in ten were unemployed, another tenth were pupils or students and a further 15% were not part of the labour market for various other reasons (e.g. long-term illness).

As regards those members of the population in work, 20% still have man-ual jobs, 18% are managers or hold equivalent jobs, and no less than 53% do either administrative or low-level management tasks (see Table 3.2). In the French case, what is important to note first here is the rapid fall experi-enced in farming employment between 1955 and 1990 (down from 27% to 5% of the working population, then to 1.6% in 2017). If the timing of France's 'rural exodus' has similarities in countries such as Italy, it occurred much later than in the UK and Germany.[1] As for the decline in industrial jobs, however, this trend is not only more recent, but also the object of more frequent social and political comment and debate. Although the industrial heritage of France is no doubt less famous in the rest of the world than that of the UK or Germany, today's French population is heavily socialized by the education system, the mass media and a range of politicians from both left

Table 3.1 Work and other forms of activity, 2009 and 2014

	2009	2014
Potential working population (PWP)	41,713,368	41,786,338
PWP as ratio of total population %	71.7	73.5
Of which:		
Those in work	63.3	63.2
Currently unemployed	8.4	10.3
Students	10.4	10.3
The semi-retired	8.7	7.7
Other non-workers (invalids, etc.)	9.1	8.5

Source: INSEE, www.insee.fr/fr/statistiques/4277653?sommaire=4318291, consulted 10th May 2020.

Table 3.2 Employment by profession and gender, 2016

	%	% Men	% Women
Farming	1.8	2.6	1
Artisans, shopkeepers, small business owners	6.6	9	4
Managers, teachers	17.8	20.4	14.9
Intermediary professions	25.8	23.6	28.2
Office workers	27.4	12.6	43.2
Manual workers	20.3	31.5	8.3
Others	0.4	0.4	0.4
Total	26,584,000	13,761,000	12,823,000

Source: INSEE, www.insee.fr/fr/statistiques/2381478, consulted 10th May 2020.

and right into believing in the might of French-made products in industries ranging from cars (Renault, Peugeot, Citroën) and aircraft (the Concorde, the Mirage, the Rafale) to nuclear power. Although the commercial success of many of these products is debatable, the mythology that surrounds them is crushingly consensual. Part of its resonance stems from the cult of the engineer that has been promoted, in particular by the *grandes écoles*, since at least the Enlightenment, the Revolution and the Napoleonic era. But the meaning still attached to 'national' industrial products has also been deeply affected by the role many of them played within France's post-war economic boom. Indeed, numerous sectors in France industrialized during a period that is very much still within living memory of many of its citizens. This is important because it also explains the salience of evidence and debate over the 'industrial decline' the country is repeatedly said to have experienced since the mid-1970s. As Table 3.3 highlights, whilst it is still ahead of the UK, France now has fewer industrial workers than Italy and, above all, Germany. In their place, a range of tertiary jobs have developed, particularly within industries such as tourism. Just as importantly, if manual labourers still account for 20% of all French workers, no less than 27% more are low-level office workers. Moreover, of those with some kind of management responsibilities (44%), more than two-thirds are in hierarchically inferior positions.[2]

From a separate but just as important angle, the high rate of female employment in contemporary France should also be highlighted: in 2014, women accounted for no less than 48% of all jobs. This said, as already mentioned in chapter 1, it is important to supplement these figures on gender by others relating to part-time employment on the one hand, and levels of seniority on the other. From the first angle, as Table 3.4 underlines, in France 30% of employed women work part-time. As we saw in chapter 1, in many instances this figure includes women who take Wednesdays off to look after their children and who therefore work as much as 80% of the time (as do a tiny minority of men). Within this third of French female workers who are part-time, many others, of course, have much shorter working weeks. Notwithstanding these figures, however, one still needs to recall that in relative terms French women are in paid employment much more than their counterparts in countries such as Germany.

As regards senior positions in the private or public sectors, like every other country in the world bar those of Scandinavia, France continues to

Table 3.3 Share of workers by sector in five large European countries, 2016

	France	*Germany*	*Spain*	*Italy*	*UK*
Agriculture	1.1	0.7	3	2.6	0.6
Industry	15.2	22.3	15	23	12
Construction	5.4	6.1	5	5	5
Trad. services	32.4	32	42	35.5	35
Non-market services	33.5	27.9	25	24.6	33
Qualified tertiary	11	10.8	10	9	14.4

Source: DARES, 'Comparaisons européennes des durées du travail', *Document d'études* number 220, 2018.

Table 3.4 Rate of part-time employment for men and women (%)

	France	*Germany*	*Netherlands*	*Italy*	*UK*
Women	30	48	78	32	38
Men	7	9	28	8	10
Total	19	25	50	20	25

Source: DARES, 'Comparaisons européennes des durées du travail', *Document d'études* number 220, 2018.

feature very few women. Whilst it is true that in France 'only' 62% of all 'bosses' (including supervisors) are now male – a rate similar to that of the UK (60%) but which still contrasts sharply with Scandinavian countries such as Sweden (52%) (Eurofound, 2017) – a 'glass ceiling effect' still very much exists. This is because the level of gender inequality climbs dramatically as soon as one restricts the category of bosses to senior managers. In 2008, only 17% of the management of private companies and just 7% of their boards of directors were women. Meanwhile, if 57% of all civil servants are women, amongst its 4,200-strong hierarchy, only 16% were women in 2005 (Laufer, 2014).

Alongside these long-term trends, the period 1975 to 2020 has, of course, been marked just as deeply by the dramatic rise, then stabilization at high levels, of unemployment. Moreover, the very definition of 'the unemployed' has undergone significant shifts (Demazière, 2019). As the chronology set out in Table 3.5 recalls, since the mid-1980s the number of people of a working age without a job in France has oscillated between 2.3 and 3 million, i.e. 8–10%.

In addition, it is crucial to underline that the highest levels of unemployment are concentrated in certain regions (notably the north-east and the south – see Table 3.6, and especially parts thereof, e.g. the north-eastern outer suburbs of Paris, parts of Marseille).

As sociologists have explained in depth, being unemployed nearly always has deep effects both objectively in terms of revenue and subjectively in terms of self-perception and how one is seen by others (Demazière, 1995). Moreover, for much of the remainder of the population, high levels of unemployment create not only difficulties in finding a job and the fear of losing it once one has done so, but also engender a generalized sentiment of 'precariousness' as regards employment *per se*.

The latter point is particularly salient in France because, as Demazière and Zune (2016) underscore, job stability in this country is often measured against a 'golden age' when 'the permanent contract' was the norm. For instance, in 1982, 94% of wage earners had permanent contracts – a contract which, at least at that time, was very difficult to 'lose'. Today this figure has only fallen to 87%. However, what is crucial to realize is that for

Table 3.5 The number of unemployed since 1974 (millions)

1974	1977	1982	1993	2000	2006	2010	2016	2018
0.5	1	2	3	2.2	2.3	2.5	3	2.7

Source: INSEE, *Marchés de travail*, downloaded 30th November 2018, updated 10th May 2020.

Table 3.6 The ten *départements* where unemployment was highest, 2016 (%)

Pyrénées-Orientales	15.4
Hérault	13.9
Aisne	13.7
Gard	13.5
Aude	13.4
Vaucluse	12.9
Seine-Saint Denis	12.8
Aube	12.6
Nord	12.6
Pas de Calais	12.3

Source: INSEE, *Données du 3e trimestre 2016, Observatoire des inégalités*, July 2017 (at the time, the national unemployment rate was 9.7%).

persons under 25 in work, no less than 50% of them are on short-term contracts (v. 10% of the equivalent cohort thirty years ago). Indeed, the ratio is even less favourable for unskilled or low-qualified workers. Moreover, these figures need examining alongside others that pertain to the time it takes for young people to enter the job market at all. For example, a recent report highlights that as much as 9% of young people take up to three years after leaving full-time education to get a job (CEREQ, 2018).

To sum up all the important information presented above in a few words, the world of employment in France has become an extremely tough one. As elsewhere, this world is much less predictable than that experienced by cohorts born during or just after the Second World War (Demazière, 2020). Moreover, as will be shown below, in France this trend has been experienced widely as a form of social demotion (*déclassement*). In turn, this contributes to a form of generalized anxiety about the future that is rarely as prevalent in other countries.

Income, wealth and poverty

In capitalist societies where savings, investments and inheritance can also generate substantial differences in incomes, it is, of course, important not to just examine rates of hourly wages or salaries. Nevertheless, before proceeding to more sophisticated analyses of wealth, Tables 3.7 and 3.8 provide some basic data about the income that most of France's population receive in the form of wages or salaries.

As is well known, the French economist Thomas Piketty (2014) has headed up a long-term and in-depth research programme that has sought to look in more detail at wealth in capitalist societies, as well as the degrees of inequality that it encompasses. Although his dataset extends considerably beyond France, the parts pertaining to this country are of direct interest to this

Table 3.7 Hourly wage rates in 2016 by category of employment (euros)

	Total	Women	Men	ratio W/M
Total	14.7	13.0	15.8	82.3
Managers	26	22.4	27.8	80.6
Intermediate professions	14.7	13.6	15.6	87.2
Office workers	10.5	10.3	11.0	93.6
Manual workers	11.0	9.7	11.3	85.8

Source: INSEE, www.insee.fr/fr/statistiques/2021266#consulter, consulted 10th May 2020.

Table 3.8 Average annual revenue, 2016 (euros)

Total	20,666
Women	17,815
Men	23,398
Less than 25 years old	7,362
Age 25–39	18,963
Age 40–49	23,935
Age 50–54	25,367
Age 55 and over	24,598
Managers	40,455
Intermediate professions	22,944
Office workers	13,988
Manual workers	15,282
Those without the *baccalauréat*	17,529
Baccalauréat + 2	23,064
Baccalauréat + 3 or greater	36,537

Source: INSEE, www.insee.fr/fr/statistiques/2381326, consulted 10th May 2020.

chapter. His overall argument is that at the national scale aggregate levels of income inequality have certainly dropped over the last century (by 15% according to his calculations, meaning that just 1% of France's population now generate their income solely from their own capital (2014: 278)). However, this drop can chiefly be ascribed to the relative loss of earnings by the richest owners of capital (the *rentiers*) experienced essentially in the period 1914–45. In the strict sense of wage inequalities, however, their reduction has been negligible. Indeed, since the 1990s there has been a sharp rise in salaries for managers, and top managers in particular, which have reinforced overall inequalities considerably (290). Indeed, whereas by 1980 the rate of total national wage income captured by the top 10% of French earners had fallen to 31% (from 37% in 1960 and 45% in 1900), by 2010 it had crept back up to 33% (p. 323). Indeed, when one adds in earnings from capital investments of varying kinds, in 2010 the top 10% of the highest wealth holders in France owned between 60% and 65% of the country's total wealth (p. 340) (of which the top 1% accounted for no less than one-third).

Even more tellingly, France continues to feature high levels of poverty. Certainly, as Table 3.9 shows, the percentage of its population who are officially 'poor' is lower than in the UK, Italy or Spain. Moreover, there is no doubt that the level of social transfers accorded to certain categories of beneficiaries in France is higher than in all three of those countries and that this protects many of the vulnerable, and particularly those in unemployment, from abject poverty (see Table 3.10). Nevertheless, and despite these social transfers, the French ratio of the poor has remained remarkably stable over the last fifteen years.

Table 3.9 People at risk of poverty or social exclusion in the EU, 2008 and 2017

	2008	*2017*
France	18.5	17.1
Denmark	16.3	17.2
Netherlands	14.9	17
Germany	20.1	19
Belgium	20.8	20.3
UK	23.2	22.2
Ireland	23.7	24.2
Italy	25.5	28.9
Spain	23.8	26.6
Greece	28.1	34.8
Portugal	26	23

Note: Here the EU's poverty rate is used, i.e. poverty is defined as having an income less than 60% of the country's median. As Paugam (2013: 6) rightly reminds us, the way poverty is defined is critical to how it is measured. For example, changing this criterion from 60% to 50%, as many countries do in their own official statistics, lowers their publicized poverty rate dramatically.

Source: Eurostat, 'Downward trend in the share of persons at risk of poverty in the EU' (news release 16th October 2018).

Table 3.10 Rate of poverty amongst different parts of each population in 2010 after social transfers

	% of the employed	*% of the unemployed*	*% of the total population*
France	6.2	33.1	11.8
Germany	7.2	70.3	15
UK	6.8	47.4	15.7
Italy	9.4	43.6	16.8
Spain	12.7	38.7	19.7

Source: EU-SILC (EU Statistics on Income and Living Conditions), www.eui.eu/Research/Library/ResearchGuides/Economics/Statistics/DataPortal/EU-SILC, consulted 20th October 2019.

Wealth and poverty rates are, of course, the subject of in-depth research and intense debate that cannot seriously be discussed here. Their comparison across countries and regions and over time is particularly complex. Moreover, as Paugam has so convincingly shown (2013), it is even more important to generate and analyse data on how poverty is categorized and represented not only by those involved in public policymaking, but above all by the people most directly affected by it. Crucially, the same should be said more generally for employment. This is precisely why our analysis now needs to turn back to the issue of work, this time from the angle of how it is experienced and portrayed by the workers themselves.

The meaning attached to work: from collective identities to individualized 'paths'?

Indeed, simply describing where people in France work or are unemployed ultimately tells us little about why this is important to them or to the French polity and society. Of course, as we have just seen, actual earnings are vital for virtually all the population and differences between them participate strongly in social distinctions and differences. But the meaning of work goes even deeper because this touches directly upon how each person interprets their socio-economic role and even their social worth. For this reason, it is important to spend some time here examining first how people in France today perceive work in general, before focusing in particular upon how they envisage the hierarchies that this part of their lives entails. As regulationist economics has encapsulated within its key concept of 'the wage relationship', work is not just about a transaction between the employer and the employee. It also concerns the subordination of the latter to the former (Boyer, 2015; Gourges and Yon, 2018). Indeed, re-examining this relationship today is particularly heuristic because it has clearly changed considerably since the days when large factories and collective identities predominated, without, however, giving rise to a clear-cut alternative that has been successfully legitimized.

What work means to the French: money, social worth and rights

Although in France it did not last all that long, the 'Fordist' era (which featured strong divisions of labour, lifelong employment, regular wage increases and favoured security over individual freedom) continues to strongly mark the social imagination of much of this country's population. Featuring large units of creation or assembly, strong 'Taylorist' divisions of labour, relatively high trade union membership and a hands-on form of management, Fordism lay at the centre of French capitalism from at least 1945 to 1985 (and in certain sectors had predominated since the 1920s). Moreover, in many instances (e.g. for steel) production was organized in such a way as to accentuate concentrations of not only working-class jobs, but neighbourhoods, schools and other services. In this way Fordism was not just an economic phenomenon, it also strongly structured the social fabric of an urbanizing France and its quest for a new socio-political model. In a word, work within Fordist companies was a guiding light. Given the centrality of its institutions, when they began to break down as of the mid-1970s, the consequences were deep and largely uncontrolled. Indeed, the dramatic shift that has ensued is one from a world where work provided clear paths towards social mobility and self-acceptance, to one where it is *the* source of uncertainty, self-doubt and distrust of the rest of society (Dubet, 2019). As Bigi *et al.* put it, for most workers they are no longer asked 'to scrupulously follow a script, but to be adaptable and able to confront a range of risks' (2015: 11).

Public opinion data on perceptions of work provide an initial illustration of both this trend and its effects. Méda and Vendramin (2013: 94–104), for example, highlight 'the French paradox' as regards work: if respondents in France declare that it is important to them markedly more than their colleagues in other European countries (67% v. 50% in UK and Sweden), 65% of them are also more likely to wish that work took up less of their lives than other activities (a figure that is again around 50% in the UK and Sweden).

The most recent European Working Conditions Survey (EWCS) upon which those figures were drawn also includes 'work intensity' and 'social environment' indexes. These highlight that although France is just below the EU average in terms of perceptions of how hard work is, perceptions of hierarchies in the workplace are the worst in the EU (Eurofound, 2017: 47, 65). We return to that finding below, but here it is important to supplement it with data on how respondents to the survey see the fit between their work and commitments elsewhere in their lives. Here only 76% of French responses consider that this fit is satisfactory, a rate that is amongst the lowest in Europe alongside that of Montenegro and Serbia. In contrast, 89% of Norwegians interviewed considered that their work fitted well with the rest of their lives (Eurofound, 2017: 114). A final set of data concerning 'self-reported ability to work until the age of 60' will be used to complete this sketch of how workers in France perceive their own working lives. Here, and once again, France has the lowest figure, with only 53% of women and 56% of men considering that they could go on being workers until the age of 60. These figures contrast sharply with the 84% of German women and 86% of men, or 75% and 77% of their British counterparts, who make equivalent projections (Eurofound, 2017: 121).

Qualitative data derived from longer, face-to-face interviews or ethno-graphic observation provide a means of deepening analysis of why such a high proportion of workers in France are so dissatisfied with where they work and what they experience whilst they are there. For example, Bigi *et al.*'s detailed study used just such research methods. It reveals many of the reasons why recognition in the workplace is today seen as so important, together with why so many of those in employment consider that their efforts are insufficiently recognized by their managers, or even their imme-diate colleagues (2015). This research shows first that recognition has become such an important criterion in France largely because of the break-ing down of collective identities which enabled many workers to experience their time at work positively during the Fordist era. In so doing, they add more support to Castel's thesis that the replacement of Fordism by a diverse, less predictable pattern of working arrangements, together with the 'chroni-cization' of unemployment, has generated a widespread perception that work has been individualized. This perception has in turn encouraged indi-vidualistic thought and action (Castel, 2009).

Secondly, Bigi *et al.*'s interviews also show that because many workers now consider that their jobs are precarious (either because their company might fold or because staff cuts are a latent threat), they have become par-ticularly sensitive to how they think they are being evaluated. Indeed, this trend is exacerbated by the rise in the rate of temporary work. Other effects of this trend will be examined below, but here it is important to stress that this has not just produced more uncertainty for those actually on short-term contracts, it has also often sapped solidarity between those with permanent jobs and those without. Indeed, Bigi *et al.* relate in detail how the status-affecting impact of contracts, which can even last a year or more, affects many workers. During such periods, many 'colleagues' on permanent con-tracts often make the life of the temporarily employed uncomfortable, and frequently downright unpleasant (2015: 148).

Standing back from the trends sketched out above, Méda and Vendramin heuristically conclude upon their combined impact around the three dimen-sions of work classically studied in the social sciences (2013: chapter 1). First, as regards work as income and security, they highlight once again that although judged in quantitative terms (and allowing for inflation) income for nearly all workers has continued to rise slowly since the 1990s, security levels are down. More importantly still, as we have seen above, perceptions of job security are much lower than hitherto. Drawing upon Marx's axiom that work is the essence of man [sic], Méda and Vendramin's second cut on work in contemporary France concerns its 'expressive' dimension, i.e. its contribution to feelings of self-realization or social integration (Méda, 2011: 29; Bigi *et al.*, 2015: 281). They conclude here that lower 'economic' security has had a fundamental and lasting impact through lowering the self-esteem of workers and their sense of social worth. Indeed, for these authors a generalized decline in the expressive dimension of work overlaps with the destabilization of its third dimension: how work contributes to redistributing revenue, rights and protections. They argue that whereas since the nineteenth century a relationship between the workplace and the recognition of political rights had essentially been striven for collectively via the actions of trade unions, today in France many quests for rights have become individuated (see also Bigi *et al.*, 2015: 289) or limited to the mobilization of increasingly narrow professions (such as pilots in the airline industry).

Hierarchies and subordination

Before proceeding to examine what French trade unions have become, however, it is first necessary to delve a little deeper into a key aspect of perceptions of work that relate to hierarchy at the workplace. This is important because authors such as Philippon (2007) consider that France does not suffer from 'a crisis of work' but rather from strong dissatisfaction with the form of management that is so predominant in its companies and organizations. The result is not 'a crisis of work' but 'a crisis in the capacity to work together' of workers and managers (2007: 20). Philippon's argument is that this management is typically highly concentrated, hierarchical and top-down – a trait attributed to the nomination and promotion of managers based either upon nepotism (within family firms) or upon the primary role accorded to higher education and exam results (exacerbated by the effects of the *grandes écoles* and *concours*, see chapter 2). Moreover, in many workplaces, this trait dovetails with an institutionalized penchant for the strict following of procedures and lines of management (resulting from the transposition of public bureaucracy norms to the private sector). Here we examine this thesis using data on perceptions from both managers and workers derived from public opinion polls, together with other information from more targeted, qualitative studies.

A way into this subject is first to note that according to the European Working Conditions Survey, in France relations between workers and their managers are perceived as being relatively bad: only 52% of respondents in France consider these relations to be good, compared to 60% for the EU as a whole and nearly 80% in Germany, Ireland and Portugal. The survey then goes on to pose more specific questions, such as the extent to which workers consider that they are usually consulted about any reorganization of their work. Here again France scores badly, because only 51% of respondents in this country consider that they are, compared to between 62% and 65% in countries such as the Netherlands, Ireland or Denmark. Similarly, perceptions of stress levels are again much higher in France (at 27%) than in the

Netherlands (10%) or Denmark (12%). Meanwhile, 'fatigue' related to work is a condition regularly experienced by 54% of respondents in France, whereas the EU average is only 35%. Finally, the survey also reveals high disappointment levels amongst the young as regards work satisfaction: in 2010, 31% of young French respondents considered that their level of qualifications meant they ought to be doing something more demanding (EWCS figures quoted by Méda and Vendramin, 2013: 98–99).

In order to better explain these figures, another study, the Third European Company Survey, provides more detail about worker–management relations. It shows first that as regards decision-making, this is only done jointly according to 34% of French respondents, thereby placing France firmly in a group with countries such as Spain, Latvia and Italy. Joint decision-making is reportedly much higher in Finland at 59%, and even higher in the UK at 41% (Eurofound, 2015: 52). But this study goes a stage further in defining a typology of company decision-making, then calculating the ratio of companies per type by country. As Table 3.11 highlights once again, the situation in France is dominated by perceptions of 'distant' management (50% in total) on the one hand, and 'involving' and 'interactive' approaches on the other (39%). It is therefore more accurate to conclude that there is a significant dualism within the way companies are managed in this country which is similar to Germany (40 v. 43%) and the UK (44 v. 43%), but quite different from the case of Finland (25% 'distant' v. 73% 'interactive and involving').

Moreover, if one returns to Bigi *et al.*'s qualitative analysis, in France a good manager is seen as showing recognition by being attentive, close to their staff and, in particular, never humiliating individual workers in public (2015: 187). However, their evidence shows that distance between management and workers is now the norm, thereby deepening a top-down operating mode, making the manager 'more a transmitter of decisions and choices' from the board to the workplace and thus not seen as accessible. Moreover, they have become more 'administrative' than actually engaged in the substantive issues which financing, producing or selling goods and services entails (2015: 197). Indeed, the general conclusion drawn from this research is even stronger:

Table 3.11 Workplace decision-making

	Systematic & involving	Interactive & involving	Externally orientated	Top-down, intern-orientated	Passive management
France	29	10	32	18	12
Finland	52	21	15	10	2
UK	29	14	26	18	13
Germany	27	16	22	18	17

Source: Eurofound (2015: 127).

'Work, its content and its modalities are the responsibility of companies and organizations which, in the French case have shown themselves to be particularly un-innovative in this respect. Most of them have joined in the universe of global competition without changing their ways of managing and accompanying their workers' (Bigi *et al.*, 2015: 295).

Some caution is necessary in interpreting the data presented above, first because there are obviously considerable differences within the thousands of workplaces that make up the French economic field. More fundamentally still, when examining perceptions of work and its management in any country, it is vital to recall that objectively there has never been 'a golden age of work' (Méda, 2010: xii). This is particularly important in contemporary France because nostalgia for the *'trente glorieuses'* often blurs analysis and debate, and this despite the fact that many studies have shown that work during the 1945–75 period was often far from 'glorious'. Nevertheless, as Méda underlines, it is particularly heuristic to analyse the extent to which French socio-economic life has moved towards what she calls 'sustainable work' (2010: xv, 325–328), i.e. a social practice and set of norms that gives work significance but not all-importance. Certain actors have sought and are seeking to achieve this very goal by reorganizing not only work but French society as a whole. It is now time to take a closer look at who some of them are and how they have gone about tackling this task over recent years.

Representing the interests of labour and capital

As we have just seen, the rules, norms and conventions which structure work and unemployment in France have been seriously destabilized and challenged since the 1970s. Some have changed considerably (e.g. rights to unemployment benefits), whereas others have evolved more slowly (e.g. access to professional training, individualization in the workplace) or hardly at all (e.g. the distance between managers and workers). How have the formal representatives of labour (trade unions) and of management (business organizations) adapted to these shifts and either accelerated or altered them through political work? By looking at each side in turn, some answers to the deeper question of what has caused change or reproduction will progressively be developed.

A fragmented and troubled trade union movement

France's reputation for strikes and demonstrations where trade unions are highly present is legendary. Many an outside observer can conjure up images of May 1968, the steel strikes of 1975–85, those of the winter of 1995 against the Juppé pension reform, or more recently the sustained resistance to the employment laws of 2016 and 2017 or the pension plans of 2019–20. Indeed, in France itself there is a generalized expectation that *les syndicats* will be at the forefront of resisting virtually all governmental policies which affect not only pay and working conditions, but also a wide swathe of social protection and economic intervention institutions. However, the mediatized dramatization of the most visible moments of trade union activity tends to hide two key aspects of the very structuration of French industrial relations. The first is their long history that has produced a particularly fragmented trade union movement whose fundamental divisions continue to this day. The second is that trade union membership in France fell dramatically in the 1980s, indeed experiencing the biggest fall of this kind in the world: 'in France a fundamental transformation of trade unionism occurred, not just a shrinking or a miniaturization' (Andolfatto and Labbé, 2006: 322, 350). Yes, this decline stopped in the 1990s. Indeed, it has even been reversed to some degree in certain sectors and companies (Allal *et al.*, 2018; Quijoux, 2018). However, the puzzle of how such low overall union membership still coexists with considerable political capital can only be understood by recalling how the movement as a whole developed historically, then retracing why this rich history continues to have such resonance within French society to this day.

As in many other Western countries, trade unions first emerged in France in the mid- to late nineteenth century. However, unlike in the UK for example, the movement immediately developed two contrasting strands. On the one hand, a range of militants committed to socialism or communism developed organizations by sectorial 'branch' and by region designed to directly confront the managers and other representatives of capital in order to initiate a visible and binary power relationship. In 1895, this movement coalesced into the *Confédération générale du travail* (CGT) which, as we will see below, remains a key part of the contemporary French union movement. Although clearly positioned firmly on the left, and often linked in practice to the *Parti communiste français* (PCF), the CGT's legendary *Charte d'Amiens* signed in 1906 has meant that, unlike British trade unions, it has no direct link to any political party. By contrast, the second major strand of the French trade union movement was, at least initially, strongly linked to a bastion of French conservatism: the Catholic Church. Although the activists in the *Confédération française de travailleurs catholiques* (CFTC) strongly tended to position themselves in the centre or on the centre-left of the political spectrum, their linkages to the church nevertheless had durable impacts upon their goals and repertoire of action. More committed to sustained dialogue than to open confrontation, the *CFTC* thus inaugurated a moderate approach to the labour–capital relationship which, again, exists to this day.

Having begun along these two seemingly incompatible lines, French trade unionism institutionalized itself and grew in terms of membership in the years immediately prior to, during and just after the Second World War. The 1930s were particularly important for this movement (e.g. in the late 1930s the *CGT* grew from 800,000 members to four times that number). This was also when it began to have significant institutional impacts, in particular during the government known as the *Front Populaire* from 1936 to 1938 (the first of the Third Republic to be headed in part by members of the Socialist Party). During this short but intense period of national politics, the unions were at the forefront of the adoption of legislation which initiated compulsory two-weeks' paid holidays for all workers, the codification of union rights, a significant rise in wages and a reduction in the working week from forty-eight to forty hours.

Union membership rose still further just after the war to an all-time high of 43% in 1948. Moreover, and more surprisingly, in 1940 then again in 1944–45 moves were made to merge the *CGT* and the *CFTC*. Key members of the latter closest to the Catholic Church ended up vetoing this project. Indeed, what happened instead was the splitting of the *CGT* in 1948 due to the departure of many of its members to form *Force Ouvrière* (*FO*), a more federal organization and entirely separate from the *PCF*, and thus create a third strand of unionism in France. Just as importantly, in setting up a national social security system for the first time, trade unions which had a sufficient number of members were given a place at a new 'negotiating table' around which the management of different aspects of the new social protection system was now to be managed. More precisely, the policy concept of *paritarism* was introduced, which ensured that equal numbers of representatives from unions and business organizations would participate in this permanent negotiating arena. The hope initially expressed was that this system would help pacify labour–capital relations and encourage greater solidarity as regards the decisions taken. To this day, this arrangement continues to have significant impacts upon the way policies on unemployment, sickness pay and even professional training are governed in France. Moreover, it clearly participates in legitimizing trade unions as key parts of the French economic field.

However, despite the sustained growth of the French economy as of the late 1940s, membership levels of all three of the unions just mentioned fell to 25% by 1953. Nevertheless, this level then stabilized and remained relatively high into the 1960s, when the next key moment was a split within the *CFTC*. This generated a new, non-confessional and centre-left *Confédération française démocratique de travail* (*CFDT*), which rapidly soon attracted more members than the *CFTC* and, partly as a consequence, became a central player in French labour–capital relations.

Table 3.12 The rise, fall, then rebooting of trade union membership, 1977–2014 (thousands)

	1973	1983	1993	2003	2014	2018
CGT	1870	1070	639	685	686	653
CFDT	655	613	473	889	860	624
CFTC	86	108	93	128	140	na
FO	430	460	370	950	500	500

Source: figures declared by each trade union.

Thereafter, however, and despite May 1968 providing another moment for recruiting members to all unions and achieving concessions from both the state and company management (the rate of union membership rose to 28–30% in 1968–70), a massive fall in trade union membership began in the mid- to late 1970s. Whereas since the early 1950s, the rate of union membership had remained relatively high at between 25% and 30% of the total workforce, by 1990 it had fallen as low as 6–7%.

This sharp decline was caused in part by fall-out from displacements within France's economy, and in particular a swathe of factory closures – notably those linked to steel in the Lorraine region (Nezosi, 1999) – which destroyed many bastions of unionism. Indeed, as Table 3.12 highlights, this challenge affected the *CGT* in particular. More generally, the rise in unemployment and the pressure this placed upon those in work to toe the line also contributed strongly to falls in union membership. The increasing power of financialized capitalism during the first decades of the twenty-first century has also created a strong tendency for personnel and employment issues to be dealt with wholly at the level of each firm, i.e. not at the level of sectorial '*branchs*' or nationally, where trade unions have often been stronger. In a word, because the definition of the public problem of employment has shifted in this direction, trade unions have often experienced great difficulty in retaining a significant voice (Gourges and Yon, 2018).

However, specialists of this subject area also point to two more 'endogenous' causes of this fall. First, some claim that fierce competition between the different main unions discouraged many potential members from joining. It also took up much of the time and energy of their respective leaders, thereby sapping their capacity to impact upon substantive issues. Second, a more detailed thesis is that the professionalization and the bureaucratization of shop stewards produced a type of unionism that was detached from the concerns of shop-floor members (notably those regarding management–employee relations as discussed in the previous section) and, ultimately, was undemocratic (Andolfatto and Labbé, 2006: 351).

Today, other specialists of trade unions have emerged in France who, through conducting ethnographic research and targeting less the national scale and more what happens within specific organizations and companies, have highlighted instead a slight rise in union membership since the nadir of 1990. Stimulated in particular by a series of national-scale mobilizations which began with the 1995 strikes, trade union membership is now estimated to cover 11% of the working population. More fundamentally still, these researchers stress that a modification of union priorities and repertoires of action has occurred which makes France's unions today much more akin to social movements than hitherto (Allal *et al.*, 2018; Giraud *et al.*, 2018). This type of research has generated valuable knowledge about efforts to relaunch the *CGT* (Piotet, 2009), the *CFDT* (Guillaume and Pochic, 2009) and *FO* (Yon, 2009). Notwithstanding this renewal of unionism, it is important to underline that it has been highly uneven by *branch* (e.g. at 18%, union membership is highest in the transport sector) and as regards the public–private divide (20% of union membership for the former, less than 10% for the latter). One has to be careful when comparing union membership across countries (for example, with Scandinavian nations, where such rates continue to reach 70% or more, but where unions also provide more services to their members and participate directly in professional training or even unemployment systems). Nevertheless, France's union membership rate is clearly extremely low.

More generally, the shifts related above confirm that one cannot fully understand work in France, the institutions which structure it, or how they have been made without taking firmly into account the nation's trade unions. Nevertheless, the enigma set out in the introduction to this section continues to hold true: why do unions in France continue to not only attract media attention, but to affect the economic field's institutions despite their low membership levels and the individualization of work more generally? Indeed, the uncertainty that surrounds the very role of trade unionism in France both needs explaining and, perhaps, provides some explanation of why social mobilization takes the forms that it does in this country (see chapter 6).

A business community also far from united

As underlined earlier, the representatives of labour have also been shaped by their relationship with those of capital. But who are the latter in France? And how have they been shaped by their own organizations? As Offerlé highlights, in this country the term 'bosses' (*les patrons*) certainly has a great deal of social resonance. However, he warns, 'it is important to reflect upon the differences and cleavages which both criss-cross and unite the business world' (2017: 6). Indeed, amongst the three million companies in France, there are, of course, considerable differences which first need taking into account before discovering the permanent challenge of aggregating and defending their interests this diversity has generated.

As in any national economy, the first thing that separates companies is the sector or industry within which their respective activity takes place. As Table 3.13 sets out, certain industries are more predominant that others. One should also grasp the sheer number of 'micro-enterprises' there are in France today (3.9 million employing 19% of the working population), as well as the importance of very large firms (292 of these employ 29% of that population), as well as their high level of concentration in certain sectors (notably building and transport).[3]

Focusing upon who manages these firms provides an initial means of moving from meso to micro analysis. As Hugrée (2017: 32–33) has shown and Tables 3.14–3.16 summarize, the biggest change over the last twenty years has been in the formal qualifications held by company CEOs. In 2010, half of them had a diploma that is *bac+2* or above, whereas the corresponding figure in the 1990s was only 37%.

This rise in the level of qualifications amongst the people who run firms in France is considerable. Yet one notes at the same time that for artisans and shopkeepers the rate of change has been less great. More precisely, along with much of the population under 55, possessing the *baccalauréat* is now relatively common (see chapter 2). However, most of the bosses in these two sectors left school well before this stage of schooling. Moreover, given that the ability to speak English is perhaps a more relevant yardstick for those in economic activity, a survey revealed that if 65% of all French managers admitted they were non-English speakers, this rises to 82–84% for artisans and shopkeepers (Coulangeon and Lamel, 2009).

Even more striking is Hugrée's second finding that the percentage of women in senior positions within business has barely gone up at all over the last twenty to thirty years (see Table 3.17). Indeed, the only significant rise

Table 3.13 French workplaces by sector, 2018

	Number	%
Industry	376,033	7
Building	651,842	12.2
Commerce, transport, hotels and restaurants	1,592,446	29.7
Business services	1,618,967	30.2
Services for individuals	1,118,142	20.9
Total	5,357,430	100

Source: INSEE, Démographie des entreprises en 2018, www.insee.fr/fr/statistiques/3973005, consulted 10th May 2020.

Table 3.14 Managers possessing the '*bac*' and at least two years of higher education

	1990s	*2010s*
Artisans	5	13
Shopkeepers	14	32
Managers of 10+ workers	37	50

Source: derived from Hugrée (2017: 33), his source being INSEE, *Les enquêtes emploi*.

Table 3.15 Managers possessing the '*bac*'

	1990s	*2010s*
Artisans	10	23
Shopkeepers	14	22
Managers of 10+ workers	19	22

Source: derived from Hugrée (2017: 33), his source being INSEE, *Les enquêtes emploi*.

Table 3.16 Managers with no diploma whatsoever

	1990s	*2010s*
Artisans	30	15
Shopkeepers	32	15
Managers of 10+ workers	13	5

Source: derived from Hugrée (2017: 33), his source being INSEE, *Les enquêtes emploi*.

Table 3.17 Percentage of managers who are women

	1990s	*2010s*
Artisans without employees	11	23
Shopkeepers without employees	38	42
Artisans with 1–9 employees	14	22
Shopkeepers with 1–9 employees	30	30
Managers of 10–49 workers (building, transport & industry)	15	11
Managers of 10–49 workers (commercial, services)	20	25
Managers of 50–499 workers	15	13
Managers of 500+ workers	12	20
Total	23	25

Source: derived from Hugrée (2017: 36), his source being INSEE, *Les enquêtes emploi*.

here has been for artisans who work on their own (from 11% to 23%) and managers of very large companies (from 12% to 20%).

Hugrée (2017: 38) also presents key data on the social origins of the businessmen and women of interest to us here. First, Table 3.18 sets out the

Table 3.18 The social origin of businessmen and women, 2010s (%)

	Profession of their father		
	Farmers or independents	*Administrators or manual workers*	*Managers, teachers and 'intermediates'*
Artisans without employees	31	49	20
Shopkeepers without employees	33	35	32
Artisans with 1–9 employees	37	47	16
Shopkeepers with 1–9 employees	40	32	27
Managers of 10–49 workers (building, transport and industry)	58	25	17
Managers of 10–49 workers (commercial, services)	38	26	36
Managers of 50–499 workers	35	24	41
Managers of 500+ workers	22	29	49
Total	35	40	25

Source: derived from Hugrée (2017: 38), his source being INSEE, *Les enquêtes emploi*.

relevant figures for the 2010s (which are the average for the years 2010–16). Amongst the wealth of information resumed in this table, one immediately notes that no fewer than 49% of managers of large companies and 41% of SMEs have fathers who were also managers or came from a socially equivalent category. By contrast, only 29% and 24% of the managers of these sized firms had a father who was a manual labourer or an office worker (the remainder being farmers or other 'independent' workers). Similarly, most of today's French artisans rarely had a father who was a manager. If this data is not in itself surprising, when compared with figures from the 1990s (see Table 3.19), it provides a stark insight into the slow rate of French social mobility over the last three decades. For example, the impact of becoming a manager of a large company or SME when one has a father who is or was a manager or equivalent has risen by 6–10% from an already high level. Meanwhile the likelihood that one can reach this level of seniority in a company if one's father is or was a farmer, an independent worker, an administrator or a manual worker has decreased by up to 9%!

Table 3.19 Change in the social origin of businessmen and women between the 1990s and 2010s (%)

	Profession of their father		
	Farmers or independents	*Administrators or manual workers*	*Managers, teachers and 'intermediates'*
Artisans without employees	−9	−1	+11
Shopkeepers without employees	−7	−7	+2
Artisans with 1–9 employees	−10	+3	+7
Shopkeepers with 1–9 employees	−6	+4	+9
Managers of 10–49 workers (building, transport and industry)	+7	−7	No change
Managers of 10–49 workers (commercial, services)	−9	−12	+10
Managers of 50–499 workers	−9	−1	+10
Managers of 500+ workers	−7	+2	+6
Total	−8	+13	+10

Source: derived from Hugrée (2017: 38), his source being INSEE, *Les enquêtes emploi*.

In summary, as the data presented above underlines, there has been relatively little change towards greater equality in the sociological composition of management in France over the last three decades. Instead, the social mobility that has occurred in this respect is one where, in general, a pre-existing dualization of French society has only deepened further. Indeed, in most cases this trend has been fuelled by the ever-increasing emphasis placed upon formal qualifications highlighted earlier in this chapter and in chapter 2.

It follows that an additional question that can now be asked concerns the extent to which this high level of social reproduction can be attributed to the way business represents itself and, in turn, is represented by the remainder of the population. As regards the 'peak' business representative, chronologically, a *Confédération générale du patronat français* (CGPF) was first established as late as 1919.[4] After the Second World War, it was renamed and recast in 1946 as the *Confédération nationale du patronat français* (CNPF). Finally, in 1998, a change of name to the *Mouvement des Entreprises de France* (MEDEF) was made to symbolize a further relaunching and 'modernization' of the same

Table 3.20 Key participants in the space of French business representation, 2013

Organization[1]	Members	Who it represents	Head-office staff (2009)
MEDEF	74 federations[2]	All companies	180
CGPME	69 federations	SMEs	35
UPA	51 federations	Artisans	15
ACFCI	147 regional, municipal, *départemental* entities	Chambers of commerce	185
AFEP	92 large companies	Big joint-stock companies	30

[1] The *CGPME* is the confederation of SMEs, the *Union Professionnelle Artisanale* (UPA) represents artisans and the *Association française des entreprises privées* (AFEP) represents large companies.
[2] The term 'federation' is used loosely here to include a range of 'sub-organizations'.

Source: Offerlé (2013).

organization (Offerlé, 2013). What is extremely important to understand, however, is that, like its predecessors, the *MEDEF* is very much a confederation of federations. As Michel Offerlé underlines, it is more heuristic to consider that in France there is a business representation 'space' within which the organizations set out in Table 3.20 all play a specific role.

What is important to retain here first is that each of these organizations participates in defining, aggregating and defending not only 'the interests' of French company owners and managers, but in defining 'the public problems' they consider affect their activity. Not surprisingly, the confederation of SMEs (*Confédération générale des petites et moyennes entreprises: CGPME*), the *Union Professionnelle Artisanale* (*UPA*) and the *Association française des entreprises privées* (*AFEP*) do not always see eye to eye on a range of issues. Indeed, on some of them they are clearly in competition in order to convince representatives of the state in particular to listen most closely to them and fight their respective corner in Paris or Brussels. In this respect, speaking for business in France is difficult because of the fragmentation of organizations which claim to do so within a space of essentially Paris-based actors (Offerlé, 2013: 102, 2009). But being a legitimate and recognized representative of business is also a challenge because each of the above-mentioned organizations, with the exception perhaps of *AFEP*, are themselves ultimately quite loose assemblages of either sectorial or territorial organizations which, by contrast, tend to feature greater solidarity, coherence and durability. In the case of the *MEDEF* in particular, on a daily basis its leadership and permanent staff consider they have to manage this organization's own internal contradictions – for example, when it produces 'expertise' for the state and MPs in the form of briefing papers (Offerlé, 2013: 326).

Indeed, it is precisely this pressing need to mediate internal tensions which explains in part both the 'lateness' of the emergence of a peak business organization in this country and, above all, its relatively low membership. For example, assessed in terms of membership rates as regards the total number of companies, even at its highest-ever point in the period 1936–46, the representativeness of the *MEDEF* (i.e. its historical antecedent) was estimated at only 13–14%. By 1975, this figure was down to 8.5%, then fell as low as 6% by 2005 (Offerlé, 2009: 21). Indeed, because today these figures are comparable to those of the trade unions presented earlier in this chapter, a similar question arises: just why are these organizations, and the *MEDEF* in particular, given so much importance by the government of the day and the media?

Unfortunately, to date social science has generated relatively little data with which to reply to this question. What the pioneering work of Michel Offerlé has done, however, is clearly identify what such data production could and should be focused upon. Moreover, it highlights how and why representatives of capital have developed three different but reinforcing types of capital: the social, the economic and the informational (Offerlé, 2009: 101). As regards social capital, leaders of the peak business organizations are clearly key players amongst French society's elites. Family background and therefore social class is important here, but it is as important to realize that most of these actors attended the select groups of schools and higher education establishments described in the previous chapter. From the point of view of economic capital, the vast majority of these same actors are not only wealthy themselves, but also work or have worked for the nation's largest and most affluent companies. Finally, as will be highlighted in the following chapter, their informational capital is high because so many have either worked for the state early in their careers, work with it because their company is partly state-owned, or simply know personally key persons within the civil service because of their social or economic capital.

In summary, it would be a mistake to conclude that the *MEDEF* and its sister organizations are simply the mouthpieces of 'capital' or of right-wing, *libéral* political parties. As we have just seen, they have great difficulty in speaking for capital precisely because its thinking is not homogenous and is rarely even clear. Secondly, although they rarely position themselves 'on the left', many powerful members of even the *MEDEF* are not necessarily positioned on the right of the political spectrum (Offerlé, 2017: 570). Indeed, again rather like the trade unions, and as, of course, also occurs in many other countries, *MEDEF* members tend strongly to avoid the taking up of durable political positions in order to have more freedom to act either with or against the government of the day, depending upon the issue at hand.

Conclusion

As stressed from the beginning of this chapter, what structures work in any country is an institutionally dense social relationship between labour and capital. As in any relationship between two phenomena, both are responsible for their patterns of interaction, interdependence and their substantive outcomes. Of course, French representatives of capital benefit from possessing a range of social, economic and political resources which their opposite numbers in the trade unions and equivalent bodies simply do not have to the same extent. Nevertheless, the traits which mark the way French companies and organizations are managed – notably their penchant for hierarchy and the avoidance of sustained employer–employee dialogue – need explaining not only around what empowers managers in this country (notably their social origins, education and training). Explanation also needs to take into account the persistent traits of labour representation, in particular its rhetoric of distrust and its repertoire of hostile discourse and radical or even violent action. Indeed, it is from this angle that the theme of social mobility and its impacts can usefully be readdressed. Changes in workplaces and their practices over the last forty years have certainly contributed to increasing individualization in France. Indeed, they have also participated in a deepening of the dualization of French society as a whole – one that divides those who have resources and thus good life chances from those who patently do not. But it is too simplistic to reduce explanation of these shifts merely to the strengthening of capital and its representatives over those of labour. Instead, what better explains the world of work in France and how it is experienced is that most employees now find themselves relatively alone and isolated. This is particularly because many of those immediately around them, people previously seen either as partners or adversaries, have now so often been accorded other, less straightforward, roles (Cousin, 2019).

Moreover, as we have repeatedly seen, this relationship between labour and capital can only be fully understood if the state is brought into the equation. At least in France, statist actors not only structure industrial relations indirectly, many are direct participants in the management of key companies. Indeed, it is notably from this angle that questions regarding the impact of neo-liberalism and 'globalization' take on particular resonance in the French economic and bureaucratic fields. Although both these terms, and the arguments for change they condense, have certainly been deployed in order to change societal structures regarding work in this country, neither have had significant direct effects. Instead, today's institutions in this issue area, together with the asymmetric power relations that accompany them, are much better explained as the result of webs of propositions, powering and compromises, all of which have been strongly shaped by the fields within which they have taken place. Put another way, work in France as elsewhere is an integral part of business and, as such, is inextricably linked to the politics of economic activity (Smith, 2016). Indeed, this is precisely why it is now time to discover how business as a whole is conducted in France and by the French.

Notes

1 Amongst other things, this has meant that even during the expansion years of 1950–80, linkages between town and country remained strong as many urban workers regularly returned 'home' to the places where they were brought up. Indeed, this trait of French historical geography continues to impact upon the relatively high rate of second home possession (according to INSEE, 10% of housing in France fits this category) – and where people spend their holidays and, indeed, much of their leisure time and retirement.
2 INSEE, *Les entreprises en France*, 2018. www.insee.fr/fr/statistiques/2381478, consulted 10th May 2020.
3 INSEE, *Les entreprises en France*, 2018: 66. NB. Since 2003, the European classification has been: 0–9 employees = microenterprise, 0–19 = very small enterprise; 0–250 = small and medium enterprise; 250 + = large enterprise.
4 From 1919 to 1936 it was called the *Confédération générale de la production française*.

4

Business time within neo-*dirigiste* capitalism

Introduction

The previous chapter presented a good deal of information on the relationship between capital and labour. But how does this actually impact upon the way business is done in contemporary France? How are goods and services produced, marketed and sold in this country? More generally, what structures the economic field in this country? In order to answer these questions – and, more importantly still, the underlying puzzle regarding why French business is conducted as it is – this chapter will focus in part upon the scale of the individual company, but more upon that of the meso (industry) and macro (trans-industry) power relations and institutions which impinge upon them, i.e. the rules, norms and conventions that not only constrain how goods are made and sold, but also those that provide the conditions for individual companies to engage durably in economic activity at all (Smith, 2016).

Over and above the presentation of information about the structuring of business activity that is essential for anyone seeking to understand France and the French, this national case of the politics of economic activity is of wider import for at least two reasons. The first is that despite the liberalism that has dominated most of France's economic history, today this country's 'variety of capitalism' (Hall and Soskice, 2001) remains indelibly marked by the form of state interventionism that structured government policy, collective action and many company strategies from 1940 until the late 1980s. Commonly known as *dirigiste* (loosely translated as 'directive'), this approach to economics combined a soft but influential form of state planning, nationalizations, an emphasis on large 'national champions' in each industry and governmental intervention in markets through instruments such as price controls, quotas, subsidies and import tariffs. Legitimated by a desire to break with the socio-economic and political elites of the 1930s and 40s (Hall, 1986; Cohen, 1992: 20), the post-war expansion of the French economy and by the electoral success of the politicians who maintained it in place, *dirigisme* came under sustained attack during the 1980s. We now know, however, that by then it had already been sapped over two decades by a range of measures pushed by liberal-minded technocrats and business leaders (Lemoine, 2016). For all these reasons, together with the complexity of clashes between *dirigiste*, liberal and neo-liberal problem definitions and proposed policy instruments, comparative political economy has been particularly interested in what the French model has become. Three competing theses currently dominate this area of research.

The first considers quite simply that ever since a relaunching of *dirigisme* was abandoned by the first Mitterrand government in 1983–84, 'globalization' has made the French economy undergo a comprehensive neo-liberalization of its structures (Culpepper, 2006; Denord, 2007). From this angle, *dirigisme* has been dead and buried for more than three decades. The second thesis concurs that much has changed in France but argues instead that parts of the state continue to possess significant 'post-*dirigiste*' traits, reflexes and tendencies (Levy, 1999; Clift, 2002; Schmidt, 2003). In particular, the continued presence of the state on major company boards is frequently highlighted. Thirdly and finally, together with Matthieu Ansaloni (Ansaloni and Smith, 2018), we have recently developed an alternative line of argument which considers that French *dirigisme* is very much alive, and indeed considerably more so than post-*dirigisme* scholarship would have us believe. Specifically, the first section of the chapter accepts in part the claim, made by authors such as Culpepper and Goyer, that the financing of French capitalism has changed considerably over the last thirty to forty years. However, as its second and third sections subsequently relate, *dirigisme* has nevertheless largely been reproduced and renewed as neo-*dirigisme*. Specifically, this reinvention has essentially taken place around the institutions and power relations which structure how goods and services are actually produced then sold in contemporary France. Crucially, state representatives continue to support these societal structures through their daily engagement in socio-economics. Indeed, we argue it is only by re-examining how business as a whole is conducted in any country, and thus by going beyond the crucial but not all-determining labour–capital nexus, that France's brand of capitalism and positioning within global trends can be fully grasped. The key question that can then be reframed is whether or not neo-*dirigisme* has actually changed the way state actors think about their purpose and objectives? Moreover, in so doing, has it reconfigured their role and positions within the economic and bureaucratic fields?

To answer these questions and illustrate my overall argument, three industries will be examined in particular. That of defence provides a means of discovering how *grands projets*, such as the Rafale fighter jet, are financed, produced and sold by large companies like Dassault, but also a range of small sub-contractors. By contrast, although a couple of giant wine merchants have emerged over the last thirty years (Grands Chais de France and Castel), the wine industry in France remains dominated by a plethora of small producers and, once again, considerable state intervention. Finally, the chapter also takes a close look at the housing industry as a mixture of goods and services within which, over the last three decades, public authorities have involved themselves in a structurally different way to the model of 1945–85, without however sidelining representatives of the state.

By mobilizing illustrations from these three industries,[1] throughout the chapter the argument that French capitalism remains highly structured by neo-*dirigisme* will be bolstered by a second contribution the chapter seeks to make to wider debates in political economy: the impact the European Union (EU) has had since the 1950s (Jullien and Smith, 2014). As will be shown, particularly since the late 1980s, the significance of EU membership upon French capitalism has clearly been direct and massive. Nevertheless, French influences upon the EU itself have translated, and in many cases attenuated or even orientated, this impact. Indeed, it is precisely through working politically at the European scale of regulation that certain key French actors have actually enabled their national capitalism to retain many of its most significant institutions and power relations.

Financing business: banks, the stock market and the state

As in any capitalist society, French firms seek the financing they need from five different sources: personal or family savings, banks and other credit organizations, private equity investors, the stock market and public authorities. In each country and at different historical periods, the dominant mix between these five sources varies considerably and has given rise to a sharp distinction between 'patient' and 'impatient' capital (Offer, 2018). As these adjectives imply, the first category is typically dominated by long-term bank, personal or private equity loans, whereas the latter denotes more 'footloose' investment, notably the trading of shares often caricatured as 'speculation'. Long dominated by patient capital, since the 1980s the French economy has tilted increasingly towards shorter-term financing. However, in documenting this shift, the first part of this section also seeks to avoid binary analysis, notably because 'patient' and 'impatient' are ideal types between which lies a continuum of capitalization practices. Moreover, as will be shown subsequently when we examine what these approaches to finance mean for specific industries, the role of the state and its neo-*dirigiste* practices often cuts across the patient–impatient divide.

From patient to impatient capital?

Obtaining capital from one's family is clearly not specific to France. However, partly due to a structural bias within French inheritance laws (see chapter 7), in this country the passing down of capital is still particularly important. Indeed, in *Le capitalisme d'héritiers* Philippon (2007: 14) has argued strongly that if around 80% of all French firms are family owned, this practice extends right up to the ownership of large firms essentially financed through the stock market. This said, and despite their being used by the majority of the population only since the 1970s, banks have been the dominant lender of credit to French businesses since at least the mid-nineteenth century. Indeed, as recently as 1976 the ratio of bank loans to stocks and shares in France was 85:15 (as in West Germany), figures in sharp contrast to the UK's 58:42 and the US's 51:49 ratios (Levy, 1999). However, at that time the big difference between France and West Germany was that French banks were not independent from the state. Indeed, as Jonah Levy highlighted, until the 1980s, the state even fixed the price of credit, 'and because it usually set that price quite low', it created 'an excess of demand over supply'. Moreover, the three dominant banks of that period (Crédit Lyonnais, Société Générale and BNP) 'were not called upon to provide long-term loans or take up an equity stake in risky infant industries' (Levy, 1999: 259). When French banks did lend to industry, they were very cautious and risk averse (Zysman, 1983). Consequently, 'French banks related to industry less as partners than as casual acquaintances' in 'an arms-length relationship' (Levy, 1999: 260, 38). In practical terms, French SMEs in particular suffered from this institutionalized banking relationship because they had to pay much more than their German counterparts to reimburse short-term loans and overdrafts. More generally, as Lazarus (2012: 8) has underlined with a focus upon credit to individuals, for a long time the French banking sector had an image of being a non-competitive, quasi-administrative, service to the public. 'Stability' was the key criterion for loan decisions, a criterion judged in terms of the perceived permanency of the client in question (whereas in the US greater accent has long been placed upon the client's history of lending and reimbursement) (Lazarus: 2012: 268–269). Moreover, within virtually all banks the amount of delegation to each banker was low. This meant that being a successful banker was essentially about applying the rules imposed by head office and covering oneself as regards one's hierarchy. Indeed, as Goyer has underlined (2006), before 1984 the state's instruments as regards banking included controls on capital movements, administered interest rates (including subsidized low-interest credit) and even ceilings on bank loans.

All these traits can only be fully grasped, however, by first understanding how, particularly since the Second World War, the French state has so frequently substituted itself for the banks as a lender to industry, whilst controlling the capital of these very organizations. This money-lender state has essentially taken the form of a variety of state agencies, above all *la Caisse des Dépôts et Consignations* (CDC). We return below to this engagement within the financial sector by the state. But what needs underlining at this stage is that this trait also had a knock-on effect upon the stock market. Before the Second World War, France had a 'lively' stock market, but after the war the equity markets were eroded by 'negative bond yields and competition from cheap state-allocated credit' (Levy, 1999: 258–259; Lagneau-Ymonet and Riva, 2015).

As regards actual bank ownership, it is important to recall that in France this remains highly protected by the state. Indeed, even since it reprivatized key banks in 1986, the state has always sought concentration of the sector through retaining a power of veto as regards takeovers and by orchestrating mergers (e.g. Banque Populaire-Caisse d'Epargne in 2009, or that of Crédit Lyonnais and Crédit Agricole in 2003). Indeed, one of the aims sought here has been to limit foreign ownership of such organizations (a policy that from this respect has been very successful: in 2009 only 12% of bank assets in France were foreign-owned: Goyer and Valdivielso des Real, 2014). The overall result has been that since 2014, four big banks have dominated the French banking industry: BNP-Paribas, Société Générale, Crédit Agricole and Banque Populaire-Caisse d'Epargne.

Notwithstanding the sustained engagement of state actors in this industry, since the 1980s French capital as a whole has nevertheless experienced a relatively rapid shift towards a model of financialized capital. This can be seen first within the domain of banking itself and its lending practices in particular. Baud and Chiapello (2015), for example, have analysed a shift within bank practices towards the primacy of 'financial' management and decision-making tools over 'economic' ones. This in turn has had an impact on the way SMEs are supposed to report to their banks, keep their accounts and manage themselves more generally (2015: 455). According to Goyer (2006), such a shift began when controls on capital were dropped as of the mid-1980s because of pressure on the state applied by SMEs. Meanwhile, ceilings on loans were abandoned too, to be replaced by higher interest rates imposed by the central bank to control inflation.

As regards the Paris-based stock market, a move towards wider shareholding also began in the 1980s and was followed by institutional reform thereafter (Levy, 1999: 258). This was fuelled in particular by the privatization in 1993 of the major insurance companies and the arrival in France of Anglo-US pension funds which followed. Fierce competition between financial services and an often booming stock market has since eventuated as part of a quest for what Levy calls 'cheaper and deeper capital markets'. Indeed, the French experience meshed with a more global one of change in numerous capital markets and the internationalization of shareholding worldwide. Partly as a consequence, Anglo-American investors began to geographically diversify their portfolios. Indeed, by 2001 foreign investors possessed 41% of the capital of France's top 40 companies (*le CAC 40*). In particular, this internationalization largely put an end to the cross-holding of shares amongst large French companies that had been favoured by the state in the 1970s and 1980s (Goyer, 2006).

This said, as new research now tells us, it is important to understand that a series of subtle changes made within the financing of the state since the late 1960s largely prepared the ground for the more evident transformations observed in the 1980s. As Benjamin Lemoine in particular has revealed (2016), what is key is 'the placing on the marketplace' of the state's own debt. This is important because from 1945 to the mid-1960s this debt had been considered to be 'outside the market' since it was part of a purely administrative circuit of intra-state financing. Specifically, liberal civil servants within the state itself began to contest the very legitimacy of this 'circuit', nationalized banks and, more generally, Keynesian capitalization policies. Indeed, as of the late 1960s, seeking finance for the state from private investors had already come to be depoliticized and institutionalized as 'a technical necessity' that even technocrats belonging to the *Parti Socialiste* now shared (Lemoine, 2016: 106). Throughout the 1970s this shift was shored up by a convergence of views with key senior civil servants working in the European Commission's economic and finance Directorate General II (renamed DG ECFIN in 1999). In practical terms, this shift in doctrine was accompanied by new policy instruments in the shape of statistical categories and ways of measuring what public authorities owe to private creditors (Lemoine, 2016: 158).

This said, the state as a financer of business activity in France continues to show considerable resilience. This is reflected partly in the high level of shareholding that the state still holds in a number of large companies and key industries. Managed today through the *Agence des participations de l'Etat*, this holding of shares amounted to over 77 billion euros in June 2018. The energy sector constituted 49% of this figure and that of defence a further 27%. Nevertheless, it is important to note that the state still possesses considerable amounts of shares in the automobile sector (via Renault in particular) and even that of telecommunications (via Orange). Moreover, one also needs to take into account the role played on the boards of all these companies by no fewer than 761 formal representatives of the state. To that figure a swathe of ex-civil servants must also be added, most of whom continue to embed their activity in networks joined during their training in *grandes écoles*, together with the years they each initially spent working directly for the state itself.

Three industries and their modes of capitalization: defence, wine and housing

In the domain of defence, the continued importance of state financing is perhaps unsurprising given 'the national interest' so easily evoked in this domain and that the industry's primary customer remains the French armed forces. Moreover, analysis also needs to recognize the domination of this industry in France by companies that most often were once nationalized, and within which the state retains high levels of shares – notably Thales, Safran and Naval Group. Nevertheless, even here state resilience needs explaining in at least three ways.

First, the impact of a profound mistrust of private capital, and therefore the stock market, is quite simply omnipresent amongst actors in French defence companies and administrations. Secondly, and as a consequence, the state has repeatedly engaged in structuring the very supply of defence equipment by encouraging 'strategic' mergers between domestic operators. In so doing, a neo-*dirigiste* strategy of preserving the tissue of sub-contractors which are vital to these large firms has been adopted, aided and abetted not only by contracts to participate in specific arms programmes, but also by low interest loans from the state's funding agencies.

Thirdly, as alluded to above, the omnipresence of state or ex-state officials on the boards of the firms themselves is crucial. As Table 4.1 sets out in detail, the state is very much part and parcel of the companies involved. In the case of Safran, this involvement notably takes the form of a board of directors upon which as much as 41% of its members over the period 2007–17 were representatives or ex-officials of the state, a figure even surpassed by Thales with 53% (Faure *et al.*, 2019).

Overall, it is, of course, true that during the last twenty to thirty years, new and increasingly foreign investors have bought sizeable shareholdings within France's key defence companies. However, it is simply meaningless to

Table 4.1 Safran and Thales's board members' experience of working within the state (%)

		2007	2012	2017	Total (2007–17)
Safran	Private	17	20	53	28
	Still state official	28	20	17.5	24
	State > Private	22	13.3	6	13
	State > Private > State	0	13.3	0	4
	In house	22	20	17.5	20
	Other	11	13.3	6	11
Thales	Private	50	45	50	38
	Still state official	12.5	16.5	12.5	14.5
	State > Private	25	16.5	25	25.5
	State > Private > State	6.25	11	6.25	13
	In-house	6.25	11	6.25	7
	Other	0	0	0	2

Source: Faure *et al.* (2019).

note this change, then assume that it has had deep effects upon the way these companies are run in this country. In practice, many if not most of the institutions and power relations which lay at the heart of 'high *dirigisme*' in the defence industry are still firmly in place.

As regards financing the wine industry in France, one dominated by SMEs and small farms, the banks have been the key player, often working together with the state and the EU. In keeping with other parts of French agriculture (Muller, 1984), the expansion and 'modernization' of France's vineyards took place in particular between 1950 and the 1980s. For example, it was during the first decade of this period that in the region of Bordeaux, the area which has provided most of its generic wines – the Entre-Deux-Mers – converted from white to red wine, and away from wine in bulk delivered to merchants or co-operatives to bottled wine from individual chateaux. Within this process, the role of the Crédit Agricole was highly important (Bonin, 1992). Indeed, to this day this bank is the main lender to an estimated 70% of all French growers and farmers. This said, it is important to grasp that in the wine industry bank loans frequently supplement grants or interest-free loans given by the state or the EU to assist growers and merchants to improve 'the quality' of their production, and this through either renewing their vines or revamping their wine-making plant (Itçaina *et al.*, 2016). By contrast, the arrival in French vineyards of large investors, such as the Californian firm Mondavi in the Midi, has often been unsuccessful and even racked with controversy (Torrès, 2005). Indeed, even here statist neo-*dirigisme* plays a role given that all sales of agricultural land outside the family concerned still have to go before the local board of a national organization – *Les Sociétés d'aménagement foncier et d'établissement rural* (the SAFER) – which can veto acquisitions of land it deems inappropriate.

Overall, of course, the increased financialization of capital throughout the French economy and society has had knock-on effects upon its wine growers and merchants. Loans and grants are not as straightforward to obtain as they once were. Nevertheless, in this industry as in numerous others, producers and company managers are hardly 'at the mercy of the markets' or of 'big capital', as too many knee-jerk critics and commentators would have it. Instead, the impact of financialization has been more subtle and insidious. This is because it has affected the way business strategies are examined by banks and state administrations, together with the accountancy systems used. Indeed, financialization has had a pervasive impact upon the very way capital is even thought about by the growers and merchants themselves.

Such an impact has not surprisingly been more direct and visible in the case of the housing industry, and this because of financialization's inextricable relationship with the construction of flats, houses, offices and other commercial edifices – an activity which in 2016 accounted for no less than 209 billion euros.[2] In the case of France, however, this relationship cannot begin to be understood if one omits to take into account how the French state intervened so heavily in it between 1950 and the mid-1970s. In the nine-teenth century, previous regimes had, of course, been highly active in clear-ing intricate webs of streets and inner-city 'slum' housing by replacing them with boulevards and blocks of flats. In particular, under Napoleon III, during the 1860s Baron Haussmann led the charge in Paris by transforming much of the city, whilst similar changes were made in a number of provincial cap-itals such as Bordeaux and Lyon. However, during the Third Republic the building of housing slowed dramatically, a trend obviously worsened by the Second World War. Indeed, hampered by the reticence of banks to lend and of the state to intervene in the market, the number of housing units built in 1950 was as low as 70,000.

However, this liberal and conservative model changed dramatically there-after. In quantitative terms, the number of housing units built reached 400,000 a year by 1965, and this due to the combined effects of post-war national planning, the active involvement of senior civil servant-engineers from the *corps des ponts et chaussées* (Thoenig, 1987) and state subsidies (Topalov, 1987; Bourdieu, 2000; Pollard, 2018). Indeed, what is important to stress here is the impact of a reform of the key state agency mentioned earlier – *la Caisse des Dépôts et Consignations* (CDC) – which, from 1953 until the mid-1970s, was the principal organizational instrument through which state investment in land and building was channelled (Frétigny, 2015). However, as will be explained more fully in the next two sections, three key developments have since modified the housing industry as a whole and the state's involvement within it in particular: the rise of mortgage-based house buying since a change in the law in 1968; the state's retreat from social housing since the mid-1970s in favour of private real estate development; and the increased role played by municipal governments and, more gener-ally, decentralization *à la française*.

In summary, since at least the 1980s, capital in France has clearly meta-morphosed from the 'patient' end of the spectrum towards more 'impatient' forms of financing business activity. In this regard, neo-liberal policy reci-pes have clearly influenced their thought and action. In the light of the ecological and COVID-19 crises, in recent years an increasing number of actors and commentators have called for a shift in the other direction, one they consider the French state is well placed to catalyse (e.g. Terra Nova, 2016). For the moment at least, however, most indicators suggest that state actors have yet to work politically in this direction. Most prefer instead to continue intervening in how capital is allocated within the French economy by using instruments that do not fundamentally challenge the primacy of 'the impatient'.

Production and its sourcing: not just a-political 'management'

In France the theme of industrial decline has been constantly at the forefront of business and political debates since the mid-1970s (Cohen and Buigues, 2014). To give just one quantitative indicator of this trend, between 1980 and 2008 this country lost more than 2 million manufacturing jobs. Initially, a generalized slowdown in the performance and profitability of French firms was ascribed either to the sudden arrival of cheaper and more reliable products on the market, particularly from Japan, or to even deeper difficulties regarding competitiveness experienced by French steel and textile producers. In the first case, the French state responded with a range of protectionist measures, then used bilateral and EU–Japan diplomacy (Carter *et al.*, 2014). In the latter, a series of national 'social plans' was implemented in order to organize a retreat from these industries in the least painful way possible. If that strategy failed in many ways (Nezosi, 1999), it also institutionalized an expectation in France that the state could always be called upon to act as the 'stretcher-bearer' (Cohen, 1989) in cases where plant closures and large-scale redundancies have been imposed by company owners. Indeed, regardless of whether a right- or left-leaning party is in government, a central feature of French neo-*dirigisme* has always been this reflex by the state to mediate change in the national productive system.

Of course, this trait has not only been reflected in cases where companies or entire industries have been in great financial difficulty. Neo-*dirigisme* has also authorized and pushed representatives of the French state to intervene more or less heavily in a range of economic activities that are seen as 'the stars' of French industry. Here their aim is to bolster the perceived comparative advantages of firms and encourage their expansion. In focusing successively upon the defence, wine and housing industries, my intention is therefore to show just how the state is an omnipresent feature of French business strategizing over production-related issues – ones which, in many other countries, occur with less public authority involvement. Throughout, it will be shown that French neo-*dirigisme* is marked by constant governmental support for premium products, but also by repeated failings to evaluate the economic, political and social costs of their actual realization.

Defence: striving for performance or perfection?

As in many other countries, between the Second World War and the fall of the Berlin Wall in 1989, defence companies in France were largely able to produce, and often expand, safe in the knowledge that most of their revenue would come from their national defence ministry. Indeed, during this period relatively large defence budgets, a reluctance to open up markets to foreign competitors and low levels of importance attached to exports were common traits in capitalisms ranging from the US to Sweden. Symmetrically, since 1989 most of these same countries have reduced the amount of public money spent on armaments, opened up their defence markets to external companies and strongly encouraged their domestic producers 'to get out more' so as to find customers for their products overseas (and thus reduce their price overall). In the French case, however, this shift has been much less wholesale than in countries such as the UK. Indeed, it is precisely because neo-*dirigisme* continues to hold sway in this country that the buying of arms is still highly structured by institutions and power relations which reproduce and bolster the national 'defence industrial base'.

In order to substantiate this argument, let us examine first how key weapon systems are developed then chosen in the French case. The first point that needs underlining is that although most such products are now designed in France by companies that are formally 'private', the senior engineers involved have almost all been trained within a relevant *grande école* (most often *Polytechnique*). Moreover, in many instances this linkage to the state has been reinforced during periods of work spent by these engineers within the Ministry of Defence and its procurement wing – the powerful *Direction générale de l'armement (DGA)* – in particular. On the one hand, this elitist approach to engineering has strongly encouraged the development of arms and weapons systems that are amongst the most sophisticated on the market (for example the Leclerc tank was repeatedly legitimized as 'the best in the world': Genieys and Michel, 2006) – and this despite the problems such products repeatedly have in living within their budgets and finding customers (as testified in an adjacent field by the Concorde aircraft). Indeed, this brings us to a second point: the extent to which the French state has been accommodating in picking up the tab of cost over-runs, many of which ultimately have been linked to its own 'quest for performance'. To illustrate this twofold characteristic of arms production in France, Samuel Faure's (2016) comparison of how the Rafale fighter jet and the A400M airlifter were conceptualized, designed and bought is particularly instructive.

In the case of the Rafale, events began in the mid-1970s when plans to replace France's previous generation of fighters (the Mirage) were initiated and when, crucially, a choice was made not to participate in the European consortium which eventually produced the Eurofighter (often know as 'the Typhoon'). More specifically, for several years the possibility of participating in this European project was mooted and indeed supported by certain actors within the French decision-making process. From this perspective, a series of discussions was held aimed at producing a common specification acceptable to representatives of Germany, the UK, Italy and Spain. However, by 1985 this European option was officially abandoned, formally because in France it was deemed impossible to reach agreement on precisely what this fighter would be designed to do (air–ground or air–air combat?), and therefore on its weight, capabilities and cost. However, as Faure relates in detail (2016: 189–191), a deeper reason for rejecting the Eurofighter was that many key French actors wanted the future fighter to be built by the French manufacturer Dassault. Not surprisingly this company, which always promotes itself as a family-owned private one despite the state owning up to 20% of its shares, was itself a prime mover in shaping the French decision to go it alone. Indeed, to a large extent Dassault shaped the very demand for this aircraft through not only proposing its initial specifications, but also underlining how it would participate in generating new technology and skills in France, as well as jobs within its own walls and the range of sub-contractors with which it would network to produce the Rafale. But these arguments alone do not suffice to explain why successive French governments have backed this option of 'autarsic' production. Instead, one needs to take into account the legitimacy Dassault had developed since the 1960s around the Mirage programme (seen as a success in terms of both military interventions and exports – see next section), as well as the high levels of social proximity this production had generated between the company itself, the *Armée de l'air* and the *DGA*. Indeed, not only had many senior personnel in the latter two bodies actually spent part of their careers flying Mirages, many Dassault senior managers had previously served in one or both of these organizations. When one adds into the equation that the main French aviation engine manufacturer SNECMA (now Safran) pushed strongly to equip the Rafale and thus establish a key partnership with Dassault, and that Jacques Chirac (a leading Gaullist, Prime Minister 1974–76 and 1986–88, then President 1995–2007) was a consistent supporter of Dassault, the choice eventually made now seems totally unsurprising. It is important to recall, however, that given the high costs of this arms programme (46 billion euros for 180 aircraft finally ordered), its destabilization by the abrupt ending of the Cold War in 1989, the fact that a European alternative was being developed and that a US-built option already had been (the F-18), a radical choice was made which certainly did not convince or please all concerned. Right to the end of the decision-making process, for example, the French navy clearly came out in favour of the F-18. Meanwhile, concerns about costs were raised strongly in Parliament and the press. Ultimately, therefore, it is only by taking into account key industrial policy and sociological aspects of neo-*dirigisme* that one can fully understand the choice of the Rafale and the dismissal of alternative courses of action.

Although this may appear paradoxical, neo-*dirigisme* also explains why over a very different military aircraft – the strategic airlifter known today as the A400M – French decision-makers chose the option of a European con-sortium-generated product. Indeed, on the surface, the case of the A400M appears to be strikingly different from that of the Rafale: it was conceived jointly by four European states (France, Germany, the UK and Spain), built by a 'European' company (now an integral part of Airbus) and bought using a 'commercial approach' which was supposed to avoid vacillation, tinkering by defence ministries and cost overruns by the manufacturer (Joana and Smith, 2006). Although in this instance French actors never seriously considered building this aircraft alone, a significant number of them would have pre-ferred to buy already existing aircraft 'off the shelf' either from Boeing (in the shape of C130s or C130Js) or even Russia or Ukraine. These alternatives were finally abandoned in 2000 after nearly twenty-five years of discussions and, above all, a 'harmonization' of European needs sealed in 1995. Indeed, the key decision-making period as regards this aircraft extends from that year, when Airbus Military was created, until 2003 when a contract to build 180 aircraft was signed between what is now Airbus and the four European states involved (plus Turkey). Ultimately, the key to understanding the devel-opment of this aircraft despite its cost, the choice of its manufacturer and how it would be made and sold is to grasp its role in consolidating and expanding Airbus as a corporation. Whilst the latter had developed initially in the 1970s and 1980s as a civil aerospace joint venture between French, German and British actors (Muller, 1989), in the mid-1990s heads of gov-ernment from these countries decided together to assist the development of a military dimension. Incarnated as of 1997 by the European Aeronautical and Defence Company (EADS – formally merged within Airbus in 2014), this organization envisaged the A400M as both a means of financing its establishment costs and its symbolic 'flagship'. Although Airbus remains dependant upon its different national components to produce its aircraft and foster its political support, its European character and imagery has proven just as vital. This is clearly the case for the A400M where French support has been constantly legitimated by discourse and practices designed to bolster Airbus as a European champion. Indeed, as regards the ordering and payment for this aircraft, French actors have openly and successfully sought to extend their neo-*dirigiste* approach to the European scale.

That said, the consistency of this French support has also been tempered not only by drives to ensure that a maximum of 'workshare' on producing the A400M comes to France (as in Germany, the UK and Spain) but also by how France's A400Ms have subsequently been maintained and updated. Indeed, to understand fully how and why defence procurement takes place in France, it is just as important to grasp the ways in which, once in opera-tion, weapons systems are 'supported', i.e. what provision is made for their maintenance and updating, together with the personnel and training needs this entails. Here the case of the A400M is again highly instructive (Giry and Smith, 2019a). Indeed, although designed, built and financed via high levels of European co-operation, similar synergies have not been sustained when it comes to in-service support for this aircraft. Despite the massive cost of maintenance, spare parts and training, this activity has been almost totally renationalized by the French *Armée de l'air*. The first reason is that the French actors involved have chosen a model which is essentially one of in-house support where Airbus has instead been contracted in to supply spares and undertake only major repairs. All support work is run by a specific squadron of the *Armée de l'air* based in Orléans. Consequently, if a small set of Airbus personnel are present on this base, they only occasionally give advice or actually intervene over very specific matters or major repairs. But the deeper cause of this way of conducting aircraft support is that company–state–armed forces relations in France are still structured by highly symbolic commitments to not only retain in-house support capacity, but also to continue to favour national firms whenever possible. In short, all this constitutes an industrial policy which is quite explicit. This means that although, in the last few years, in-service support has also become a key issue for the French state and air force, and even been formalized in the form of a policy concept – *le Maintien en Condition opérationnelle (MCO)* – certain ways of going to market and contracting remain taboo. Over the last few years, attempts have been made within the French state to loosen the linkages between defence procurement and industrial policy. Indeed, those in favour of such a change have targeted in-service support in particular. However, defenders of governmental interventionism have thus far prevailed.

In conclusion, neo-*dirigiste* institutions and power relations continue to heavily structure how French armaments are designed, produced, bought and supported by the state. The sociological proximity between company-based engineers and the hierarchies of both the Ministry of Defence and the air force, their collective commitment to industrial policy, as well as the autonomy their political work has achieved as regards the rest of French economic policymaking, have all contributed to the success of this long-standing political enterprise.

Wine: when 'quality' is linked to territory and 'tradition'

Although, in contrast to armaments, French wine is nearly all produced by small and medium-sized growers, industrial policy of the neo-*dirigiste* type has also heavily marked it in the past and continues to do so to this day (Smith *et al.*, 2007). Its history began in the early twentieth century when the first steps were taken to control by law and by force what could be produced and sold as wine (only the result of unadulterated fermented grapes), then what place names could figure upon its labelling (thereby protecting and consecrating vineyards such as 'Bordeaux' and 'Burgundy'). These nationally imposed steps were then supplemented by the emergence within each wine region of guilds charged with defining specifications for their respective wines (concerning authorized varietals, densities of planting, modes of 'assembling' during vinification, etc.) (Stanziani, 2005). Indeed, following prompting by state-trained agricultural engineers and from the Ministry of Agriculture itself, in 1935 these disparate sets of product norms were codified around the term *Appellation d'origine controlée* (*AOC*) and came to be governed by a new national institute on geographical indications, the *Institut national des appellations d'origine* (*INAO*). Specifically, even if this agency was not formally part of the Ministry of Agriculture, members of the latter sat on its board and the Minister themself had to sign off its most important decisions. These concerned any updating of each *AOC* (of which for wine there are 313 at the time of writing), but also how *AOC* wines as a whole planned nationally to fit with other categories of wine, most notably non-geographically linked 'table wine' until the 1970s, then this category and newly established *vins de pays* (territory-specific wines initially seen as of lower quality than *AOCs*). Moreover, the French Ministry of Agriculture has always controlled how many and where vines for winemaking can be planted through a system of plantation rights. Moreover, it successfully negotiated to extend these rights to the European Community (EC) level in the 1970s.

Barring the Second World War, from the 1930s until the 1970s this wine policy based upon a combination of *AOC* institutions and those of table wine strongly orientated a development of the wine industry in France which witnessed production increase slowly, a stabilization of domestic consumption, the beginnings of a rise in exports but also a considerable fall in the number of growers. However, in the mid-1970s this institutional ordering experienced a series of upheavals with separate but overlapping causes. As of 1970, it also developed a European scale of regulation as the EC's agricultural policy extended itself into the wine sector. First, domestic demand for table wine fell sharply, thereby generating an unsold surplus which not only drove down prices, but also greatly increased the EC's budget (obliged as it then was to 'intervene' in the market to make up for the shortfall between an officially set minimum price for wine and that at which consumers actually bought it). Secondly, when wine became part of the EC's general agricultural policy, this also meant that product from elsewhere in the Community could now enter France tariff-free. The threat of Italian wine taking up this opportunity led the French government to act first by limiting cross-border trade in this commodity (despite this contravening EC law), and a Community-wide system of 'plantation rights' which, as I flagged earlier, effectively put a cap on each member state's production levels. Moreover, this episode also gave rise to a new category of wine, *le vin de pays*. Initially designed for wine areas without *AOCs*, this category enabled local wine bodies to collectively develop specifications like those of their prestigious cousins. It was hoped this move would not only improve wine quality, but also attract interest from a new, supposedly more discerning, consumer.

Adjusting to this revised institutional order caused considerable disruption not only for individual growers and wine merchants, but also at the level of regional and local vineyards, in particular that of the Midi. In this part of what became the Languedoc-Roussillon region, hundreds of growers sold up, farms amalgamated, as did dozens of local co-operatives which eventually became part of large corporate groups (Roger, 2010a). But from the point of view of the argument being made here, what is crucial to retain is that this shift was very much structured by policies worked for politically by state officials, once again hand in hand with the dominant representatives of growers and merchants. Moreover, as of the mid-1980s when prices stabilized and subsidies diminished, the new institutional order was credited with improving French wine quality as a whole and even facilitating the opening up of export markets. In short, during the late 1980s and 1990s, the neo-*dirigiste* government of the French wine industry was widely seen as having soothed the path towards economic rebirth by keeping its social costs relatively low.

Whether this evaluation stands the test of time can, of course, be questioned. In any event, the durability of the new mode of production and its government soon came under fire from a source often too rapidly reduced to the word 'globalization'. In the early 2000s as the expansion of French wine production, fuelled largely by exports to northern Europe and the conversion of many domestic consumers to more expensive wines, began to slow, criticism of government and producer organization policies started to emerge. Initiated separately by large producers and merchants, neo-classical economists and marketing specialists, this critique essentially considered that these policies were stifling growers and processors who wanted to take on the challenge of competing directly with wines from the New World (Australia, South Africa, Chile, California, New Zealand). Specifically, the latter were seen as winning new swathes of market share, particularly in the UK, by concentrating upon varietal wines that were consistent from year to year and sold using strong brands and high marketing budgets. French wines in particular were seen as handicapped not only by plantation rights and the fragmentation of supply, but also by the constraints imposed on production methods by the *AOC* and *vin de pays* system of rules and norms. If, at that time, these New World wines were certainly destabilizing French access to northern European markets, no conclusive evidence was ever produced to demonstrate that it was such rules which were the root of their weakness to fight back. Nonetheless, by 2007 the coalition of actors using the banner of globalization, and the concomitant 'need' to meet the needs of a mythical 'new consumer' (Roger, 2010b), convinced not only the European Commission but also the French Ministry of Agriculture itself to change tack and dilute a number of its key institutions (Itçaina *et al.*, 2016). In particular, a new category of 'wines with geographical indications' was introduced in order to replace that of 'table wines' and thereby allow large European producers to compete more directly with their New World counterparts. In so doing, the value-added of AOCs was increasingly questioned and, at least initially, plantation rights were set to be abandoned. During implementation of the 2007–08 reform, however, it is revealing to note that this termination of a policy instrument never actually eventuated.

More generally, since that reform the legitimacy of AOCs has been largely reinstated. Indeed, although it is unquestionable that the EU's wine policy today is more liberal than it was in, say, 2006, the footprint of French neo-*dirigisme* is still very much present throughout the wine industry as a whole. On paper, individual producers now have more options open to them as regards how they categorize and label their wine. But the industry as a whole is still heavily structured by institutions and power relations that sink their roots in long-standing state- (and EU-) backed understandings and compromises over how wine should be produced, processed and governed.

Housing: production norms designed to suit producers

As in many other countries, in grouping together 500,000 companies and 1.3 million workers, the building industry in France is actually made up of companies and business strategies of three broad types. Small firms of up to nine employees account for 95% of businesses, but only 25% of the industry's total turnover. SMEs with between ten and 250 workers account for 4% of companies and 38% of turnover, meaning that less than 1% of building firms generate the remaining 37% of this business activity.[3] This basic information about the organizations which actually build housing units is important not only because it outlines economic power distribution within the production dimension of the housing industry, but also because it indirectly affects the three others: finance, the bureaucratic and the political.

This claim will be illustrated here using the case of the introduction of stricter 'thermic' norms designed to improve the insulation levels of all buildings in France, and thus their capacity to reduce energy waste – an objective stimulated by the fact that around 45% of energy consumption in France takes place in the home. After the first oil crisis, maximal limits on energy consumption were first introduced in 1974. Driven by international and EU-scale commitments, these were then tightened in 2005 before becoming part of a government-orchestrated national debate in 2012: *le Grenelle de l'environnement*. This round of meetings between representatives of the state, building firms, developers and NGOs generated a national plan on sustainable building. According to research by Halpern and Pollard (2017), the '*Grenelle*' exchanges were a consensual experience, largely because they consolidated the existing network of actors in the housing industry and, secondly, because any actual debate was concentrated on intensifying and speeding up the implementation of existing norms. This was particularly the case of renovations of existing housing stock, where an ambitious commitment was made to reduce energy consumption for this category by as much as 38% by 2020 (notably via additional insulation, double glazing and technologies which reuse the heat generated within buildings: Christen and Hamman, 2017). The consensual character of the *Grenelle* was also fostered by the decision only to re-instrument through the provision of 'labels', training and other non-coercive measures. In accordance with a wider change in state intervention in this industry presented in the next section, new 'greened' fiscal measures were also introduced to incentivize investors to favour building projects which respected the thermic norms in full (Halpern and Pollard, 2017: 119). Nevertheless, and even if more visibility was accorded to the issue of energy consumption within buildings, and indeed is now presented clearly as a public problem in the general and specialized press, environmental protection has clearly not managed to position itself at the centre of how housing is produced in France. Indeed, in contrast to countries such as Germany where most new apartment blocks feature high levels of insulation and even their own solar panels, proponents of more energy saving through improving the thermic quality of housing remain marginalized in this country.

To date analysis of this phenomenon in France has been limited. Hamman and Christen have suggested that eco-building and renovation 'disrupts the routines of builders', in particular their relations with suppliers and, quite simply, their very ways of building (2015: 58). Moreover, despite the subsidies and grants now made available, changing such practices can often increase the end-price of the housing unit. Finally, in any case, with others Hamman has also shown that many French consumers are still not convinced by many of the technical innovations upon which eco-building depends, in particular the increased use of wood (Hamman *et al.*, 2014). Far from being simply a technological challenge and a matter of economics, shifting consumption practices as regards housing is clearly a deeply political and societal challenge that the French polity as a whole has singularly failed to tackle head-on. Here the state has generally kept a low profile, providing evidence that in this industry neo-*dirigisme* has much less hold than in defence or wine.

In summary, the production and sourcing of goods and services ranging from weapons to wine and to housing has clearly changed over the last thirty years. If the state's involvement in housing shows the most signs of having been reduced using neo-liberal policy recipes, in the other two industries discussed here, as elsewhere in the French economy, not only do institutions that structure the very production of goods and services continue to strongly structure each of them. The state is still very much active in producing and reproducing these rules, norms and conventions in a decidedly neo-*dirigiste* manner.

Marketing and selling: the Achilles heel of French business?

Despite the prestige attributed to many French brands (Yves Saint Laurent, Givenchy, Lacoste, etc.), getting customers to actually buy many products made, or services provided, in France is rarely seen as the strong point of this country's businesses. Indeed, many critics even see this as a structural weakness. In particular, compared to Germany and Italy, exports are relatively low, the big difference being the lack of French SMEs which export compared to those located in these two neighbouring countries (Cohen and Buigues, 2014: 98). More generally, this difference between the selling practices of France's large companies and its SMEs reflects the dualization of the French economy mentioned on several occasions earlier in this chapter: on the one hand, it features large companies such as l'Oréal and Sanofi which export a large proportion of their production; on the other, it contains a myriad of small firms embedded in national, and often local, markets. In presenting how sales and marketing are tackled by French companies in the defence, wine and housing industries, two general claims will be made. The first is that for such companies the brand 'France' is both a strength and a weakness. On the one hand, it clearly positions the source and history of their product whilst, on the other, discouraging new efforts to update the imagery and resonance it condenses. The second claim is that as much for industrialized *grands projets* such as military aircraft as for many wines or types of housing, pushed by the state and 'negotiated too early' during their respective development by actors trained essentially as engineers, French products and services frequently run the risk of becoming 'technically perfect objects without markets' (Cohen, 1992: 16).

Selling planes, guns and ammunition

The selling of defence equipment often makes the headlines for one of three reasons. The first concerns controversies sparked by announcements of sales to autocratic regimes and/or those with bad human rights records. The second concerns suspicions or proof of malpractice and even corruption in order to reach a deal with a buyer nation. Finally, and more prosaically, defence sales attract journalistic interest simply because of the sums of money involved, as well as the jobs at home the contracts involved can safeguard or even create. Although the first two of these reasons are of undoubted interest, the French case presents no specificity of note. One should simply know that corruption has haunted this domain in the past and that the national Parliament has only recently been associated in regulating the exporting practices of actors from defence industry (Béraud-Sudreau, 2014). Instead, what will be tackled directly here are the more banal, but also more revealing, sets of practices through which manufacturers of defence products in France sell their respective wares.

The first thing to underline here is that although one spontaneously thinks of defence sales as occurring abroad, and despite its annual defence exports oscillating between 7 billion and 14 billion euros, in France most selling is actually to the nation's Ministry of Defence and thence to its armed forces. As we have seen earlier in the chapter, these sales are essentially 'administrative' in the sense that arms programmes are generally commissioned by the Ministry of Defence on the basis of a specification and budget co-set by civil servants, senior military officers and company managers, then validated or not by key politicians. Indeed, as a mode of government and of commerce, in many ways this administered encounter between supply and demand, which are both far from spontaneous, has repeatedly been rolled on since at least the Second World War. That said, considerable change has nevertheless occurred within this model, largely prompted by the end of the Cold War and its knock-on effects upon the global defence industry and its markets.

The first of these effects was initially the widespread cutting of national defence budgets and, therefore, pressure upon defence manufacturers to find new clients outside their respective national borders. In many countries, including France to some extent, this change went hand in hand with attempts to make procurement more cost-efficient and 'commercial'. In the French case, for example, the *DGA* in particular was reformed internally in the late 1990s by a CEO, Jean-Yves Helmer, who had previously made his reputation as a cost-cutter within the car manufacturer Peugeot (Hoeffler, 2013).

In the wake of the wars in the former Yugoslavia, then the terrorist attacks of 2001 and those that have followed, defence spending has since risen considerably. However, the markets for equipment have become increasingly competitive, first because the US and Russia are now prepared to sell arms almost anywhere in the world (in contrast to what happened during the Cold War). Secondly, new and often aggressively commercial sellers have emerged based in countries such as Israel, Turkey and South Korea. Indeed, to a large extent buyer's markets have been generated, meaning that purchasing states are now often in a good position to not only knock down prices, but also to insist that some of the actual manufacturing takes place within their own frontiers (in the name of 'offsets' and technology transfers).

In the French case, these shifts in market conditions have encouraged defence companies to reorganize themselves both internally and as a trade. From the first angle, 'international relations' have taken on more importance in terms of both corporate organization charts and budgets. From the second, a number of trade associations are important to take into account, notably the *Conseil des industries de défense* formed in 1990 and, for aeronautical operators, the relaunched *Groupement des industries françaises aéronautiques et spatiales (GIFAS)*. These bodies, together with their most powerful individual members, have pushed the French state to be less 'modest' in supporting their efforts to sell defence equipment overseas. In turn, the state has been receptive to this request, notably by supplementing the reform of the *DGA* mentioned above by giving increased importance within the Ministry of Defence to its *Direction générale des relations internationales et de la stratégie (DGRIS)*. Indeed, in a report to Parliament in 2018, *Sur les exportations d'armement de la France*, this ministry underlined that exports were not only the job of an *'équipe France'* (team France) that included actors ranging from components manufacturers to ambassadors. They were vital to safeguarding the nation's 'defence industrial and technological base'. Specifically, exports were seen as a means of compensating for fluctuations in domestic recruitment, extending production series so as to benefit from economies of scale and enabling French companies to self-finance their R and D.[4]

To illustrate the ways in which the French state participates in the exporting of French-built defence equipment, let's take a closer look at how this issue has been handled within one emblematic equipment programme, that of the Rafale fighter aircraft. Although, as outlined earlier, the Rafale was essentially designed and financed to meet the needs of the national air force and navy, in the course of this programme's development a requirement to export the aircraft was introduced. To some extent this aspect had largely been neglected because nearly 300 of the Rafale's predecessor, the Mirage 2000, had been exported (68 to the UAE, 60 to Taiwan, 59 to India, 55 to Greece). Similar levels of success were thus expected without, however, this question having been paid rigorous attention. In the interim, however, the market situation, together with the cost of producing the Rafale itself, had changed drastically. Exports thus became increasingly important but also increasingly difficult to achieve. Indeed, to date only 84 of these aircraft have been sold overseas: 24 to Egypt, 24 to Qatar (possibly to be extended to 36) and 36 to India. Indeed, the sale to India has been particularly revealing of contemporary market conditions: the Indian government has successfully negotiated that part of each plane be manufactured within its borders as part of its 'Make in India' policy.

If the commercial and political work carried out by the manufacturer Dassault, the Ministry of Defence's *DGA* and *DGRIS*, successive defence ministers and even heads of government has all clearly participated in this modest level of exporting success, it is just as revealing to examine other cases where the Rafale has ended up not being selected by foreign buyers. Here the case of Belgium is of particular interest. Culminating in October 2017, this country had been looking to replace its ageing fleet of fighters for a number of years. Indeed, through a tendering process, it was seeking to buy no fewer than fifty new fighters. What is most surprising here is not that ultimately the Belgian government chose to buy F-35s from the US (a decision officially justified for reasons of retaining American bases in their country, obtaining some workshare and reductions in price: Hoeffler and Mérand, 2015). Instead, the most striking feature of this decisional process was that the French actors chose not to even participate formally in the competitive tender. Specifically, rather than respond to a detailed set of requirements and questions raised by the buyer, 'team France' chose to send a letter, in French, from the Minister of Defence offering 'a deep partnership' should the Belgians choose the Rafale.[5] Not only were Belgian ministers unable to compare this offer to that of its competitors, they could not even present a serious case for the French option to their parliamentarians.

Putting aside the possibility that this episode was affected by stereotypical French condescendence as regards Belgium and the Belgians, the commercial approach adopted by the negotiators concerned is baffling to say the least, and very different to that developed by countries such as the UK (Giry and Smith, 2019b). Indeed, more generally, the statist reflex is still clearly at the heart of how defence equipment is marketed and sold by actors from the French defence industry.

Selling wine that no longer 'sells itself'

Many might think that given its overall reputation, French wine literally sells itself. Indeed, depending on harvest sizes, each year France is either the country that sells the most wine in the world, or concedes this position temporarily to Italy or Spain (although France always comes first in terms of value, helped by its Champagnes in particular). However, nothing, of course, actually sells itself. First, there is strong competition between and within regional vineyards to attract French domestic customers. Although many are loyal to, say, Bordeaux or the Languedoc, others pick and choose much more often than in the past. Secondly, although in France few consumers

buy foreign wine, as mentioned earlier, since the early 2000s French producers and merchants have had to work much harder to export their wines than
hitherto. Consequently, from both the domestic and international angles,
it is particularly interesting to unpack how this increased effort to market
and sell French wine has been gone about, as well as the structural obstacles
that so often stand in its way.

The first of these obstacles is the highly fragmented character of the wine
industry in this country. If in terms of imagery having 85,000 individual
wine producers can be a strength, what this also means is that virtually all
of them have very little resources for actually getting their product known
and sold. Brands of individual wines, or for that matter of wine companies,
are weak because most such firms are small and, moreover, sell a wide range
of wines. Whereas, as in other industries and as Australian producers have
recognized in particular, brands identify a product, legally protect it and
allow one to create value, apart from Mouton-Cadet and perhaps J. P. Chenet,
French wine brands are virtually inexistent (Smith *et al.*, 2007).

The second challenge for sellers of French wine is having to work against
the tide of images that French wine is too expensive and that even if its quality is generally good, it is still uneven because of the accent placed upon
territorial specificity and the year of production. For *connaisseurs*, these two
features are still good reasons for buying French wine. But most contemporary consumers are occasional drinkers little interested in the social meaning
of this drink. Rather they purchase it in a supermarket chiefly because of the
price and the label on the product.

Finally, the reputation of many French professionals whose job is to actually sell wine is often far from good. As one merchant from New Zealand
put it to me on interview in 2002, 'they sit around waiting for a miracle –
waiting for God and expecting him to be French!'

Whether this last point has any veracity is open to question. But as a consequence of the first two points, most marketing of French wine is done by
regional collective action organizations such as the *Conseil interprofession-
nel du vin de Bordeaux* (*CIVB*). Funded and run jointly by producer and
merchant levies, over the past twenty years most of these 'interprofessions'
have increasingly engaged in marketing activities of varying types: collective
branding, advertising, participation in trade shows, market research, etc.
However, as our research on Bordeaux underlines, such collective marketing
raises a number of challenges (Smith *et al.*, 2007, chapter 6). First, it is particularly difficult to define a precise and widely accepted strategy. Conciliat-
ing the interests and preferences of large and small producers and merchants,
together with those of high-end (Chauvin, 2010) and more basic wines, is
always extremely difficult. But this is often intensified by debates heavily
affected by the territorial and professional identities which criss-cross this

industry (for example, Bordeaux possesses no fewer than fifty-seven *AOCs*). Indeed, the very image one seeks to attach to the product can rapidly become a subject of controversy that can sap the legitimacy of the interprofession (e.g. tensions within the Bordelais over the symbol of the bow tie that dominated the *CIVB*'s marketing actions in the 1990s).

Here, once again, institutions and power relations are key. In the case of the *CIVB*, its marketing committee has become a key arena for the formulation of policy instruments, their reproduction over time and change at the margins. Specifically, this is where medium-sized merchants, not big enough to have their own large marketing budgets but hopeful they can coat-tail on the *CIVB*'s efforts, are particularly active in ensuring that a wide range of markets are targeted using the most consensual tools available. This risk-averse strategy has certainly enabled the organization as a whole to avoid spending all its money on costly, one-shot advertising campaigns. However, it has also prevented the 'interprofession' from reducing its support to a biannual wine fair held in Bordeaux – VinExpo – that most producers, and even many merchants, now see as largely obsolete and even in contradiction to their own interests. Launched in 1981 by Bordeaux's chamber of commerce using a logic of '*grand projet*', VinExpo has certainly succeeded in becoming a meeting point for actors in the wine trade from around the globe. For example, the 2017 edition had 5,600 participants from 150 countries. However, during this expansion, any emphasis on marketing and selling Bordeaux's own wines has taken a back seat. Indeed, this trend is now so apparent that many actors from the region barely visit the four-day show. They concentrate instead upon others where, according to them, more actual business is done (such as ProWein in Düsseldorf).

In conclusion, the changing structure and meaning attached to VinExpo is as indicative of how wine producers in France consider they need to improve and reinvent their marketing practices, as it is of how public authorities, such as those of the Bordelais, still appear wedded to a largely obsolescent commercial model. Indeed, this example, like that of French wine more generally, highlights some of the limits of neo-*dirigiste* approaches to business itself. More generally, it also underlines how the state in this country remains wedded to acting through interprofessions and *INAO* as the key vehicles through which to support the selling of French wine – despite evidence that both find it more and more difficult to generate increases in either sales or prices.

Housing: when selling is financing

As Pierre Bourdieu in particular has underlined, there is a strong symbolic dimension to buying a house or a flat because most people see them as much more than material goods. Not only have they become a sign of where one stands in terms of social success, these housing units are also intrinsic parts of a family's immediate plans, and even of their long-term future, because of the inheritance rights they involve (Bourdieu, 2000: 33). This symbolic dimension is thus a key aspect of how housing is sold in France, but one that is nevertheless inextricably linked to the issues of finance which we touched upon earlier in this chapter.[6] Indeed, more than thirty years ago, Topalov identified three forms of selling housing, each strongly linked to different ways in which this industry as a whole relates to French capitalism: building without a developer, via a private developer, or by one specialized in social housing that essentially involved public organizations (1987: 236). Specifically, Topalov claimed that there were at least three housing markets in France, each marked by 'class relations' (p. 349). Although since then the protagonists in each market have changed a little, the institutions and power relations that structure this industry have remained remarkably stable. Moreover – and notwithstanding some liberalization that has certainly taken place – far from disappearing, representatives of the state and their respective public policies continue to play a role that is at least as important as in the period 1950–80.

It is therefore important to begin here by understanding the commercial model which emerged during that very period. Its sales and marketing practices were largely shaped first by the public control of credit and, secondly, by the state's new-found commitment to, and engagement within, the market for social housing. On the one hand, this translated notably into low interest loans for new building, thereby financing production (*aide à la pierre*). On the other, more general controls on credit were imposed both on the state itself and on the banks (in order to encourage both saving and orientate the purchasing of housing). Such controls were loosened by a radical mortgage law of 1966 which had immediate and significant effects: in 1962 French banks only distributed 22% of loans for house building, but by 1972 this figure had already reached 65%, meaning that state lending had dropped from 60% to 30% over the same period (Bourdieu, 2000: 114). However, at nearly one-third, state involvement in credit for housing still remained considerable. Moreover, the state remained directly involved in the building of social housing via its agency the *CDC* and, more generally, the *dirigisme financier* it practised at that time (Frétigny, 2015).

According to Julie Pollard (2018: 7), this model has changed the most because real estate developers have since become central actors within an institutional order where the state seeks to govern real estate development through tax incentives which affect the capitalization of house building. Between 2009 and 2014, no fewer than 30–36% of all housing units built annually in France were initiated by developers, a figure that rose to 60–65%

in the Île-de-France region around Paris. However, this shift cannot simply be attributed to more activism on the part of developers themselves. Sustained collective action is highly difficult for developers who in France are a particularly heterogeneous group (some of the biggest are part of building groups, others part of banks). Moreover, they compete too much with each other to be seen as reliable partners by state actors. Instead, it is public actors themselves who have changed the structuring of the industry through two shifts in policy and political responsibility (Pollard, 2018: 15).

First, since the early 1990s the state has switched to providing 'fiscal niches' (tax breaks) within which the rich and the relatively wealthy have been encouraged to invest in the building of properties subsequently rented to the less well-off. Reduction in sales tax on the materials used for new housing has also been introduced. This has enabled the state to reduce its housing budget and thus better respect both the Maastricht criteria on budget deficits and its own commitment to 'austerity' following the 2008 financial crisis.

Secondly, in each local area, developers have long cultivated links with local government and mayors in particular. Most of the latter are vigilant in avoiding oligopolistic relationships with one or two developers (because this would lay them open to accusations of corruption). They nevertheless prefer to build up trust-based linkages with a limited number of different types of developer (and blacklist those they distrust).

Pollard concludes that the retreat of the state in the housing industry has thus been low and, partly as a consequence, 'the market' has not been the ultimate victor. Instead, there has been a shift to 'regulation by delegation' (2018: 188). As she then goes on to underline, the more stimulating question which remains, however, is that if local mayors continue to occupy the most powerful positions regarding this industry, what is it exactly that they are seeking to achieve through intervening in it (Pollard, 2018: 193)? If one recalls their equivocation over stricter environmental norms discussed in the previous section, the commitment and willingness of these public actors to achieving societal goals does indeed need seriously questioning in many, if not most, French localities.

Conclusion

As Elie Cohen put it so cogently nearly thirty years ago, in France analysis must always be careful not to confuse effusive rhetoric over industrial policy with actual practice as regards the societal structuring of business (1992: 385). Indeed, the ending of nationalizations and *grands projets* led from the top down by the state seems to substantiate the claim that business in France is now conducted in a liberal market economy which, at best, is post-*dirigiste* (Levy, 1999; Clift, 2002). There is further support for this thesis from changes wrought in the past forty years to the institutions and power relations which now structure the financing and capitalization of contemporary French business. In addition, as the example of housing illustrates, in the name of neo-liberalism the state has largely withdrawn from not only financing industry, but also orientating what it actually produces and how.

Nevertheless, as this chapter's evidence on actual production and marketing practices underlines, interventionist rules, norms and expectations continue to play a major role. Moreover, state representatives are still heavily involved in setting and implementing these societal structures. Indeed, recent research on the career trajectories of these state officials shows that through increasingly favouring business schools during their training, these actors are even more intertwined with the world of French business than hitherto (Dudouet and Grémont, 2010; Kolopp, 2018). In so doing, their view of why the state should intervene in the economy has undoubtedly shifted from that of their predecessors of the 1945–90 period. Nevertheless, they still clearly believe in certain forms of public interventionism. Consequently, and across a wide variety of industries that extend beyond the examples of defence, wine and housing developed here, or even those of pharmaceuticals and agro-food analysed elsewhere, I maintain that our claim of the advent of neo-*dirigisme* (Ansaloni and Smith, 2018) largely holds true. Indeed, as the following chapter will illustrate, it even deeply affects how sport and culture are made in today's France.

Notes

1 Previous research on this topic has also encompassed the pharmaceutical and agro-food industries (Ansaloni and Smith, 2018).
2 INSEE, 'Caracteristiques de la construction selon la taille des entreprises en 2016', www.insee.fr/fr/statistiques/2015246, p. 1, consulted 18th January 2019.
3 INSEE, *Tableaux de l'économie française*, 2018, www.insee.fr/fr/statistiques/3353488, p. 170, consulted 18th January 2019.
4 http://www.defense.gouv.fr/actualites/articles/rapport-au-parlement-2018-sur-les-exportations-d-armement, p. 9, consulted 18th January 2019.
5 'Rafale: la Belgique claque la porte à la France', *La Tribune*, 4th October 2017.
6 Here the multidimensional role played by the corporation Bouygues is highlighted by certain authors. Not only is Bouygues one of the largest building companies and real estate developers in France, but since 1987 it has also owned the most popular TV channel in France – TF1 – and thus has constantly been able to disseminate the ideal of individual property owning (Bourdieu, 2000: 230).

5

That's entertainment! 'Culture', sport and elitism

Introduction

If the vast majority of France's inhabitants below retirement age spend a good deal of their time at work, in places of education and training, or travelling to and from them, most, of course, engage in leisure pursuits of various types. For example, the French are the most frequent cinema-goers in Europe: in 2015, 29% went four or more times in the year, as compared to 20% of the UK population (Coulangeon, 2016).[1] In France, however, many such activities are not just seen as hedonistic 'entertainment' which is purely a private matter. For a start, many of these pursuits are often framed as 'public goods' that are part and parcel of French traditions, or indeed of being French itself. Indeed, as most anthropologists would rightly underline for any social space, such activity is, of course, a key component of the very *culture* of France understood in the deepest sense of the word. But what is nevertheless more specific to the French case is the degree to which the state, and public authorities more generally, have involved themselves directly in the provision and consumption of a range of social endeavours which this chapter analyses successively under the headings of 'cultural affairs' and sport. Crucially, the intensity of this involvement was initiated once again during the period of high *dirigisme* which, as with so many other aspects of French contemporary life, structured the period from 1950 to 1980. Indeed, encouraged by President François Mitterrand in particular,[2] over the following fifteen years years state involvement in culture, but also sport, became even more intense and deeply institutionalized. As will be shown below, since then the French state's engagement with culture and sport has tended to take on new forms and operate alongside, rather than against, actors from the private sector. Nevertheless, notably in comparison to other liberal democracies, the implication of French public bodies and representatives in both cultural affairs and sport has remained exceptionally high.

Indeed, these domains of activity are good testing grounds for the three central themes developed throughout this book. Since the 1980s, 'globalization' is a term that has repeatedly been used to redefine and justify public intervention over both culture and sport. Nevertheless, by mutating into what I defined in the previous chapter as neo-*dirigisme* (Ansaloni and Smith, 2018), French public authorities continue to participate strongly in reproducing the power relations and institutions which structure even the non-work-related dimension of life in this country. In so doing, neo-liberal references and policy instruments have also been proposed, debated, sometimes discarded and sometimes adopted in a variety of new guises. Moreover, in terms of substantive outcomes, in the domains of both culture and sport, the fostering of elitist practices has often tended to trump all other social and political objectives. Indeed, to a significant degree, Laferté's thesis on *embourgeoisement* (2018) takes considerable nourishment from what French cultural and sporting practices have become over the last few decades. This said, at the very least that term needs refining by delving deeper into the trends of individualization and materialism, already touched upon in earlier chapters, which have also participated in the way culture and sport have come to be societally structured in contemporary France.

'Cultural affairs', policies and practices

For many outside observers who even vaguely followed European affairs in the 1980s and early 1990s, the association between France, culture and state policy made above would come as no surprise. Throughout the two Mitterrand presidencies, and led by their media-friendly Minister of Culture, Jack Lang, French representatives were vociferous in defending what they called 'cultural exceptionalism' as a means of 'sanctuarizing' the governing of culture from the rest of the economy. Labelled 'the cultural imperative' by Philippe Poirrier (2016: 5), this political programme was centred upon defending the right of the French state to protect the French cinema industry from initiatives to deregulate both cinematic production and its diffusion by television, first at the scale of the EU (Polo, 2003) and subsequently at that of the WTO. This episode will be returned to below, but here the key point to retain is that it has often been presented as evidence that the French 'interventionist' and 'protectionist' state has always been heavily involved in its society's cultural activity. What social science research shows, however, is that this is simply not so: such a degree of state involvement dates only from the end of the 1950s. Moreover, this research also shows that far from being consistently centre-stage, French cinema is only one industry amongst a range of others in the cultural field which have been deeply reshaped by *dirigisme*.

In what follows, I first retrace how and why this level and mode of governmental involvement was established then consolidated around a range of interwoven institutions and public policies. I then move on to focus more specifically upon the widening of public actors that has occurred since the mid-1990s, together with what many commentators depict as the 'depoliticization' of cultural policy they argue has take place over this period. Rather than buy into the latter argument, and whilst agreeing that much has indeed changed over the last quarter-century, the central claim made below is that throughout the years 1958–2019 an elitist approach to culture has consistently been maintained. Indeed, the overall outcome has been the highly political reproduction of the power relations and institutions that have dominated France's cultural field since the 1960s. As will be highlighted, these practices and their outcomes are quite different from the openly elitist arts policy of the UK, or indeed from German *Kulturpolitik* which, on the contrary, has linked culture to education and even to sport (Dubois, 1999).

The late victory of culture with a capital 'C': une affaire d'Etat

In order to understand the cultural field and what continues to structure it, one first needs to grasp that until the late 1950s, French public authority was positioned at its periphery. Explanation of the weakness of state engagement in the cultural field lies partly in the liberalism which had dominated France's elites until the Second World War. Economically, liberals considered that cultural affairs should be left to the private sector and the play of market forces. More generally, most liberals also considered that it was not up to the state to privilege certain types of cultural activity over others. Additional explanation also highlights the reticence of many artists as regards the state intervening in 'their affairs'. Dubois (1999) in particular shows that 1870 to 1959 was a period when much of art and most artists positioned it and themselves 'against the state' and 'for the people'. Part of this opposition was, of course, to the art establishment, then essentially run and backed financially by upper- and upper-middle-class patrons. However, after the First World War and the Bolshevik Revolution in Russia, opposition to these proponents of 'high culture' intensified, led increasingly by Marxists and a range of other left-of-centre militants. They proposed instead a movement of *éducation populaire* through which the aim of art was not only to entertain the working classes, but also to enlighten them about the causes of their social conditions, then promote a socialist alternative. This was encouraged essentially without state support by many municipalities which, particularly when run by left-of-centre local councils, built halls, theatres and *maisons des jeunes et de la culture* (MJC) within which they encouraged associations to enact the *éducation populaire* agenda.

Although convincing, such analysis should not lead one to think that prior to the 1950s the state was not involved at all in cultural affairs.

Notwithstanding the general beliefs and discourse of its representatives, during the nineteenth century, and indeed beforehand to a lesser extent, the French state had intervened in the development and the orientation of cultural activities through its financial contribution to the building and upkeep of theatres, opera houses and concert halls, not to mention a range of museums and monuments. However, categorized as governmental assistance to '*les beaux arts*', these measures were never presented as constituting a public policy. Instead, they were technicized as funding that simply needed administering by a small unit of unspecialized civil servants and a junior minister.

As Philippe Urfalino underlines in his seminal book *L'invention de la politique culturelle* (1996), things changed dramatically as of 1959. Just a year after General de Gaulle's election and the advent of the Fifth Republic, one of the new president's closest associates, André Malraux, was nominated Minister for Cultural Affairs. Although this nomination owes something to chance, what is crucial to grasp is that it organized, and above all symbolized, a three-dimensional rupture with the past. In terms of ideology, the state broke clearly with liberalism to place itself at the centre of the cultural field as a vector for what Malraux labelled a 'cultural progressivism' that was no longer the preserve of the left. In so doing, he and his colleagues also sought to break with the didactivism of *éducation populaire*. As Urfalino underlines, priority was given instead to 'encouraging people to like culture, not to teach it'. In so doing, a sharp break away from the world of education was facilitated (1996: 36–39).

From the point of view of cultural creation, most artists themselves now came to accept that they no longer stood outside society, but rather that they existed within a sector of subsidized art. This change in artist perceptions is explained in terms of an expansion of both the 'supply' of cultural activities and their consumption by a population, many of whom had by then stayed on longer at school. More generally, this shift reflected a growth of the middle class, thereby engendering what Dubois calls the 'crystallization of the space of cultural production' (1999: 150).

Finally, from then on, this sector developed greater administrative and budgetary autonomy which, in turn, translated into much higher governmental grants, together with more prestige and power for the new ministry's growing set of senior civil servants (Urfalino, 1996: 19). Indeed, this new organization was not staffed by a *corps d'Etat* but rather by a heterogeneous set of driven, generally young, people trained in different professions and skills, all animated by 'a missionary spirit' (Dubois, 1999: 177).

In terms of policy substance, as elsewhere in the new Fifth Republic, the action of the state in the field of cultural affairs was legitimized by a 'programme', the '*planification*' of infrastructures and by the overriding aim, so dear to de Gaulle himself, of promoting *la grandeur* of France. Although the mission statement, and even the very title, of this ministry was widely perceived as vague, crucially it was not restricted to 'the arts' or to 'leisure'. Indeed, in the early years of the Ministry of Cultural Affairs, much work was undertaken to distinguish its mandate from not only the Ministry of Education's, but also that of Youth and Sport. Indeed, much of this work entailed the setting up of specific policies for different sectors within the cultural field.

As regards the traditional purview of *les beaux arts*, notably theatre, opera and classical music, Malraux and his civil servants sought first to systematize the allocation of grants through sharpening the distinction between 'professional' and 'amateur' cultural activities. In particular, this took the form of the certification of artists, troupes and orchestras. Moreover, a new range of subsidies were put in place for the public purchasing of works of art, as well as for the encouragement of operatic (Urfalino, 1990) and baroque music (François, 2007). In short, this part of the new cultural policy essentially sought to institutionalize, and in many ways standardize, the way the state now gave assistance to types of cultural activity which it had aided in the past, but via a more haphazard and less predictable mode of governmental intervention. In this way, numerous markets for cultural activity were stabilized (François, 2007, 2008). This contributed to the consolidation of their place within the field of culture, whilst empowering the state representatives involved.

But the cultural policy launched as of 1959 also progressively came to affect other parts of the field which until then had been virtually autonomous from state intervention. This was notably the case for the publishing sector in general, and that of books in particular. Indeed, notwithstanding the world-renowned status of French literature and non-fiction, well into the 1970s not only did no governmental policy exist in this sector, but no 'paradigm' had even emerged around which such intervention could have been built and legitimized (Surel, 1997: 119). This absence is particularly interesting because the 1960s witnessed an expansion of book-buying in France by a growing, longer-educated middle class. Indeed, in the early 1970s a wide range of publishers were thriving. As this boom started to tail off, however, a series of takeovers and mergers generated concentrations of power, a sharp cleavage between large companies and small, then increased emphasis being place upon the distribution of books and therefore their points of sale. As Surel put it, the very identity of the industry was shaken (1997: 155). Crucially, the issue of distribution spilled over into the emergence of a 'public problem' concerning the pricing of books or, more specifically, how each distributor was authorized to price their products as regards the 'recommended price' set by each publisher. As early as 1974, a new entrant to the market, the *Fédération nationale d'achats des cadres* (FNAC) had begun to sell books at up to 20% less than the recommended price. This was followed by large supermarket chains, as well as a major mail order firm, *France Loisirs*, which also cut prices, often even further than the *FNAC*. Importantly, these practices not only angered the publishers and many of their authors but were also seen as endangering a symbolic player in French cities and towns: the small, independent bookshop. Specifically, a movement of resistance emerged which highlighted the actual and probable disappearance of such shops. In so doing, it found allies within and around the Ministry of Cultural Affairs itself.

What is crucial to retain here is that this definition of book pricing as both a cultural and an economic problem was taken on board wholesale by the first Mitterrand government, politicized by the minister Jack Lang and translated into French law as of 1981. Symbolized as 'a single price for books' (*le prix unique du livre*), the policy instrument adopted in fact forbade any book being sold at over 5% less than the publishers' recommended price. Backed by the courts, including the European Court of Justice, what this episode reveals above all is how a sector that had hitherto been structured by highly liberal institutions suddenly came to be deeply regulated by the state. Indeed, as Surel concludes (1997: 334), what this extension of French *dirigisme* underlines is how legitimation in the name of 'books not being a product like any other' came to mean recognition that books are first and foremost a product whose material production must be stabilized, and this whilst conserving their exceptional status.

The third example developed here of the cultural policy launched as of 1959 concerns what had previously been labelled *éducation populaire* (Arnaud, 2018). Recall first that during the period 1918–60 'popular culture' had been widely celebrated by the whole of the French left, together with being seen as a means of strengthening its political 'family' and electoral base. Specifically, this movement had given rise to a wide range of activities, notably 'the animation' of young people and adult education, which its proponents saw as deeply 'cultural'. Instead of confronting this movement directly, Malraux and his close collaborators first sought to channel it towards the fields of education and youth, then to create an alternative path centred upon an entirely new set of *maisons de la culture* (MDC). The original intention here was to build an MDC in each *département* as a 'cathedral of modern times' for hosting professional artists from across the field of culture and its specialized sectors. In practical terms, the spearhead of this initiative was theatre. However, the underlying goal throughout was to promote artists who incarnated the 'universal' and therefore 'republican' meaning of culture, and this as opposed to the more partisan or sectarian character attributed to *éducation populaire* (Urfalino, 1996: 118). By the end of the 1960s, fourteen MDCs had been built in large towns and cities ranging from Le Havre to

Saint-Etienne and even the Parisian suburb of Nanterre. However, the policy as a whole ground to a halt at this point. This was partly because its instruments were denounced as 'anti-democratizing' during the social upheaval around May 1968. But it also produced fewer outcomes because each *MDC* developed a large budget to which municipalities were increasingly required to contribute. Put briefly, these two sources of tension contributed greatly to a significant downsizing of the initiative led by Malraux's successor, Jacques Duhamel, and to the building instead of a much larger number of *centres d'animation culturelles*. Not only did the state contribute much less to the budgets of the latter but, as the next section sets out more fully, sub-national authorities were encouraged to assert much greater control in the name of *local* cultural *and* economic development.

Indeed, this concern for not only economizing on state spending but also fostering national and local economic growth also affected a fourth and final example of what the first three decades of French policy constituted: the highly publicized and state-led defence of the exception of culture as regards global and European markets and their institutions. As alluded to at the beginning of this section, the stance taken up by the French state under the presidencies of François Mitterrand was legitimated in the name of the national protection of cultural heritage and goods against what was stigmatized as the encroachment of an alien and threatening 'commercial logic' into this field (Saez, 2012: 31). Indeed, the threat initially identified was very specific: the United States and Hollywood's approach to cinematic production and distribution in particular. As Jean-François Polo (2003) explains, what the Ministry of Culture under Jack Lang sought to do in fact was to 'reconcile' culture with economics, but this from the angle of *dirigiste* governmental intervention and in the name of the 'radiance' (*rayonnement*) of France and its objection to American 'imperialism'. Concretely, this goal was sought after using a new range of public investments, directing these not only to cinema *per se*, but also to the production of films for television (therefore widening the state's target to 'the audiovisual sector') and quotas on the diffusion of European-made programmes (set at a minimum of 50%). This interventionism clashed directly with neo-liberal economic doctrine in general, and that purveyed by many actors in the European Commission and the European Court of Justice. Nevertheless, by taking support from a range of artists from the cultural field, Lang and his entourage managed to prevail, institutionalizing the notion of 'cultural exceptionalism' and winning court cases at the EU scale with the help of Commission President, Jacques Delors. Indeed, EU support even protected French policy from an American attempt to outlaw it during the 1993 GATT negotiations.

To sum up, as regards the invention of cultural policy in France, it is no accident that this occurred in the 1960s during a period of high *dirigisme* and that it was backed from the top by the country's president of the day. Rather than being merely a somewhat marginal catalogue of disparate public policies, during this period, then again during the Mitterrand presidencies, France clearly developed a cultural policy which had considerable specific and combined effects not only upon French artistic life, but also on much of the citizenry. By the early 1990s, some criticism persisted of this policy supporting 'bourgeois' culture and state paternalism. Although there have been many grounds for supporting such claims, as the following section will now relate, a range of other tensions have since emerged which have had much greater influence in sapping both the initial policy and the state's legitimacy to apply it.

Beyond the depoliticization through decentralization thesis: neo-dirigisme rides again

Since the heyday of Jack Lang's first two terms as minister of culture, the French state's cultural policy has hit the headlines much less. One explanation is that as the innovations and budget increases introduced in the 1989s have bedded down, an expanded cultural field and set of public policies has simply become an institutionalized routine, and therefore a less visible part of France's public life. Indeed, Dubois closes his history of cultural policy in this country with the hypothesis that by the end of the 1990s it was already becoming 'depoliticized', i.e. justified in the name of technicized objectives rather than mediatized values (1999: 258). A second explanation is that since the mid-1990s, in line with an ongoing process of decentralization, much of cultural policy has actually shifted to cities and regions. Consequently, the tensions that do arise around it are more likely to be local than national – the most glaring example being when *Front National* mayors of towns such as Orange have sacked the director of their *centre d'animation culturelle* or drastically cut its budget. In short, as Urfalino concluded rather dramatically as early as 1996 (1999: 360), 'cultural policy was brought to an end by the triumph of culture public policies'. Indeed, in the postface added to the 2009 re-edition of this book, he goes so far as to conclude that 'cultural policy is no longer, long live public support to the economics of artistic life!' (406).

As I acknowledge in the first part of what follows, there is much to be said for both these explanations. However, I then go on to argue that they have also tended to create a blind spot as regards how the state continues to affect the cultural field as a whole. As will be highlighted below, the state is still very much present in this field and this largely because here too it has shifted towards more neo-*dirigiste* modes of operating. Indeed, despite appearances to the contrary, these remain highly political.

The narrative that cultural policy has decentralized is compelling, notably because it is one that has been developed across the Western world and even beyond. Symbolized by how the American geographer Richard Florida's notion of 'the creative class' (2002) mutated over time into that of 'the creative city' (2005), this movement has been driven in part by the linkages made between how a locality 'supplies' cultural goods and services and its respective economic development. More precisely, the underlying economic theory of action is as follows: the more a locality attracts and retains highly educated and relatively young inhabitants via its cultural 'supply', the more they they will contribute to the local economy and tax base. Propagated by geographers like Florida, but also by a range of private consultants and through the use of 'success stories', such as the regeneration of cities like Bilbao around its Guggenheim Museum (Dubois, 2012: 157), this narrative reproblematized culture as a key form of public investment (Dubois, 1999: 245).

However, for this reframing of the public problem to take root, it also had to find the appropriate 'soil' and 'climatic conditions'. In France these have been provided by the shift in centre–periphery relations sparked by the municipal elections of 1977, the decentralization laws of 1982, the emergence of autonomous regional councils as of 1986, then the establishment and consolidation of a new metropolitan scale of government beginning a decade later (Négrier, 2005; Saez, 2012). Across France, the 1977 local elections brought to power a large number of new and leftist mayors, many of whom were particularly keen to be more ambitious in the municipal provision of cultural equipment, services and events. In particular, they financed a range of *MDCs*, partly to modernize traditional libraries but also, and more generally, to provide a focal point for the cultural field in their respective town or city. The decentralization launched by the first Mitterrand government reinforced this shift, first by providing more autonomy to the renewed elected bodies in each *département* (then called the *Conseils généraux*) to also support cultural activity, and subsequently by enabling a similar shift to take place for the now elected *Conseils régionaux*. Indeed, one of the ways the latter sought to legitimize themselves was to provide subsidies for cultural activities not only in urban areas, but also in rural ones. In the case of Rhône-Alpes, for example, as early as 1991, a policy was launched to incite groupings of communes to build projects around travelling cinemas, taking theatre into schools, festivals and book fairs (Faure and Smith, 1994). However, as Table 5.1 underlines, the most ambitious attempts to make local cultural policy have clearly occurred at the scale of the large city and their agglomerations. Indeed, alongside new moves to join forces across urban communes to provide services in general, those pertaining to culture have received a massive boost since the mid-1990s (Bonet and Négrier, 2008). Moreover, this was further reinforced by the new decentralization law of

Table 5.1 Spending on culture by different types of local authority
(millions of euros)

	2006	*2010*	*2014*
Régions	556	661	773
Départements	1,292	1,390	1,355
Communes	4,357	4,606	3,463
Inter-communal groupings	842	1,061	1,612[1]
Total	7,047	7,718	7,203

[1] This figure covers only groupings that include a commune with more than 10,000 inhabitants.

Source: Département des études, de la prospective et des statistiques (DEPS) du Ministère de la Culture, 2014 and 2019.

2015 which not only amalgamated many regions and made them more powerful in many ways, but also further legitimized and empowered intercommunal groupings which contain a commune of more than 10,000 inhabitants. Specifically, this has further consolidated the capacity of cities to strengthen their cultural policies and share costs with their surrounding communes.

Indeed, if in 2014 each region devoted on average 35 million euros annually to cultural affairs and each *département* around 13 million euros, each commune spent only 3,500. Given the vast difference in size between communes, however, the latter figure means virtually nothing. It is much more telling to examine the budget of largish cities such as Bordeaux. In 2016, the city council proudly proclaimed that it spent no less than 333 euros a year per inhabitant on culture. Indeed, at over 80 million euros in total, this sector was the one the council supported the most.[3] Moreover, not only do such cities spend large sums of money each year on culture, but what they spend it on is also highly revealing. The largest proportion by far is spent upon the building and upkeep of museums and venues, whereas relatively little is devoted to artistic creation itself (for Bordeaux this budget was only 22 million euros in 2016). Indeed, for local authorities more generally, Table 5.2 provides some useful data. It shows in particular that *départements*, and many small or medium-sized communes, are largely prisoners of year-on-year spending on heritage sites; their upkeep is costly and leaves little room for other initiatives. Interestingly, intercommunal groupings also have had to take on some of these expenses, often in the name of 'mutualizing' the costs (and benefits) of sites which contribute to the touristic development of not only their communes but of those around them. Nevertheless, these groupings, the regions and the larger communes have the most leeway for spending on cultural activities *per se*, and thus of developing public policies that are chiefly of a cultural, rather than a touristic, type.

Table 5.2 Total budgets by type of authority and type of expenditure, 2010 (millions of euros)

	Total budget	%	Cultural activities	%	Heritage sites	%
Regions	657	9	501	12	146	5
Départements	1,375	18	526	12	807	28
Communes > 10.000 inhab.	4,453	60	2,701	63	1,609	55
Groupings	986	13	597	13	367	12
Total	7,472	100	4,325	100	2,930	100

Source: Département des études, de la prospective et des statistiques (DEPS) du Ministère de la Culture, 2014, www.culture.gouv.fr/Sites-thematiques/Etudes-et-statistiques/Publications/Depenses-des-collectivites-territoriales, consulted 10th May 2020.

Table 5.3 How cultural activities were financed in four regions, 2008

	Communes	Groupings	Départements	Region	State
Lorraine	45	18	15	7	15
Poitou-Charente	35	18	18	12	17
PACA	56	13	14	7	10
Rhône-Alpes	54	7	19	6	14

Note: Operating budget only (excludes buildings maintenance).

Source: Inter-regional Study, 2013, cited in Dupuis (2017: 47).

This said, it is important to recognize too that spending on cultural policies varies considerably from region to region. As Table 5.3 underlines using data on four such areas, in relative terms certain regional councils fund culture more than others (e.g. Poitou-Charente), whereas in some areas intercommunal groupings hardly fund it at all (e.g. Rhône-Alpes). Moreover, although the state's contribution to funding cultural action is now relatively low (at 10–17% for each of these regions), it varies considerably.

More fundamentally, although the figures in Table 5.3 all tend to suggest that the state is no longer a major player in the cultural field, in fact this is simply not the case. To begin with, one has to recall that expenditure by local authorities in this domain includes money they receive each year in the form of global grants from the state (Dupuis, 2017: 47). Although this argument might seem formalistic, it does serve as a reminder that because French local authorities are not totally free to self-fund, their margin for manoeuvre to make policy is limited. More fundamentally, the state remains highly active in the field of cultural affairs, as the following three points all testify.

First, throughout France the state is very much still there through its network of field offices. Indeed, as of 1977, *Directions régionales des affaires culturelles* (*DRACs*) were established in each region, ostensibly to implement national policy and to provide 'expert advice' to local authorities. Nearly forty years on, Négrier and Teillet (2014) consider the *DRACs* have lost power because their resources have been cut, due to the rise of the regional councils and cities in terms of expertise, together with what they label 'the instrumental turn' experienced by France's cultural policies. Specifically, they identify the latter as stemming from a generalized 'managerialization' common to all of the state and its field offices. In particular, this has taken the form of new methods of accounting. Notwithstanding these changes, in most areas state involvement in cultural policy remains strong, notably because the *DRACs'* certification process is still firmly in place. Indeed, recent developments in the cultural sector provide further evidence for Renaud Epstein's (2015) overarching claim that the power of the state has not been reduced. Rather it has been recalibrated through the state acting more 'at a distance' from the actual implementation of policies: *l'Etat à distance*. Indeed, this is precisely the positioning that a leading expert on cultural affairs, Claude Patriat has recommended for this sector: 'the time has come for a "strategist state", one that is a pilot and an expert, and which channels its competence into collective projects alongside local authorities' (2017: 34).

My second reason for underlining the continued importance of the state is quite simply the overall budget that it devotes to culture. Although put under pressure by 'the great recession', as Table 5.4 highlights, this budget is still high and accounts for 30% of all public spending on cultural affairs in France (Ministère de la culture, 2018: 10–11).

It is certainly true that there is a massive concentration of spending in Paris and its surrounding region (Île-de-France) where most monuments and much cultural activity is concentrated (Dupuis, 2017: 43). Indeed, in terms of budget per inhabitant, Île-de-France received 202 euros per head from the Ministry of Culture in 2017, whilst other regions received only between 17 and 30 euros (the lowest being Pays de la Loire) (Ministère de la culture, 2018: 11). Indeed, all regions with large rural areas are put at a distinct disadvantage in this respect, one which local authorities struggle to compensate for. Moreover, it is obviously difficult to push an agenda on live performance when there are 240 theatres in Île-de-France and only seventeen in the region of Centre Val de Loire or twenty-four in Pays de la Loire.

Nevertheless, what needs stressing is the continuity that marks the French state's actions over culture in general. As a recent book edited by Poirrier sets out clearly (2017), the French state continues to intervene heavily across the cultural sector in issue areas ranging from the art market, to cinema,

Table 5.4 The Ministry of Culture's budget, 2006–16 (millions of euros)

Budget lines	2006	2007	2008	2009	2010	2011	2012	2013	2014	2015	2016
Heritage	1,024	1,154	1,183	1,260	1,300	902	801	797	727	769	877
Creation	787	795	811	821	830	776	787	761	765	740	748
'Education'	821	826	823	820	855	1,075	1,060	1,058	1,061	1,091	1,111
'Cultural industries'						284	262	258	250	250	276
Research on culture	144	148	144	154	152	123	118	114	110	110	122
Total	2,776	2,923	2,961	3,058	3,138	3,162	3,031	2,991	2,916	2,960	3,134

Source: Loi des finances (2016), cited in Dupuis (2017: 40).

television and even video games. Indeed, as we have seen earlier in the case
of cinema and TV, in order to defend its interventionist approach, the French
government has often had to seek allies in order to protect its positions at
the EU scale. Recently, issues such as authors' rights have been challenged
not only by the internet but also by giants of the digital age such as Amazon
and Netflix. So whilst it is certainly valid to criticize the French state for
trying to cover too much and, partly as a consequence, for not doing so
deeply enough or having contradictions within its own policy (Bouquillion,
2017: 171), one has to admit that it affects cultural activities in France considerably. As François underlines in his economic sociology of the development of baroque music in France, 'just because the artists themselves
consider they constantly have to "juggle" between several sources of financing does not mean there is no underlying logic ... The link between the
market and politics remains strong' (2007: 647).

More deeply still, as research in the 1990s had already underlined, cultural policy in France has certainly entailed very little 'democratization'
(Dubois, 1999). Rather it has accompanied an extension and diffusion of
bourgeois values and practices via the education system. Indeed, one of the
paradoxes of all the political activity in France over culture since the 1960s
is that, when compared to other European countries, the actual practising of
artistic activities in this country is relatively low: in a 2015 survey, only 11%
of respondents said they engaged in such pursuits at least once a week
(whereas this figure is 22% in the UK and 30% in Germany).[4] More fundamentally still, as Urfalino highlighted, as regards social stratification, 'the
impact of art is limited, at most, indirect ... [Cultural policy] has not changed
social stratification as regards "cultural practices", but it has engendered
convergence between two elements of growth: the supply of professional
artistic activity and equipment, together with a larger cultivated middle
class' (1996: 394).

This vast question regarding the social impact of French cultural policy
has yet to be tackled head-on and in depth by social science. In the absence
of robust data and analysis, I clearly cannot come to any firm conclusion on
this form of impact either. What this section has sought to show instead is
the ambition of public policies in the cultural field in France, as well as the
political meanings attached to them, and the conflicts to which they have
given rise. Arnaud, for example, rightly raises the question as to whether
cultural policy in France today is much less about linking culture and social
justice than it was in the period 1920–90, and much more about 'territorial
marketing' and even 'cultural washing' (2018: 215). More generally, as
Dubois underlines, what is certain is that as a vague category of public
action 'culture' has been a remarkable success (1999: 299). Indeed, where
my own analysis goes a stage further is to highlight how the neo-*dirigiste*

state has made the most of this vagueness to appear very active – an appearance of activity that sub-national and local public authorities have copied and, in many instances, gone beyond. Critics of today's cultural interventionism may well be right to pinpoint examples where the actors involved have lost sight of the policy's initial objectives and fallen into the trap of routinized administration of unreflexive programmes and budget lines. Moreover, politicized controversies over their substantive content clearly merit more study. What is certain, however, is that in France the very existence of cultural policy is rarely questioned. Neither is the extent to which it has become an institutionalized part of both public affairs and state–society relations.

Sport or sporting achievement?

If research has shown how culture in France has become an issue of both political and economic importance, the same can also be said about another activity previously consigned to the private sphere: sport. Indeed, just as Pierre François has underlined in the case of culture, if the social scientist poses 'disenchanted', 'vulgar' questions to a field which is constantly 'enchanted' by its own protagonists, this applies equally to sport – another 'enchanted world' which, to paraphrase a famous manager of Liverpool Football Club (Bill Shankly), 'is much more important than life'. What is perhaps most intriguing in the French case is that, like culture, sport has only become the sustained object of public and political debate since the 1960s. More precisely, although sport played a role in the lives of many inhabitants of France way before this period, it is only over the past six decades that it has become a legitimate object of public intervention and political investment.

As in the cultural field, explanation for this development and the depths of its contemporary institutionalization comes largely from the manner through which *dirigiste* elements in the early Fifth Republic worked politically to make sport, and sporting achievement in particular, a national priority. In so doing, alliances between state representatives, those of the federations of certain individual sports, together with the leaders of major clubs, are key to understanding how sport became and has remained a French 'public problem'. Moreover, as the second part of what follows will stress, although this problem, together with the policy instruments devised to tackle it, has been deeply shaken since the early 2000s, the basic foundations of France's sporting model are still very much in place. Throughout, what will be highlighted is how those who dominate sport in France so rarely frame it as a leisure activity and source of fun 'for all'. Instead, emphasis has consistently been placed upon the production of a sporting elite capable of not only winning trophies and medals, but also generating jobs and wealth.

The institutionalization of sporting achievement as a national problem and priority

Understanding how, as of the 1960s, the state came to be at the centre of a relatively ambitious national sports policy cannot simply be reached by following what its own representatives did in the opening years of the Fifth Republic. Those actions are important, but they only 'made sense' and had effects because of how sport had hitherto been framed as a social and public activity.

A better place to start is thus with the history of how sport in general initially developed in the French case. This occurred in a way that ran contrary to what occurred in countries such as the UK where schools, and in particular prestigious private schools, were key vectors of developing and encouraging sporting activity. As underlined in chapters 1 and 2, schooling in France was traditionally linked to the 'instruction' of a precise set of discipline-driven subjects, one within which sport or even physical education had no place. Although structured physical activity began to be introduced into curricula as of the 1920s in an effort to 'regenerate' French youth in the aftermath of the traumas of the First World War (Callède, 2002), sport as a whole remained framed as a private and leisure activity. Indeed, this framing had a second set of roots in the emergence of sporting federations by discipline as of the 1880s. Formalized by law in 1901 as 'associations', ever since, these federations have structured what is known as *le mouvement sportif*. This vague term condenses those who actually play organized sport and, above all, those who have been elected to run it. More specifically, for more than 140 years, the basic unit of sport in France has been the club, an entity most often linked to a commune and always a member of its respective national federation.

Indeed, an initial move by representatives of the state to encourage sport in France beyond schools also began in the 1920s. Initially pushed by actors within the Ministry of War eager to encourage young people to become fit and active, the baton then passed to representatives of the *Ministère de l'instruction publique* (renamed the *Ministère de l'Education nationale* in 1932). Whether an increase in sporting activity was encouraged by the modest levels of this initial state intervention is open to debate, but by 1930 a million people in France were registered to play organized sport and certain large municipalities, notably Lyon, had begun programmes of infrastructure construction. Further impetus was given by parliamentary debates in 1930 and, in particular, by the *Front Populaire* government of 1936–38. Indeed, during the latter, an under-secretary of state for leisure and sport, Léo Legrange, was highly active in commissioning an inventory of sports infrastructure, launching state subsidies for its construction and, more generally, legitimizing the state 'as a guide' for the sporting movement as a whole (Callède, 2002: 443–444).

Although this government was short-lived and, above all, was followed by a Vichy regime more committed to physical education for hygienist and military reasons than to sport itself (Callède, 2000, chapter 3), it nevertheless provided some ideological and symbolic foundations upon which post-war state representatives gradually built a more ambitious policy. Given the many other priorities and preoccupations of the Fourth Republic, the groundwork for this took a considerable amount of time. Indeed, it was not until the advent of the Fifth Republic and the nomination, in 1958, of Maurice Herzog as *Haut Commissaire à la jeunesse et aux sports* that any significant change became apparent. Subsequently elevated to the rank of secretary of state, like André Malraux in the field of culture, this *résistant* who first became famous as a pioneering mountain-climber entered politics with a precise mission and with the personal backing of President de Gaulle (Martin, 1999). Taking further motivation from the poor showing of French athletes at 1960's Rome Olympics (five medals, none of which were gold), Herzog was able to build his team within a growing *Ministère de la jeunesse et des sports*. Together they embarked upon a systematically planned expansion of infrastructures across France, the building of renewed relations with the federations and pushed the Ministry of Education to reprioritize physical education within all French schools. As regards the first objective, a multitude of swimming pools, athletics facilities and sports pitches were funded in association with individual communes. Spilling over well into the 1970s and 1980s, this plan to make the most of France's then expanding urban demographics also fitted with the initiation of new contracts with clubs and associations which took the form of the state 'delegating' them 'a mission of public service'. Indeed, as Table 5.5 highlights, by 1995 there were no fewer than 13 million sports 'licences' taken out each year. A total of 160,000 clubs now existed, all linked to over 100 national sports federations (up from just fifty-seven in 1954). Remarkably, since then these figures have remained stable.[5]

What is perhaps even more important to retain from this brief summary of the institutionalization of what practitioners still call 'the French sports model' is that it has consistently prioritized sporting achievement, and thus elitism, over sport for all. This primary objective has been striven for through the state's monopoly of qualifications to teach and coach sport, its employment of up to 7,000 persons to do just that and their being 'placed at the disposition

Table 5.5 The number of sports registrations in France, 1949–2019 (millions)

Year	Total registrations
1949	1
1959	2.5
1969	5
1979	9
1989	13
1999	14
2014	16
2018	16.4

Source: Nys (2011: 217); Ministère des sports, www.sports.gouv.fr/organisation/publications/statistiques/Donnees-detaillees/Donnees-detaillees-2018, consulted 10th May 2020.

of' a limited range of elite federations, associations and clubs. In addition, in 1975 a new category – *les sportifs de haut niveau* (high-level sportspeople) – was defined by the Ministry of Sport. Ever since, this category has been used to attribute funding to a select set of athletes who have either already represented France, or who are earmarked as likely to do so. Today, the total number of these sportspeople is around 7,000, each of whom benefits from monthly payments and access to training facilities granted by the state (Fleuriel and Schotté, 2015). Although, as we will see subsequently, the status of these two policy measures has been destabilized over the last twenty years, they have both constituted a key means through which the state has sought to improve the performance of individuals and teams who might one day represent France. This strategy has met with some success if, for example, one looks at the Olympic Games or recalls the two football world cups won by French teams in 1998 and 2018. The other side of this model has nevertheless been the continued low emphasis placed upon sport in schools, for women[6] and for disabled people. Indeed, an imperfect but nevertheless revealing indicator of French sport's elitism is that whereas in Finland, Denmark, Sweden and Austria more than 70% of their inhabitants over the age of 15 do some sport or fitness activity at least once a week, this figure is only 50% in France (just above Spain and just below the UK at 55%).[7]

Meeting the challenges of decentralization and austerity: a model refined but not recast

As with *dirigisme* in many if not all other sectors (Ansaloni and Smith, 2018), that of French sport has experienced a series of challenges since the early 1980s. First, it has had to face up to the budgetary cuts and reduction in state personnel that have been imposed from above in the name of a succession of 'economic imperatives'. More precisely, in order to reduce the country's budget deficit, meet the criteria of monetary union then of the European Central Bank and, more generally, fit in with the increasing recourse made to neo-liberal policy recipes in the Ministry of Finance (Lemoine, 2016) and other key state elites, decision-makers within the Ministry of Youth and Sport have had to discover new ways of organizing and acting.[8] Alongside this change, adapting to decentralization has constituted an additional challenge. If, before 1982, communes, but also *départements* and regions, were already strongly present in the regulation and financing of sport throughout France, since then their omnipresence has been legitimated and the scope for territorialized initiatives vastly enhanced (Honta, 2010). In purely budgetary terms, in 2007, two-thirds of public spending on sport was by the communes, 6% by the *départements* and 4% by the regions, leaving just around 20% for the state (Del Prete, 2011: 162). By 2016, at 12 billion euros per year, local authorities had become responsible for no less than 92% of public expenditure on sport, and the state's Ministry of Sport only 8%.[9] Indeed, it is important to consider that in many cases managing, and adapting to, the twin challenges of top-down restrictions and decentralization has frequently gone hand in hand. Nevertheless, now acting using instruments that are neo-*dirigiste* and enable it to 'govern at a distance' (Epstein, 2015), and despite being challenged more systematically than hitherto, the state is still very much involved at both national and local levels. Three examples will illustrate this claim.

The first concerns the state employees who are paid to train and advise not only sportspeople, but also the federations and clubs: the *conseillers techniques sportifs* (CTFs). A study by Honta and Julhe (2013) highlights that since the 1980s the expertise of these actors has been 'demonopolized' by two types of privatization, as well as a more general trend in the governing of sport in France. The first type of privatization derives from the emergence of privately paid personal trainers for many top athletes. Firmly linked to the worldwide professionalization of the latters' respective sports since the mid-1980s, and notably that of athletics, many such sportspeople now consider themselves as small enterprises who do not need or desire the 'interference' of CTFs. Similarly, the second mode of privatization concerns a limited number of wealthy sports – notably football and rugby – which have chosen to develop their own centres for elite training and development.

More deeply still, however, the legitimacy of CTFs has been sapped by a change in the very framing of their work which has given ever-increasing importance to a logic of results produced in the short term, rather than to one of putting in place programmes where the achievement of such results is made more likely. Honta and Julhe trace this trend to a perceived slide in the results of French teams at the Olympics: fifth in the medals table in

1996, sixth in 2000, seventh in 2004, tenth in 2008 – a slide halted at the London Olympics in 2012 (seventh) then in Rio in 2016 (seventh). Indeed, their research shows that the very model of the *CTF* has been questioned since the mid-1990s (Honta and Julhe, 2013: 70). Nevertheless, in 2012, more than 75% of the Ministry of Sport's budget was concentrated on the highest level, leaving little money for the promotion of 'sport for all' (just 3.3%), public health through sport (8%), or the promotion of sport professions (14%). Indeed, this example is particularly interesting because whilst it shows how one of the pillars of *dirigisme* – the *CTF* – has been deeply questioned, it also underlines that the state as a whole is now seeking to pilot sport as a sector 'from the top'. This has meant reasserting its legitimacy as 'the sole defender of the national interest' (now defined essentially as the performance of teams and individuals wearing *le coq sportif* – French sport's national emblem).

Examining directly how other roles given to sport are handled provides us here with a second example which illustrates how French sport is structured: the case of the linkage between sport and health. In line with international medical findings about this linkage, in 2012 the French state launched its plan *Sport, Santé, Bien-être* (Sport, Health, Well-being). Its implementation requires civil servants across France working for both the ministries of youth and sport and of health to work together on the one hand, and establish partnerships with local authorities on the other. Here it is important to note that notwithstanding the role accorded to local bodies, the state is supposed to be the overall 'pilot' of this programme. However, as Honta and Illivi underline (2017: 875), in most instances the state's actors 'have great difficulty in imposing its priorities and establishing network dynamics'. According to them, part of this difficulty stems from 'the plethoric character of the missions that its agents have to cover' (877). But more fundamentally the problem lies in the fact that despite decentralization, the state considers it is, and must always be, the prime actor who frames the very problem of encouraging sport to improve public health. Specifically, 'local actors are not associated directly enough with formulating the national plan in order for them to co-produce, alongside the state, the meaning and the goals of a shared programme dedicated to this policy objective' (884). In short, and once again, despite the state's budget on the sport–health linkage remaining decidedly modest, as well as interministerial co-ordination being one of its structural weaknesses, its representatives have positioned themselves to remain at the centre of policy making and administration.

A final example of how decentralization and restrictions upon the state's budget have affected how sport is now regulated in France concerns the building of new stadia in general, and those of the country's most popular sport in particular: football. Despite the fact that the inhabitants of France attend live sporting events much less than their neighbours in other European countries,[10] and that the average attendance at a French first division football match in 2018–19 was only 20,000, public authorities have been strongly linked to each professional club since at least the 1930s. Specifically, in most instances each municipality concerned was actually a shareholder in its local club, sometimes to the tune of 80% or more (e.g. Lille: Sawicki, 2012b). This arrangement was destabilized first in the 1990s, by the introduction of a law putting French practice in line with that of the rest of the EU by outlawing such shareholding as of the year 2000. Alongside this change, and under the influence of American and British examples in particular (Segas, 2018), many clubs themselves began to seek new locations, thereby enabling not only the expansion and modernization of their stadia, but also to combine them with shopping centres or hotels. Seen by many supporters and leftist militants as an example of gentrification and as a means of expelling 'traditional' modes of 'supporterdom' (Smith, 2002: chapter 2), these costly projects have more fundamentally challenged the relationship between major French football clubs, 'their' local authorities and, indirectly, the state itself. However, as Segas perceptively shows (2018), it would be a mistake to consider that the construction of these new stadia is simply one more example of 'rabid neo-liberalism' gone rife. Rather, certain neo-liberal recipes have been injected into a 'hybrid' French model within which both 'the market' and the state continue to play singular roles.

The best-documented instance of this development is the case of Lille and its football club, the *Lille Olympique Sporting Club* (*LOSC*). As Frédéric Sawicki has painstakingly documented, in the late 1990s plans were initially made to enlarge its stadium situated in the centre of the city. Relatively quickly this firmed up into an initiative to transform the existing 18,000-seater stadium into a 32,000 one, essentially by rebuilding and enlarging its grandstands. However, in the face of protests by local residents concerned that a larger stadium would devalue a local and protected architectural site, as well as generating numerous difficulties on match days as regards parking, and in the face of the highly publicized court case which ensued, in the early 2000s the plan changed to one of building an entirely new ground on the outskirts of the city that could contain 50,000 spectators. Although this change in tack enabled the city council to placate many of its residents, it both angered many *LOSC* supporters and required this municipality to consult and financially involve the other communes of Lille's metropolitan area. In the end, the new ground was built but at a cost four times over budget, and through involving not only funding from the regional and *département*-level councils, but also from the state's budget set aside for financing the 2016 'Euro' championship (Sawicki, 2012b, 2016). Indeed, from the point of view of this chapter, what this illustration shows is not only that the state has kept itself outside local controversies over stadia, as in other cases such as those of Grenoble and Rennes, but nevertheless it still remains within the decision-making configuration through contributing relatively modest, but often indispensable, sums of money to the projects at issue. More generally, the state has also participated in the rise in public–private partnerships through which urban projects involving stadia have been realized by legitimizing this mode of government and relationship to businesses in general, and to real estate promoters in particular (see chapter 4).

In summary, the practice and governing of sport in France has clearly undergone some significant shifts over the last two decades. However, particularly when one compares these changes with what has occurred at the same time in equivalent countries, one is immediately struck by the continued presence of a neo-*dirigiste* state in this domain. As I underlined in the previous chapter, neo-*dirigisme* does not depend upon funding alone to ensure that state representatives remain central within priority and decision-making. From this angle, over the last two decades, the central state has clearly reduced its rate of contribution to financing French sport. What is more important, however, is that state representatives have retained a central role in setting 'the rules of the game', i.e. impacting upon the institutions that structure the field in question. Indeed, it is from this position that, allied to a range of other public, collective and private actors, state officials have participated fully in reproducing, and often deepening, the elitism that dominates sport in France.

Conclusion

Be it within sport or the field of culture, concluding that elitism predominates does not, of course, mean that other ways of engaging in these domains are precluded in this country. Thousands of France's inhabitants engage frequently in a wide variety of sporting and cultural practices that are scarcely affected by formal governing at all (e.g. jogging, rap music or hip-hop dance). In this way, they largely escape from the effects of elitism. In so doing, they can, of course, participate in other deep societal trends, notably that of individualization or high levels of spending on material goods (e.g. when taking up kite-surfing). Nonetheless, as we have seen in this chapter, wide swathes of sporting and cultural activity in this country clearly are still strongly orientated by the institutions and asymmetric power relations which structure these two fields – fields within which state officials continue to play a major role. Indeed, the very legitimacy of public action in both is rarely questioned by their respective professions, associations, clubs and interest groups. To understand this recurrent phenomenon better, it is now time to examine French engagement in such organizations more generally.

Notes

1 Eurostat, Culture statistics – frequency and obstacles in participation, October 2018. https://ec.europa.eu/eurostat/statistics-explained/index.php?title=Culture_statistics_-_cultural_participation#Cultural_participation_by_country_of_birth, p. 4, consulted 23rd February 2020.
2 A 'personal' commitment symbolized by the whole budget for the Ministry of Culture being doubled during his first year in office.
3 www.bordeaux.fr/p82366/bordeaux-culture, consulted 10th January 2020. The figure of 80,000 euros constitutes about 8% of the city's total budget.
4 Eurostat, Cultural statistics – frequency and obstacles in participation, October 2018. https://ec.europa.eu/eurostat/statistics-explained/index.php?title=Culture_statistics_-_cultural_participation#Cultural_participation_by_country_of_birth, p. 9, consulted 23rd February 2020.
5 In 2017 there were 166,000 sports clubs in France. Meanwhile, a university-conducted public opinion survey concludes that 41% of those surveyed are members of an association, and that 19% of these memberships concerns a sport (up from 16% in 2008) (Lardeux, 2019: 76).
6 There are some signs that this inequity has recently begun to change. Although this figure alone is not sufficiently telling, note that in 2018, 38% of registrations for sport were for women. www.sports.gouv.fr/organisation/publications/statistiques/donnees-detaillees/, consulted 10th February 2019.
7 Eurostat, 'Statistics on sports participation', 2014. http://ec.europa.eu/eurostat/statisticsexplained: 2, consulted 6th November 2018.
8 In particular, in the name of the 'rationalisation généralisée des politiques publiques', in 2010 the *département* scale *Directions des jeunesse et sport* were merged into new and downsized *Directions départementales interministerielles à la cohesion sociale.*
9 *L'optimisation des dépenses publiques en faveur du sport, un rapport interministeriel*, April 2016. NB: According to this report, the state also finances sport in schools to the tune of 3.8 billion euros a year.
10 According to a survey conducted in 2015, 71% of people in France never attended any events, whilst only 12% attended four or more per year. These figures may not be so different from the UK and Germany (65/15 and 62/18 respectively), but they contrast sharply with social practices in the Netherlands where only 45% of the population never attend live sporting events and no less than 32% attend four events or more. Eurostat, 'Statistics on sports participation', 2014, http://ec.europa.eu/eurostat/statisticsexplained: 4, consulted 6th November 2018.

6

Social and political activism: State-centred but organizationally fragmented

Introduction

Nation states are, of course, not only delimitations of space within which a particular range of social, economic and cultural activities take place. They are institutionalized entities which have been deeply shaped by varying forms of collective and political action, on the one hand, and, on the other, set parameters upon how this action has developed and taken place. In order to set out how collective action takes place in contemporary France, this chapter will therefore describe the types of activism that predominate in this country, whilst seeking to explain them in terms of the recurrent rules, norms and processes which generally guide and fuel them. In so doing, however, I do not simply roll on the conventional distinction between 'social movements' and 'political' organizations. This separation dominates not only the literature in social sciences, but also their very structuration in terms of research, teaching and debate. As Erik Neveu underlines (2015: 8–24), the first reason for proceeding otherwise is that sharp distinctions between organizations and social movements simply do not hold up in the actual world of collective action. In order to mobilize, endure and have any chance of affecting public life, movements need to also become organizations. Conversely, any organization engaging in politics which loses its movement-like impetus is likely to end up reducing its societal impact and, eventually, fading away. The second reason for not drawing a thick line between social movements and organizations is that any collective mobilization becomes political whenever it calls upon public authorities and the public space to be involved in, or simply to react to, its respective cause (Neveu, 2015: 11).

Indeed, a third and final reason why movements and parties will be analysed successively yet together in this chapter is that, as regards both types of collective action, France is too often depicted as an outlier, or even as an exception which can only be explained ideosyncratically. Specifically, in the literature on social movements, academics have rushed to make too much of the 'weakness of intermediaries' between French society and its government which, they claim (Kaplan, 2001), stems originally from the outlawing of corporations after the Revolution, and has since been reproduced by the overwhelming power of the state (Barthélemy, 2000), or at best 'state pluralism' (Elgie and Griggs, 2000). As will be shown below, there is no doubt that certain types of social mobilization, such as the public demonstration or marches through city streets, are more common in France than in many other Western democracies. Similarly, French interest groups often do have to struggle harder, and often in vain, to highlight their legitimacy than they do in more 'pluralist' polities such as the United States. Nonetheless, it is simply wrong to consider that 'intermediaries' in France are necessarily weak, that the state always dominates them and that, consequently, the frequency of 'taking to the streets' sums up a polity with a powerful top, a powerless bottom and no middle. Although the protracted and much-publicized confrontation in 2018–19 between the *gilets jaunes* and Emmanuel Macron's presidency and government might appear to suggest otherwise, as the first part of this chapter will show, French society and politics as a whole is very deeply structured by the social movements and organizations it encompasses (Sawicki and Siméant, 2009). Although its state is indeed omnipresent, this certainly does not mean that non-governmental organizations and movements always lack power and legitimacy. Indeed, what has become of the *gilets jaunes* movement will be addressed as a means of validating this argument.

Similarly, much of the existing literature on French political parties tends to stress their instability and weaknesses in terms of aggregating societal demands into coherent programmes for changes in government and policy. Here emphasis is placed first upon the relatively high number of parties in France and fluctuations in their share of electoral votes, but also upon their tendency to split or simply be cleaved into a myriad of 'factions' (Seiler, 2011). Secondly, other authors highlight instead the structural weakness of the French Parliament as regards the Executive and, more generally, the state itself, thereby concluding that in any case parties matter less in France than they do elsewhere (Brouard, 2011). Once again, such analyses both caricature the French polity and render it incomparable to that of other Western democracies. Of course, the continued strength of the state in France impacts heavily upon how political parties are structured and act, just as this country's electoral system accounts for some of the heterogeneity of its range of parties. But by themselves these macro variables tell us very little about how political work takes place within and between French parties, nor about the effects they have upon France's field of professional politicans. For this reason, the second part of this chapter will also focus upon the ways in which political parties are actually structured, operate and have social meaning in this country. Indeed, it is precisely by focusing upon activism, organization, culture and networks, both within parties and their links to various social groups (Sawicki, 1999; Haegel, 2012), that it becomes possible to fully understand the societal impact of political parties within France and, by extension, in any other democracy.

More fundamentally, just as parties can and should be studied as Weberian 'political enterprises' (Offerlé, 2018: 17), so should the non-governmental actors who seek to affect the course of government and power relations within this polity (and indeed any other). In both cases, the omnipresence of the state does indeed play a heavy role. But the fragmentation of the social movements and parties made in France also have endogenous causes and deep effects.

Non-governmental organizations as political enterprises

As regards what I will label broadly here as 'non-governmental actors', it is important to clarify from the outset that what follows is interested less in the classic social science question of why individuals engage, or not, in collective action (Olsen, 1965), and much more in how its different types and forms have emerged and consolidated over time. In a nutshell, the perspective adopted here is the one opened up by Charles Tilly (1976) and like-minded colleagues in the 1970s. Their aim was to examine more closely the history of social mobilizations in order to discover the social conditions which both generated their 'repertoires'[1] and shaped their respective concretizations.

In order to demonstrate the validity of my overall claims about activism and non-governmental actors in France, two empirical examples will now be developed. Due to the salience environmental damage has developed since the 1970s, but also because France is too often caricatured as being 'behind' other countries in this matter, activism around initiatives to better protect the environment will provide a first case study. Subsequently, because the *gilets jaunes* movement was initially sparked by governmental taxes in the name of environmental protection, but also because it raises even deeper questions regarding non-governmental resources and repertoires, it will come centre stage as a second case to be explored. As will be shown, rather than reducing this movement to being an unstructured, 'populist' rabble, there is much to be gained by analysing its resources and repertoires. Throughout, a focus upon the arenas involved, as well as the political work they tend to structure and engender, will be retained. Indeed, this will be done in particular to shed light upon how in the French case, far from being an external onlooker, the state is very much part and parcel of non-governmental activism. Put succinctly, on the surface, these two examples will describe non-governmental actors which adopt either 'insider' or 'outsider' strategies, i.e. repertoires dominated by litigation and expertise on the one hand,

and public protest on the other. When examined in more depth and compared, however, it will be shown that in both cases a wider range of political work has been mobilized.

Striving to protect the environment: organizational dispersion and institutional inertia

Throughout the world, public concerns over damage to the environment have sparked various modes and degrees of activism which, in turn, provide some explanation of why the issue has intensified but rarely been tackled at its roots. In the French case at least, how activism has been structured societally has had considerable impacts upon this relationship between social mobilizations and institutional change. Consequently, the way non-governmental organizations have organized themselves as actors will first be described in some detail, then analysed as regards how and why, in this country as in many others, the environment has institutionalized as a distinctly shapeless public problem.

As regards France's environmentalist NGOs, Nathalie Berny (2019) provides a detailed, comprehensive account of their emergence, consolidation and frequently difficult relationship with public policymaking. Beginning her analysis in the 1960s, Berny traces and compares the trajectories of five national organizations in particular: *La Ligue pour la protection des oiseaux* (LPO), *France Nature Environnement* (FNE),[2] *Les Amis de la Terre* (AT), World Wildlife Fund (WWF) and Greenpeace France. As in many other countries, the movement's pioneers were either natural scientists or naturalists of various types. These were prominent in founding both the *LPO* and the *FNE* around a combination of a myriad of local groups and an initially fragile national federation. Whilst local groups linked to each organization engaged in specific battles, for example against hunting practices in Brittany and cleaning up after 1967's *Torrey Canyon* tanker disaster for the *LPO*, or a sustained protest against plans to amputate part of the Vanoise national park for the *FNE*, each national federation progressively sought to influence the state and its policies. As for *AT*, and indeed for the international Friends of the Earth movement to which it has been associated since 1970, impacting directly upon national law and policy has always been a top priority. More specifically, although *AT* also spawned a wide network of local groups, at the heart of its actions have lain a series of campaigns, notably against nuclear power, to save the whale and, more recently, to outlaw the use of genetically modified organisms (GMOs) in agriculture. Similarly, WWF and Greenpeace initially developed in France around publicized national and international campaigns, respectively over saving certain species and the testing of nuclear weapons. As Table 6.1 sets out, the membership of these

Table 6.1 Membership of French environmentalist NGOs over time

	1977	1985	1989	1995	2000	2015
LPO	2,800	3,800	8,350	20,900	30,600	46,000
FNE[1]	500,000	na	850 000	850,000	na	500,000
AT	50 local groups	3,000	3,000	800	1,000	2,100
WWF	6,000	6,000	1,000	13,0000	59,000	220,000
Greenpeace	na	5,000	0	27,000	47,000	169,200

[1] *FNE* is a federation. Its total membership has been calculated infrequently. Moreover, its figures include the *LPO* and, at certain times, even Greenpeace France.

Source: Berny (2019).

organizations has fluctuated widely and, in any case, has never been very high. For example, Berny estimates that in 2019 only 3–4% of France's population had ever been members of an environmentalist NGO (2019: 44) – a rate that one can compare to 10% of all adults in the UK in 2013.[3]

As regards the resources developed by these five groups over time, considerable differences have emerged and, in most cases, institutionalized. First, the *LPO* and the *FNE* have consistently sought to ally the scientific and legal expertise of some of their members, and particularly that of their local volunteers, to the overall number of members they each have. In the case of the *LPO*, for example, systematic counting of migratory birds is used to counteract the knowledge and arguments used by hunters in order to weaken national and European legislation regarding the amounts of birds that can be shot and when. Indeed, antagonism between the *LPO* and hunters is a central feature of French environmental politics. As regards the *FNE*, using its local associations and experience in court cases, it has often been at the forefront of efforts to better regulate, or sometimes even close, factories which pollute water systems in particular. This organization also often mobilizes over plans to build new roads or railway lines. Like the *LPO*, the *FNE* has long had privileged access to the Ministry for the Environment. Indeed, particularly when left-of-centre governments have been in power, this federation has frequently conducted studies for the state and, as a consequence, been able to employ permanent personnel using this source of income.

For shorter periods of time, the *AT* has also undertaken similar studies and benefited from its links with the Ministry. This was particularly the case when, in 1988, its ex-President and founding member, Brice Lalonde, actually became under-secretary, then Minister, of the Environment for four years within the Rocard and Cresson governments. However, since then not only has membership of *AT* declined, its remaining activists have clearly chosen instead an outsider strategy by concentrating upon publicized protests and campaigns. Here they have been rivalled, then overtaken, by Greenpeace, an organization which, of course, has always taken the outsider route. In the French case, however, it developed only in the 1990s and the size of its membership has only taken off during the twenty-first century. Paradoxically, this organization was actually hampered by the *Rainbow Warrior* incident in 1985 – the moment when the French Secret Services blew up this ship that had been used to hinder nuclear testing in the Pacific Ocean, killing a member of its crew. Although one might have thought this incident would have sparked a rise in members, in fact it precipitated a decline because of the government and media's successful stigmatization of Greenpeace as 'anti-French'. Since 2000, however, Greenpeace has regained its strength partly because that 'incident' has been largely forgotten in France, but mostly through the success of its membership drives and mediatized protests. More generally, as Berny underlines, in quantitative terms public demonstrations over environmental issues have become more frequent since the 1990s. However – and with the exception of specific, sustained 'alter-globalization' movements, such as that against a proposal to build a new airport for Nantes during the 2010s (within which the five main NGOs were not highly present) – each individual protest attracts far fewer participants than in the 1970s and 1980s (Berny, 2019: 137; Ollitrault, 2008).

In many senses, WWF both exemplifies this trend away from public demonstrations and constitutes the outlier amongst these five NGOs. For many years its membership was very low and its actions were discreet. This trait was in part a consequence of WWF's reliance upon private companies for donations, but also because many of its actions have been targeted upon urging and assisting such firms to become more 'environmentally responsible'. Indeed, its repertoire has consistently been one of developing insider-oriented expertise as regards certain species considered in danger, then campaigning on this basis. In so doing, it has been particularly active over the issue of the standards used to regulate product markets, e.g. that of tropical woods.

In short, for each of these environmentalist NGOs, managing the balance between their respective resources and repertoires has been a constant source of internal tension and one that has not facilitated their relationship with external actors in general, and those of the state in particular. Their relationship with the different permutations that green parties have taken provides a case in point. Although *AT* decided to throw its weight behind a 'green' presidential candidate as early as 1974 – René Dumont, who received only 1.3% of the vote, then Brice Lalonde in 1981 (3.8%) – environmentalist NGOs in France have strongly tended to keep their distance from the parties which share many of their values and standpoints (although of course many of their individual members vote for such parties and even campaign on their behalf). As we have seen above, however, except for Greenpeace, such distance has not been duplicated as regards the state and local authorities.

On the contrary, one of the features of environmentalist activism in France has been its close proximity to the state, a trait reflected in how the Ministry for the Environment was invented (Lascoumes, 1994; Charvolin, 2003) and has subsequently evolved (Lascoumes *et al.*, 2014). Indeed, this proximity between environmentalist NGOs and the state was particularly evident during the sustained consultations and negotiations launched by the Sarkozy presidency in 2007. Known as *le Grenelle de l'environnement*, one of this consultation's deepest impacts has been to reinforce actors within environmentalist NGOs who favour insider strategies over the repertoires of outsider mobilization (Boy *et al.*, 2012).

Indeed, this proximity has had deep effects upon the political work of defining environmental protection as a public problem in general, and that related to 'climate change' in particular. Here the groundbreaking research of Jean-Baptiste Comby (2015) is particularly stimulating because it not only delves into the NGO–state proximity, but also shows how both the media and a range of elite 'climate specialists' have also contributed in three overlapping ways to restricting the definition of the public problem of the environment to 'causes' that never challenge deep-seated socio-economic practices. He concludes that the cumulative result has been 'a conformism that preserves the capitalist social order' (2015: 16).

The first institutionalized practice which, since the 1990s, has been shared by virtually all these actors is the 'desocializing' of environmental issues. Consequently, the latter have become ones for individuals to address (e.g. through saving energy in the home or recycling), not types of social activity such as industries which require deeper, more radical change.[4] Indeed, for Comby, here the role of journalism has been key. In particular, he shows not only that the sociology of journalists specialized in environmental issues changed dramatically in the 1990s: since then they have come from the higher echelons of the middle class and were trained first as journalists before specializing in the environment, without ever having been environmental activists (2015: chapter 1). Comby also demonstrates how journalistic coverage of the environment has essentially become focused upon consequences and solutions, and rarely upon causes other than those that are vaguely labelled as 'human activity' (see Table 6.2). In so doing, illustration has become more important than explanation. Moreover, any radical alternative, such as banning cars from city centres, has been 'folklorised' (2015: 30, 158).

The second trait that has prevailed within environmentalist activism in France is the type of science that has come to dominate both environmental activism in France and its interlocutors in both the state and private companies: 'ecological modernization'. This mode of analysis considers that most environmental damage can be reduced using technological 'progress' and incentives such as carbon certificates.[5]

Table 6.2 How climate change was presented on the television news of TF1 and France 2 (%)

	1997	1999	2001	2003	2006	1997–2006
Consequences	29	56	19	51	69	44
Causes	23	33	6	22	5	15
Solutions	49	11	74	27	26	41

Source: adapted from Comby (2015: 35).

Finally, and perhaps above all, Comby highlights how a combination of NGO activism, scientific domination, state intervention and deep change in the media has successfully taken the question of social class out of problem definition. Despite social elites being the biggest individual polluters with their 4x4 cars, large homes and penchant for travel by air, in France the dominant problem definition systematically 'avoids making visible and debatable the role played by social hierarchy' (Comby, 2015: 162–168). More generally, he concludes that in this way a pacification and depoliticization of social protest has occurred – one within which any criticism that goes beyond the accepted framing is 'sterilized' (22). Consequently, the role of counter-expertise to that of the state and industry once played by French environmentalist NGOs has disappeared (150).

If I share much of Comby's analysis, what is most important to underline here is what the case of environmental activism in France as a whole shows: the positions taken up by the state have clearly and consistently played a causal role in the low levels of institutional change that environmental damage has thus far prompted. Specifically, by providing arenas for the deployment of only certain insider modes of activism, together with the NGOs that now dominate this issue area, state actors have also facilitated the building of alliances with other actors (notably polluting firms and the media) who have worked politically to limit the introduction of deeper institutional change. Indeed, as Berny (2019) has shown, precisely because of their dependence on the state, and deep-seated respect for it, the repertoires of France's major environmentalist NGOs themselves, together with their structural fragmentation, are largely responsible for the recent forms of problem shaping, instrument-making and legitimation highlighted above.

The gilets jaunes: *going beyond the 'populist' label*

Throughout much of the world, in late 2018 and early 2019 France featured on televised news programmes and newspaper front pages because of the visibility and virulence of a new social movement: *les gilets jaunes*. Known by this name due to the yellow safety vests they have worn from the outset, and initially in protest against a rise in taxes on car fuel, this movement has been seen as original for at least three reasons. First, it has deliberately avoided existing intermediaries between 'the people' and the state, notably trade unions, user groups (such as the French Automobile Association) or political parties. Instead, the movement has sought to protest directly against the government of the day without transforming itself into an organization, co-ordinating itself using the internet and social media (Bornstein, 2019). Secondly, its protests have taken the form of sit-ins and blockades on the one hand (particularly of key roundabouts and tollbooths), and on the other, demonstrations every Saturday afternoon in city centres throughout France. Finally, these demonstrations have frequently been accompanied by violence and the destruction of public and private property. This feature stems sometimes from the *gilets jaunes* themselves, more often from groups of extreme-left militants (*les black blocs*) using the demonstrations as cover for their own strategies, but also from the methods used by the police to channel and control each event. Although this is not the focus here, one should also add that the *gilets jaunes* movement has already had a number of policy effects, most notably being the government's decision to organize a 'national debate' in early 2019, then make a series of policy changes and concessions on issues ranging from tax rates to old age pensions.

Research is, of course, still producing data on this social movement and seeking to make sense of it. What is already apparent is that it has raised new challenges for specialists of this subject area, but also confirmed a number of pre-existing findings about how 'outsider' protest takes place in France.

A first line of enquiry concerns the social composition of *les gilets jaunes* and its relationship to their mode of co-ordination. Indeed, here the challenge for research has indeed been how to understand a movement which, initially at least, rejected the very term 'organization'. From this perspective, one piece of research entailing social media analysis and a questionnaire has already generated data on 5,000 members of the movement (Guerra *et al.*, 2019). In contrast to other French public protest movements, it has found in particular that of those surveyed:

- 40% live in a village or on a farm, 38% in a small town,[6] 22% in a big town or city (usually French demonstrators are from the latter);
- 60% are women;
- most *gilets jaunes* are much older than the typical French 'protester' (38% are 35–49 years old and 29% are aged between 50 and 64);
- 61% declare that they are neither 'on the left' or 'on the right'; indeed most of these respondents reject this categorization;
- only 3% voted for Emmanuel Macron in the first round of the 2017 presidential election (v. 18% of the electorate as a whole);

- Finally, the movement features an even distribution in terms of levels of education: a third each for no secondary school diploma, a diploma from this level, or having undergone at least two years in higher education.

As regards the repertoire of action adopted, it is important to note that many partakers in the roundabout or tollbooth blockades declare that they had never previously participated in public protests of any kind. Meanwhile, another detailed study shows the proportion of *gilets jaunes* on these block-ades who were new to public protesting to be as high as 46% (Collectif, 2019: 15). By contrast, many more of participants in the weekly demonstra-tions had prior experience of this type of protest, and this in particular for those who continued to demonstrate regularly after January 2019. Moreover, in part because the government reacted to the movement by launching a *grand débat* to which a vociferous minority of protesters wanted to respond, a certain degree of organization eventually emerged to co-ordinate the movement's overall claims.

From the point of view of analysis, if the occupation of roundabouts and toll stations was certainly new (for France at least), that of the demon-stration certainly was not. Particularly since the ground-breaking epi-sodes known as 'May 1968' that shook up the government of General de Gaulle and prompted not only policy changes but also wider conceptions of the political itself, the public demonstration has been normalized in France by a succession of overlapping cohorts (Mayer, 2004). Indeed, this normalization has gone hand in hand with an institutionalization of the demonstration, complete with norms over what is and is not acceptable, together with the widely shared premise that such events need 'organiza-tions that have strategies' (Filleule and Tartakowsky, 2013: 13). Given the *gilets jaunes'* reticence on this point, not surprisingly their demonstra-tions were initially difficult to structure and, from the police's point of view, 'to control'.

More fundamentally still, however, analysis has struggled to grasp the content and the vehemence of the *gilets jaunes'* criticisms of the government of the day, the procedures and norms of French representative democracy, and, more generally, the asymmetries that mark this country's distribution of wealth and power. This point links strongly to a political and scientific con-troversy concerning whether the movement is really 'populist', i.e. based upon a binary image of society as one split between a corrupt elite (anti-elitism) and a virtuous people (who ought to have more direct access to the running of the country: 'the sovereignty of the people'). From this perspective, although the research by Guerra *et al.* (2019) partly confirms that the *gilets jaunes* movement is indeed populist, it also underlines that what unites these protestors is the sentiment that they are 'the hard-working people' of France.

Galvanized by what Ivalidi and Massoleni (2019) call 'producerism', the *gilets jaunes* consider themselves to be the makers of French wealth, not the takers. This means that ideologically they have more in common than is commonly thought: 65% of those surveyed have a job, but 68% have a monthly income of less than the median net disposable income (2,480 euros per month in early 2019). Consequently, on the scale of 'precariousness' developed by Guerra *et al.* (2019), 67% of the *gilets jaunes* surveyed are indeed 'precarious', a ratio that is twice that of the population as a whole. Despite this common feature, however, most *gilets jaunes* are not against capitalism, capitalists or indeed large companies. Moreover, they are not overly concerned about unemployment (see also Collectif, 2019: 12). Instead, initial accounts by leading sociologists underline more how the movement is a reaction against the 'the social contempt' this segment of the population consider they experience on the part of the country's national governmental elites, a situation that has made them feel 'invisible' (Paugam, 2019: 37). Indeed, as François Dubet has argued, although the feeling of not being integrated into the same social space as these elites is far from new, the level of anger manifested by the *gilets jaunes* has been accentuated by the fact that they consider it is no longer possible to channel their feelings into a political form. This is because 'the regime of social class', together with its party political and trade union dimension, is no longer considered relevant by many members of this social movement (Dubet, 2019: 44–45). As such, the *gilets jaunes* movement as a whole is thus clearly anti-elitist. Moreover, most of its members consider that 'the sovereignty of the people' should be 'restored'. In short, this movement is clearly populist in many ways. However, simply reducing it to this label discourages analysis from grasping how this movement reflects the state of social activism in contemporary France, together with its underlying causes.

At the time of writing, research on the *gilets jaunes* is obviously only just beginning and we will know much more about them and their mode of activism as time goes on. What is important to 'take away' from this example of social protest is that this phenomenon is clearly in part a reaction against the institutionalization of activism in France, one that has been exemplified by what environmentalism has become in this country since the 1990s. More precisely, be it as regards environmental NGOs or trade unions, many French people who support the *gilets jaunes* cause now consider that these organizations' repertoires of protest have become excessively insider-dominated, and indeed 'elitist'. Without being totally accurate, this representation of reality clearly has some foundation in social facts and practices. Moreover, as the following section will now relate, such visions of French society have also been nourished by what its main political parties have become over the last three decades.

Political parties, their activists and limited societal reach

As signposted in the introduction to this chapter, specialized and comparative research on political parties is, of course, right to analyse the impact of a certain number of key variables which impose themselves upon the structure and processes of such organizations in any country. In the case of France, this mode of analysis usefully highlights in particular:

- The bipolarizing effects of the two-round, first past the post electoral system introduced in 1958, combined with that of presidential elections and instability within each pole (Sauger, 2009);
- How the introduction of proportional representation for European and regional elections in the 1980s allowed new parties to emerge, in particular the extreme right *Front National* (relabelled in 2018 *Rassemblement National*) and various shades of greens;
- The encouragement given since 1988 to party creation by public subsidies;[7]
- The low membership of each party and of parties in general: only *c.* 1 to 1.3 million in total in 2018;[8]
- The relative weakness of the French National Assembly as regards the Executive, together with the high importance accorded to MPs' constituency work (Costa, 2013).

All the information generated around the above points and variables must therefore be taken on board when examining political parties in France, just as they should for any other national case. However, as Frédéric Sawicki has underlined (2017: 420–421), it is important not to stop there and thus explain politics uniquely in terms of formalized definitions of politics and politicians. Instead, it is vital 'to treat parties like social facts that are explainable using other social facts'. Specifically, what Sawicki and like-minded colleagues mean by this is that the structuring and daily life of party politics also needs bringing into the light using qualitative research methods, together with a focus on at least three other variables that purely quantitative research simply cannot nourish empirically and therefore test.

The first of these additional variables is each party's internal structure and external networks. As Haegel underlines (2016: 381), 'to consider political parties as socially embedded cultural institutions is to emphasize party culture and how the behaviour of party actors is constrained by specific codes and norms'. Indeed, the structuring of a party can only be understood by studying its institutions closely, together with how members who transgress rules and norms are punished (or not). Just as importantly, studying this aspect of a party also entails analysing networks within the party itself (factions), but also those that link it to external actors, such as teachers' unions for the *Parti Socialiste* or business interest groups for *Les Républicains*.

Indeed, this is largely how electoral bases are cultivated and maintained (Sawicki, 1999). Moreover, these processes in turn provide the moments around which parties shape and update their values, the weight they attach to them and, consequently, their respective organizational culture.

The second variable concerns inter-party competition. As Offerlé underlines (2018: 87), parties exist relationally. Consequently, much of the work undergone within them to construct, then maintain, their electorates entails positioning the party, both nationally and locally, as regards its rivals. As we shall see below, the most obvious positioning of this type involves making confrontational distinctions between one's own party and what the media present as their most direct opponents (e.g. *Les Républicains* for the *Parti Socialiste* and vice versa). However, especially since the disruption of the left–right cleavage which has occurred around and since the 2017 elections, parties of all hues have devoted as much, if not more, political work to positioning themselves as regards rivals from their own side of the political spectrum (e.g. the *Parti Socialiste* v. *La France Insoumise* and *Génération.s*, or *Les Républicains* v. *Le Rassemblement National*).

Indeed, this positioning work as regards its rivals, adversaries and enemies overlaps strongly with a third and final variable that rigorous qualitative research is able to enlighten: party identity. As Offerlé has put it, ultimately the most important resource for a party is its name – a name which in many senses is its 'brand' (Offerlé, 2018: 35). By this, one of course means in part the principles, programme and, in some cases, the very ideology of the party in question. But studying identity building and maintenance within a party more generally means also producing data on how the sentiment of belonging to a group is cultivated. This is done around the characteristics of the party which, nationally but also locally, are deemed to be 'the most salient' (Sawicki, 1999: 63).

Equipped with the variables presented above, we are now ready to delve into the actual world of French political parties in a way that dovetails with the analytical framework and claims advanced throughout this book. To do so, two lines of questioning will successively be developed. The first sets out to uncover how the French right has reacted and adapted to the succession of challenges its has faced since its first series of major electoral defeats in the 1980s. Conversely, the second enigmatic set of phenomena tackled below concerns what the left in France has become since its first sustained periods in government, together with other destabilizing developments that have emerged since that time. In both instances, it will be shown that political work has certainly been engaged in to 'update' the resources and repertoires of the parties involved. Nevertheless, for the moment at least, this work has neither strengthened them as organizations, nor seriously modified the institutions which structure them.

Managing the end of hegemony: translating the French right into electable parties

Ever since formalized political parties first took shape in France in the early twentieth century, those located ideologically on the right have strongly tended to dominate French elections and thus government. Indeed, until 1981 right-wing politicians, activists and sympathisers experienced an extremely long period of hegemony during which their opponents were nearly always in a position of the challenger. Paradoxically, however, this situation was not produced by one single party, nor has it entailed the French right ever producing a party that is unified, coherent and institutionally stable. For example, Agrikoliansky describes the right under the Third and Fourth Republics as 'a federation of local political entrepreneurs with flexible, often highly decentralized structures' (2008: 21). Although, as will be shown below, the Fifth Republic has spawned right-wing parties that have become less personalized and more institutionalized, this tendency to split and secede has frequently been reproduced. Indeed, it is no accident that the term 'party' has rarely been used within the names of right-wing groupings. Instead, vaguer terms like 'movement', 'union' or '*rassemblement*' have frequently been preferred. Consequently, in order to fully understand the 'power despite disunity' that has characterized right-wing political parties in France, it is important to first briefly set out their history, before then going on to examine it as regards the variables presented above.

Agrikoliansky's depiction of the French right until 1958 is a good place to start. As he underlines, although during this period politicians self-identifying as 'conservatives' were always very strong at the national level, and particularly within the National Assembly, they almost unanimously rejected any need to develop a common ideology. Moreover, when working within Parliament, they also consistently refused to accept the discipline of party whips (Agrikoliansky, 2008: 22). Nevertheless, parties began to emerge around 1900 as soon as formal political organizations were legally authorized, the most notable being the Radical Party which at that time claimed to have around 200,000 members. From the outset, the identity of the Radicals was far from clear, other than their being firmly opposed to socialism or communism on the one hand and, on the other, committed to some key values of *La République*, such as a belief in representative democracy and a clear separation between church and state.[9] Moreover, to their right *La Fédération Républicaine* also came into being as of 1903 and attracted the support of many pro-regime Catholics, particularly in the east of France and in Normandy. More generally, however, apart from vague commitments to liberal economics, the French right as a whole developed neither a common set of economic and social policies, nor strong internal organization. Instead, its key actors continued to operate as relatively isolated individuals who, even when in government, had difficulty forging common goals and working together towards their realization. Indeed, despite its successive electoral successes, the fragmentation of the French right is one of the explanations behind the institutional inertia that marked the Third Republic, the difficulties France as a whole had in facing up to the economic crisis of the 1930s and, indeed, the debacle of 1940 and the Vichy government's collaboration with the Nazi occupier.

Not surprisingly, the more general collaboration between many supporters of the French right and Nazi Germany seriously handicapped its role in the immediate aftermath of the Second World War, and indeed for some time thereafter. At the 1946 legislative elections, for example, the Radicals only won 11% of the vote (compared to 28% for the *PCF* and 18% for the forerunner of the *PS*). Conversely, the outcome of the war strengthened the left but also the leader of 'the Free French', General de Gaulle. Indeed, alarmed by the weakness of the right and centre-right, in 1947 de Gaulle created his own 'movement', *le Rassemblement pour la France (RPF)*. This new party, which claimed to have immediately attracted 1.5 million members, won no less than 40% of the vote during the municipal elections of the same year, then 21% of the vote during the legislative elections of 1951. Despite thereby becoming the second largest party in France after the *PCF*, however, once again the *RPF* did not manage to discipline its MPs within Parliament or maintain its electoral strength over time. Indeed, as early as 1953 it lost half of its seats in municipal government and its overall membership had dropped to 100,000, a decline which prompted de Gaulle himself to announce his 'departure from politics'.

As is well known, this withdrawal proved to be short-lived. Following an attempted coup d'état linked to the Algerian war and, more fundamentally, sustained discrediting of the Fourth Republic (Gaïti, 1998), de Gaulle was 'recalled' first as prime minister, then subsequently became president. In between these two moments the *RPF* became the *Union pour la Nouvelle République (UNR)*, then won 20% of the popular vote, and thus 212 out of 552 parliamentary seats, at the elections of December 1958. Following the transition to the Fifth Republic, then de Gaulle's actual election as president, the *UNR* managed to achieve outright majorities at the legislative elections of 1962, 1967 and 1968. Indeed, it was during this period that the French right achieved its highest degree of coherence and stability, i.e. when it placed itself firmly behind a president committed to reinstating France's place as a major international power on the one hand, and 'modernizing' its economy on the other using a singular combination of liberalism and *dirigiste* policies and procedures (see chapter 4).

This stability and cohesion was soon disturbed, however, by de Gaulle's final withdrawal from politics in 1969 and its sparking of a long-standing dispute over his succession. Although his immediate successor, Georges Pompidou, easily won the 1969 presidential election, when he died in office in 1974 an intense and divisive battle to select the *UDR*'s next candidate quickly ensued. Surprisingly, the liberal and non-Gaullist Valéry Giscard d'Estaing emerged from this process as the victor, then narrowly won the presidential election itself. Indeed, this episode and result created great upheaval within the Gaullist movement which in 1976 prompted the founding of a new 'Gaullist' party led by Jacques Chirac – *Rassemblement pour la République (RPR)* (Collovald, 1999) – then, in 1978, a recomposition of centrist liberals around Giscard's new *Union pour la démocratie française (UDF)*. This open conflict between politicians, parties and activists on the right provides some explanation for the success of the left, and the *PS* in particular, as of the late 1970s (see below). For example, if in 1977 no fewer than 22% of *RPR* members were working-class, by 1979 this was down to 11% (Agrikoliansky, 2008: 104). Moreover, it is important to underline that many of the divisions within the French right that became so apparent in the mid-1970s have largely been rolled on into the twenty-first century. For example, they were particularly evident during the referendum over the Maastricht Treaty in 1992. Moreover, even when Jacques Chirac at last won a presidential election in 1995, his victory was preceded by a first round during which a fellow *RPR* politician, Edouard Balladur, stood against him.

Although, as we have just seen, by then internal conflict within the French right was far from new, the emergence of the extreme-right *Front National (FN)* over the 1980s added further fuel to this particular 'fire'. This party, led by Jean-Marie Le Pen, had begun to emerge in the 1970s, but its first electoral successes were achieved during the European elections of 1984 (11% of the vote), the legislative elections of 1986 (10%), then the presidential election of 1988 (14% in the first round).[10] In so doing, the *FN* not only took votes and voters from the 'traditional' right-wing parties, but has also provoked new divisions within them over issues such as immigration and 'national identity', cultural liberalism and European integration (Mayer, 1999). Indeed, a first organizational manifestation of such tensions was the implosion of the *UDF* in 1998, then, after the 2002 elections, the creation of a new party ostensibly designed to unite activists from the right (notably the *RPR*) and centre-right: the *Union pour un mouvement populaire (UMP)*.

As Florence Haegel has shown in detail (2012), contrary to previous attempts to federate politicians and activists from this part of the political spectrum, over the next decade a sustained effort was made to build the UMP as a coherent, more permanent organization with its own set of rules and norms. Notwithstanding its electoral successes in the 2000s, Haegel concluded in 2012 that this party remained weakly institutionalized, particularly when compared to French parties on the left, as well as to right-wing ones in other countries, especially the UK's Conservative Party. Indeed, although relaunched as *Les Républicains (LR)* in 2015, this party has subsequently suffered further due to its electoral defeats of 2012 and 2017, the continued existence of the centrist *Mouvement Démocrate (MODEM)* party,[11] and the rise of Emmanuel Macron and his *La République En Marche* party *(LRM)*. Indeed, although taken as a whole the right wing is still a major force in French politics and society, from the point of view of its translation into political parties, in many respects its contemporary situation is not that different from that of the Fourth Republic: it has a conservative extreme that attracts 15–20% of the popular vote (the *FN*), a party like the Radicals that attracts similar levels of popular support but which lacks internal cohesion *(LR)*, and two centrist movements *(MODEM* and *LRM)*, neither of which has a solid ideological rudder. Some key descriptive information has been set above which enlightens this state of affairs. But the question which remains to be answered is *why this is so?*

The first variable to be tested here concerns the structuration of the French right examined first from the angle of ideology, then from that of organizations and networks. Réné Rémond (1982) initially depicted the intra-right's ideological cleavages as reflecting three historically rooted forms of political thought: that of the *Légitimistes* (of the royal family, thus as supporters of tradition and even opponents of the 1789 Revolution), that of the *Bonapartistes* (who desire a strong leader approved by the population), and that of the *Orléanistes* (economic and cultural liberals). After the Second World War, the *Légitimistes* largely disappeared from view. However, since the end of the 1980s they have made a comeback as supporters of the *FN* or as factions of the *UMP* opposed to immigration, deeper European integration and cultural liberalism. Meanwhile, liberals have strengthened their hold within the French economy and key parts of the state, but have themselves tended to split over the weight they accord to economic and cultural liberalism. Finally, the lasting impact of Gaullism and its links to *Bonapartisme* has been considerable. As in other countries such as West Germany and Italy, by drawing upon the role of their religion during *La Résistance* and committing themselves firmly to *La République*, after 1944 some Christian Democrats did emerge in France and developed a third-way alternative to the capitalism v. collectivism divide. However, they never found their ideological anchor in France precisely because of the strength of the Gaullist movement and de Gaulle himself filled this space whilst fitting with the *Bonapartiste* ideal. Specifically, for decades thereafter it was precisely the breadth and ambiguities of the Gaullist movement which helped account for its electoral and societal successes (Gaïti, 1998; Collovald, 1999).

Moreover, one of the key ambiguities of the Gaullist movement was that as an organization, neither it nor its successors have ever demanded much either from its members or even from its politicians. As Haegel has under-lined, although each of the *UMP*'s members pays subscription fees which are only a little higher than those of other French political parties, by contrast this organization receives very little funding by taking a percentage of what its elected politicians earn in office. Instead, it relies upon much larger dona-tions from private firms (2012: 132–133).[12] One of the consequences of this organizational trait is that the party's hierarchy has a more distant relation-ship to each politician elected on a *UMP* ticket, but can also avoid having to debate how it uses its finances at party congresses. More precisely, the low level of formal rules and procedures that govern the practices of this hierarchy means that ideological divides can more easily be papered over than in many other French political parties.

Haegel's claim that the *UMP* is weakly institutionalized also provides a means of examining how this party, and its successor *Les Républicains*, has faced up to the increased inter-party competition it has experienced since 1981. Indeed, it is here that the articulation between the regulation (or its absence) of intra-party regulation overlaps with its management of increased competition on its left and right. As we saw above, in most instances the *UMP* or its equivalent has gone into the first round of presidential elections (and many others) with at least two candidates. Whereas for many parties in many countries, a way of avoiding such a situation is to organize primary elections, until 2011–12 these were rejected by nearly all French parties, and those on the right in particular. Following the 2012 defeat, Haegel (2015: 98) revisited this question and asked whether the introduction of open pri-maries into the *UMP*'s internal functioning might resolve the question that the invention of this party in 2002 'had failed to do': reunify the different strands and factions within the centre-right and right of the French political spectrum. Given the way the primary organized in 2016 turned out, how-ever (it featured no fewer than seven candidates), then what happened to its winner (François Fillon) during the presidential election of the following year – accused of corruption on several accounts, he only attracted 20% of the vote and thus missed out on the second round – it is by no means certain that such a primary will be reorganized in future. Indeed, Lefebvre's research (2016) on this point underlines that within the *UMP* primaries have led to 'the devaluation' of activists, a focus on TV appearances by candidates more than party meetings and the individualization of the preparation of party programmes.

Overall, and more fundamentally, all the above indicates that the very identity of the 'non-extremist' right in France is anything but clear, and always has been, other than between 1958 and 1968. Despite the massive influence actors on the right in France have had upon its institutions and power relations, divisions between them over how the economy should be governed, legislation on social mores and European integration are particularly flagrant. Indeed, ultimately, the French right is certainly heavily marked by a powerful yet broad political culture, one that is firmly linked to certain professions (company managers, bankers, lawyers, doctors) and social classes. This means that any outsider to these social structures certainly experiences the right in France as a 'community' whose codes they do not possess. However, as Haegel underlines, political parties on the right are not themselves 'the key sites for the production of this culture' (Haegel, 2012: 303). Ultimately, in many ways the French right is more a broad movement that has given rise to a plethora of organizations. It is definitely not an organization that has structured a cohesive set of movements. Indeed, if the relative disorganization of non-extreme right-wing parties in France explains part of their incapacity to promote institutional change, their linkages to even deeper societal structures reveal the causes of the reproduction of so many of the institutions and power relations that blossomed in the period 1945–75 – notably the considerable autonomy given to senior civil servants.

What's left? How the Parti Socialiste became an empty shell

Although this may be hard to believe following 2017's presidential election when the *PS*'s candidate, Bernard Hamon, only received 7% of the popular vote, one simply cannot understand political activism in France today without grasping the rise of this party in the late 1970s, the spreading of its influence over the following decade, but also its subsequent, and perhaps terminal, decline. As we saw in chapter 3, in contrast to countries such as the UK or Germany, the ancestry of this party did not emerge alongside a closely linked trade union movement, or without powerful rivals to its left. On the contrary, those who sought to build a socialist party in France had to do so whilst competing with a strong *Parti communiste français* (PCF) on the one hand and, on the other, unions which formally refused to link themselves to a political party, whilst informally frequently supporting the communist movement. This challenge was in many ways made stronger by socialist elites early in the nineteenth century choosing to concentrate upon the municipal scale of politics, and thus clientelistic networks linked to mayors and their respective administrations (Lefebvre and Sawicki, 2006). Indeed, taken together and compared to the then hegemonic resources of the right-wing parties described above, this explains why the predecessors of the *PS*, essentially the *Section française de l'internationale ouvrière* (SFIO), largely failed to gain office at the national scale until 1981 (with the exception of the Popular Front parenthesis of 1936–38 and other even shorter ones under the Fourth Republic).

In terms of membership, that of the *PS* only began to increase considerably in the late 1970s, before peaking at around 200,000 in the 1980s then

Table 6.3 The rise and fall of the *PS*'s membership

1970	1981	1989	1995	2000	2005	2010	2016
80,000	200,000	204,172	93,603	116,805	127,374	*c.*160,000	111,450

Sources: Lefebvre and Sawicki (2006: 56, 158); the *Bureau national des adhesions du PS* for 2010 and 2016.

declining progressively to below 100,000 after the 2017 national elections (see Table 6.3). Indeed, for decades, both in terms of its membership and its organization, the *PCF* was the strongest party on the French left and actually reached its own peak in 1979 with no fewer than 700,000 members (before declining to 380,000 by 1984, 130,000 in 2006 and 57,000 in 2016: Mischi, 2007; Pudal, 2009).[13]

As regards the rise and fall of the *PS*, most analyses begin with the refoundation of this party in 1971 at its congress in Epinay. Decisions taken at this event not only sought to restate and revise the party's ideological commitment to socialism, but also sparked a new effort to encompass and include Catholics on the left of the political spectrum, as well as other electors from the then rising middle class working within the public, social and cultural sectors (Sawicki, 2017: 8). Over the course of the 1970s, this political work entailed renewed and largely successful efforts to increase the *PS*'s share of the vote during the 1974 presidential elections (49.2% for François Mitterrand), as well as the legislative ones of 1978 (49% for the left as a whole). Moreover, at the municipal scale, 1977 constituted a watershed as the *PS* captured a wide swathe of large towns and several small cities such as Montpellier, Rennes and Nantes.

Indeed, as Sawicki (2017) has highlighted since the early 1990s, in order to understand the *PS* as an organization together with its internal and external networks, it must be studied both nationally *and* locally. Much of the national side of this story is relatively well known. Following François Mitterrand's victory in 1981's presidential elections, the *PS* won majorities in the National Assembly that year, then again in 1988. Although losing at this level in 1986 and 1993, it regained a majority for the period 1997–2002, then again for 2012–17 following François Hollande's presidential success. However, during all this time it was at sub-national levels that the party's impact was consistently the strongest. Indeed, in many senses, continuity in the *PS*'s success at the local scale into the 2000s, and even the 2010s, serves as a reminder that the party was built from the municipal scale upwards. As mentioned above, this process began in the early 1900s through the founding of electoral bastions in cities such as Grenoble, Strasbourg and Amiens. Their respective town halls became the locus of not only left-leaning policies (such as the provision of crèches and other social services). From the scale of the commune, the influence of the party also grew to that of the *département*, and seven of those in particular: Paris (Seine), Pas de Calais and Nord in the north, the Gironde in the south-west, Bouches du Rhône, the Var and Aude in the south. From these modest but solid beginnings, in the 1980s the *PS* spread its wings further using the legitimacy and resources of its national electoral successes and the opportunities opened up by the 1982 decentral-ization laws. The latter not only increased the powers of communal mayors, thereby enhancing that of the *PS* in many cities, towns and even villages (Le Galès, 1993; Faure, 1992), but also increased those of the *départements* and, perhaps above all, of the regions. Indeed, whereas beforehand the *PS* had been decidedly weak at this scale, the introduction of direct elections for regional councils enabled the party to capture the presidency of several regions, notably Nord-Pas de Calais and Aquitaine. This is not the place for an extensive description of how the electoral power of the *PS* waxed and waned over the period between 1982 and 2020. Instead, following Sawicki (2017: 13), I simply want to underline that at various points in time it has held:

- 23 presidencies at the *département* level (out of 101) in 1994, 35 in 1998, 41 in 2001, 51 in 2004 and 61 in 2010, before falling sharply to 33 in 2015 during the Hollande presidency;
- 37 cities of over 50,000 people in 1977, 28 in 1983, 42 in 1989, 57 in 2008, 30 in 2014;
- 13 'urban communities' out of 15, together with 85 out of 202 'agglom-eration communities', just before the municipal elections of 2014;
- a total of 206 regional councillor posts in 1986, 311 in 1992, 395 in 1998, 612 in 2004 and 567 in 2010, but then experienced a sharp drop to 355 in 2015.

At the time of writing, it seems likely that the election of Emmanuel Macron and the sudden growth of his party *La République En Marche* (Dolez *et al.*, 2019) will further weaken the *PS* at these subnational levels as of the municipal elections to be held in 2020.[14] Nevertheless, what this brief trip through history has shown is that local politics has been essential to the development of the *PS* as a party, and indeed the left as players in French politics more generally. From the first angle, it is strength in many local lev-els which explains both the 'nodality' of many leading *PS* politicians within local communities and networks, but also at the regional and national scales through the long-standing practice known as *cumul des mandats* (accumulation of electoral mandates). Although this practice has been curbed over the last decade by national legislation and the adoption of new intra-party norms, it undoubtedly contributed strongly to the transforma-tion of the *PS* over the 1980s into what Lefebvre and Sawicki call 'a party of elected politicians' more interested in public opinion polls than taking care of their own organization and its activists (2006: 20). At the local scale, this has often contributed to the neglect of once key networks of support within the anti-clerical movement, the teaching profession, the *CFDT* trade union and 'the student left'.

Moreover, during this process, debates over points of principle and ideology have also been pushed to the margins. Indeed, when in government, as of 1983 and particularly after 1988, *PS* ministers increasingly resorted to filling their *cabinets* with advisers employed by the state (and generally trained by the *ENA*), rather than on the basis of their commitment to the party (Mathiot and Sawicki, 1999a,b). In turn, many of these advisers were subsequently 'parachuted' into the mayorships of certain towns and cities, then rose up within the party as a whole (Laurent Fabius, Martine Aubry, Ségalène Royale, François Hollande and Pierre Moscovici all being prime examples of this practice). Indeed, when one adds François Mitterrand's mode of leadership to this 'equation', in particular the distant relationship he developed with the party as of the mid-1980s, how the *PS* lost touch with much of its activist base whilst intertwining itself further with the state becomes clearer. In a nutshell, Sawicki even goes as far as to conclude that the high level of energy devoted to local politics largely explains why, since the early 1980s, most of the *PS*'s *grands élus* have involved themselves so little in developing the party's overall programme at the national scale. Instead, this has been largely left to party bureaucrats, most of whom are *énarques* (graduates of the *ENA*) or, in any event, have no direct link to, or feeling for, the French working class (Sawicki, 2017: 19).

Of course, such analysis also needs to encompass the impact of inter-party competition, in particular upon 'sympathisers' of the *PS* who had voted for it in 1981, continued to do so to a large extent throughout the 1980s, but began to desert it thereafter. From this angle, the decline of the *PCF* clearly enabled the *PS* to continue to post decent electoral scores at the national and local scales for many years. However, this position began to be challenged to some extent by different parties from the green movement as of 1989 (Faucher, 1999),[15] then by more radically left-wing movements as of the 2000s. Indeed, in many respects the electoral support given to Jean-Luc Mélenchon's party *La France Insoumise* (*LFI*) in the 2017 presidential elections (20% in the first round) reflects a consolidation of leftist activists and voters, all of whom consider that when in government the *PS* has consistently betrayed its socialist roots and principles (Lefebvre, 2017; Sawicki, 2017).

Indeed, this competition with other parties on the left in 2011 contributed to the *PS* adopting open primary elections in order to try to build support for its candidate within 'the left' as a whole. As Lefebvre and Treille (2016: 16) have rightly underlined, as with parties on the right, the *PS*'s new strategy regarding primaries confirms that presidential elections are now the central foundation stone around which the life of all French political parties is currently organized. As regards helping understand the *PS* itself, the holding of the open primary in 2011, its definition as 'a success' in terms of turnout[16] but, above all, Hollande's electoral triumph further emphasizes the retraction of the *PS*'s membership base and the importance its leaders attribute to it.

In summary, much has clearly changed for French political parties in the second decade of the twenty-first century. However, analysis of this shift purely in terms of inter-party competition is insufficient. Instead, it is only by closely examining how each party has organized itself, worked upon its ideology and identity, and thereby strengthened or weakened its core of activists, that one can really grasp their relationship to France's key societal structures.

Conclusion

Indeed, as much for NGOs as for parties, studying activism provides an enlightening window upon what is made in France, why and by whom. Despite the unusually strong presence of the state in both fields, analysis of this activism cannot be neglected or seen as merely a residual and relatively unimportant factor. As has been shown, the causes of NGO and party fragmentation are also largely endogenous to each field and, on their own and in combination with dependence upon the state, have had deep structural effects upon participation in collective and political action, as well as upon public of perceptions of politics itself. Consequently, France is quite clearly still very distant from the pluralist ideal of a society dominated by strong interest groups and parties. Indeed, the omnipresence of the state within the fields of party politics and social activism partly explains this situation. Nevertheless, as the *gilets jaunes* movement and Emmanuel Macron's *LRM* remind us, certain types and modes of collective and political activism themselves continue to have significant impacts upon the structuring and governing of France – just as they always have done.

Notes

1 According to Tilly, actor resources are mobilized as part of five *repertoires* of action, either separately or in combination: protesting publicly, negotiating behind closed doors, taking support from science, judicialization, or politicizing from values and first principles (1976).

2 This organization was called the *Fédération française des sociétés de protection de la nature (FFSPN)* until 1989.

3 This result is drawn from a survey by the Environmental Funders Network, 2013. See *Guardian*, 27th November 2013, www.theguardian.com/environment/2013/nov/27/1-in-10-uk-adults-environmental-group, consulted 20th July 2019.

4 As Comby underlines, changing industries radically is in any case seen as 'impossible' because they are depicted as being themselves the victims of 'internationally competitive markets', and thus condemned to continue operating, and thus polluting, more or less as they always have and as their overseas competitors are said to do (2015: 114).

5 For a full critique of this theory and research tradition see Carter (2018).

6 Genestier (2019) argues that for many of the *gilets jaunes*, living outside a big city, if possible in a house rather than a flat, constitutes a goal or ideal, one which moreover sets them apart from 'elitist' city dwellers.

7 In 2016, for example, thirteen parties based in metropolitan France, together with thirty 'ultramarine' ones (based in the overseas territories), benefited from these subsidies. www.cnccfp.fr, consulted 2nd February 2020.

8 Going from left to right, in 2018 Offerlé (2018: 50) estimated party membership in France to be as follows: *Parti communiste français* (50,000), *Parti Socialiste* (50,000), *Génération.s* (20,000), *Europe Ecologie* (EELV: 5,000), *MODEM* (15,000), *Les Républicains* (150,000), *Rassemblement National* (40,000). This estimation generates a grand total of about 400,000 members to which should be added more tentative figures for *La République En Marche* (380,000) and *La France Insoumise* (550,000). However, as Offerlé stresses, the last two figures need to be handled with care because they reflect 'internet commitments' rather than more formalized acts of membership registration and payment.

9 It is important to note that 'Radicalism' as a movement had existed at least since the 1830s, in particular in opposition to the restored monarchy of 1830–48.

10 Successes which, of course, have continued since then. Notably, 15% of the voters during the first round of the 1995 presidential elections, 17% at both rounds of the 2002 ones, 18% in 2012's first round and 25% at the 2014 European elections. Finally, at the 2017 presidentials, the *FN* received 21% of the vote in the first round and 34% in the second.

11 The *Mouvement Démocrate* has had fluctuating electoral results. But one should recall in particular that its founder, François Bayrou, received no less than 18.6% of the vote in the first round of the 2007 presidential elections.

12 Julia Cagé (2018) has updated these figures. She highlights that prior to the 2017 presidential elections, by the end of 2016 *Les Républicains* had already raised 7.45 million euros from private donations, a figure much higher than the *PS* (0.676 million) but rivalled by Emmanuel Macron's *En Marche!* movement (4.9 million). The overarching claim she makes is that such donations are now a structural and structuring part of French party politics.

13 For the *PCF*, this fall in membership has mirrored a vertiginous fall in electoral results. For example, for the first round of legislative elections, in 1978 it won as much as 20.7%. However, in 1986 this was already down to 9.6% and by 2002, this figure was only 4.8%. Standard explanations of 'the fall' of this party are

dominated by the idea that it is 'natural' because its ideology and doctrine is out of sync with society, the Soviet bloc is a distant memory and, more generally, the working class has been weakened as a social category. Instead, the research of Mischi and Pudal emphasizes the impact of competition from other leftist parties and movements, together with a structural destabilization of sociabilities within the party itself and as regards its networks, particularly at the local level where the *PCF* once possessed many municipal bastions.

14 In the end the presence of *LRM* candidates most often resulted in a splitting of votes for centrist and right-of-centre candidates, as well as the consolidation of Green and *PS* coalitions. Indeed, the latter ended up winning many municipalities, including those of Bordeaux, Lyon and Marseille.

15 In purely electoral terms, 1989 is when the Green Party obtained 11.6% of the vote for the European Parliament elections. For the latter, this figure was high again in 1999 (11.2%), 2009 (19.9%) and 2019 (13.5%). Moreover, the Greens have done particularly well at two regional elections: 1992 (14.6%) and 2010 (12.2%).

16 2,661,231 participants for the first round and 2,860,000 for the second.

7

Growing old and passing on: 'Social protection' or structural reproduction?

Introduction

As with virtually all the 'developed' countries of the world, and indeed in many others too, the demography of France is such that no fewer than 18% of the 2020 population are over 64 years of age. Moreover, as Table 7.1 highlights, this figure is projected to rise to 27% by 2050. Meanwhile, 6% of people in France are already over 80 (a percentage set to double in the next thirty years).

As elsewhere, this demographic shift has a number of consequences which, when combined with various other sociological and policy changes, constitute a range of major challenges for France's social structures and polity. Indeed, given the importance of the welfare state to this country's societal and political development over the last seventy-five years, these challenges are particularly acute and evident in the French case (Guillemard, 2010). Moreover, in 2020 the COVID-19 crisis has clearly sparked a further set of controversies regarding healthcare and care of the old in particular. In this country, at the time of writing the virus has thus far caused a ratio of deaths, hospitalizations and suffering much lower than in the UK and Spain, but considerably higher than in Germany. Moreover, there have been widespread social and regional disparities as regards who has suffered and how they have been treated.[1] In short, COVID-19 has put the French health and social protection system to a severe test from which some analytical lessons can already be drawn. Indeed this crisis, together with the demographics sketched out above, justify why this final chapter will successively describe and analyse how three sets of institutions relating to caring for the elderly, pensions, then death itself, have evolved over the recent past.

The overall argument made below is that despite significant growth in calls for radical change in all three of these issue areas, the institutions established in previous, quite different, eras have proved remarkably resistant to change. However, explanation of this institutional reproduction cannot simply be reduced to the 'path-dependent' and 'veto-player' creating effects that

Table 7.1 Share of the population aged over 65 and 80, 2015 and 2050

	2015		2050	
	% over 65	*% over 80*	*% over 65*	*% over 80*
Japan	27	8	36	15
Spain	19	6	36	14
France	18	6	27	12
UK	18	5	26	10
USA	15	4	22	8

Source: OECD Health Statistics, 2017, www.oecd.org/health/health-statistics.htm: 199, consulted 11th July 2019.

historical institutionalists attribute to institutions (Hacker, 1998; Palier, 2005; Ebbinghaus and Gronwald, 2011). According to this theory – one so often mobilized over issues that affect welfare states – institutions themselves have mechanical effects upon public policy and even politics itself. As coherent as this account may be, it not only overemphasizes a distinction between moments of institutional stability and other 'critical junctures' where change becomes possible (thereby neglecting the fundamental and constant contingency of institutions). Such historical institutionalism also fails to give enough importance to the actual actors involved in defending or challenging these rules, norms and conventions. More precisely, as the case of ageing in France underlines particularly clearly, a predominance of institutional reproduction needs explaining through analysing the asymmetries of the power relations concerned, the capital of dominant actors, but also – and perhaps above all – the under-equipment of their challengers in terms of tools for conducting effective political work. In this way, and once again, evocations of 'neo-liberalism' and 'globalization' have certainly featured highly in debates over how to provide services to an ageing population in France. Moreover, trends towards individualization and increased emphasis upon the material have also frequently been drawn into such discussions. However, as will be shown, there is little evidence that any of these four variables have directly and unilaterally had causal effects upon the reproduction or moderate change that institutions and power relations in this issue area have undergone over the past three to four decades. Instead, studying distinct sets of political work carried out the long haul provides more analytical purchase.

Grey days? Caring for an ageing population

Based upon a wide-ranging study conducted in several countries of the global North, Hall and Lamont (2009) conclude that in order to be 'successful', societies must do much more than simply raise or maintain the material, and therefore budgetary, aspects of their health-related institutions. Rather, they desperately need to place emphasis upon the fundamentally social dimensions of these rules and norms, and this in particular by updating both the organization of care and the meaning which is attached to it. In the case of caring for the elderly in France, however, and particularly given the budgetary pressures it has been under since the 1980s, many specialists of this subject area would consider Hall and Lamont's positive conclusion regarding this particular country to be idealistic and even utopian. Indeed, despite generally providing a standard of care to the old that is at least as high as in other comparable countries, as the COVID-19 crisis has highlighted so frighteningly, in France glaring gaps between goals and practice clearly remain. Moreover, the social meaning attached to care is currently unclear in this country.

Accordingly, by analysing the political work that has been undertaken to adapt to demographic and budgetary pressures, first for specific policies for the elderly, then as regards those from the health issue area which particularly affect them, it will be shown that in today's France overall levels of both long-term and medical care do remain comparatively high. Political work realized in the period 1944–84 to institutionalize this mode and magnitude of public and collective intervention provides a major part of the explanation of these levels. But it also caused the gaps created and through which many of the old in this country now fall. Moreover, this safeguarding and renewal of publicly and collectively backed institutions focused on the old can only be fully explained by unpacking the defensive political work accomplished by a range of actors, most of whom fall 'under the radar' of over-hasty, actor-less analysis.

Long-term care for the old

As a number of socio-historians have rightly underlined, in virtually every country of the global North it is vital to grasp how, over the course of the period 1880–1960, 'the old' became 'the retired' (Caradec, 2015). Whereas old people had previously been seen as a private 'problem' to be dealt with by themselves, their families, the church or charities, through a long process of social construction, a different definition of the elderly as a responsibility for local and national government gradually emerged and took root via institutional development. In the French case, certain municipal governments played pioneering roles, notably that of Lyon. Meanwhile, at the national scale relatively weak and poorly implemented laws were adopted in 1905, 1910, then 1930. Ultimately, as for so many dimensions of French social policy, it was not until 1945 that a genuine set of public policies aimed at caring for the old began to emerge (Dumons and Pollet, 1994; Capuano, 2018).

More precisely, building upon welfare state institutions put in place just after the war, a more specific initiative for the elderly was launched in 1961 around the much-cited *Rapport Laroque*. Apart from the crucial question of pensions discussed in the following section, the policy instruments put in place for the old have progressively included subsidies for improvements to their housing and considerable extension of publicly subsidized care in the home. Indeed, as early as 1979, moves were made to systematize care for elderly people considered no longer able to look after themselves on their own. Using the term 'dependency' first coined within the growing discipline of geriatrics, this segment of the old has since been defined as a 'public problem'. However, as Frinault has analysed in depth (2009), it then took fifteen years before this 'problem' was clarified and gave rise to a more integrated set of policy instruments. Defined eventually as an incapacity to look after oneself (thereby creating some confusion with care for the disabled), in 1997 legislative changes led to the creation of specific pensions (*allocations personnalisées d'autonomie*) for people over 60 classified as 'dependent'. Financed in part by the social security system (in the name of dependency as 'a social risk') and in part by by the *Conseils départementaux* (in the name of their responsibility for 'social aid' and 'those in need') (Martin, 2014), by 2013 there were 1.2 million beneficiaries of this policy, 90% of whom were aged 75 and over. Forty per cent of these beneficiaries were living in an old people's home.[2]

As Tables 7.2 to 7.5 highlight, the way the elderly live out their days and are cared for in France mirrors what happens in other Western countries, but differs in some respects. In terms of the number of long-term care beds available, the French situation is quite typical of the European norm: much less capacity than two highly equipped countries (the Netherlands and Sweden), but much higher than the UK (and even more than the US). A similar comparative configuration can be observed for the extent to which long-term care is covered by government expenditure or compulsory insurance

Table 7.2 Long-term care beds in institutions and hospitals, 2015 (beds per 1,000 population aged 65 and over)

	Beds	Trend 2005–15
Netherlands	87.4	na
Sweden	66.4	−23.5
France	55.7	+1.3
Germany	54.4	+5.1
UK	47.6	−8.8
USA	36.8	−8.2

Source: OECD Health Statistics, 2017, www.oecd.org/health/health-statistics.htm: 213, consulted 11th July 2019.

Table 7.3 Long-term care expenditure by government and compulsory insurance, 2015

	% of GDP	*Ratio of health v. social care*
Netherlands	3.7	59/41
Sweden	3.2	81/19
France	1.7	65/35
UK	1.5	73/27
USA	0.5	100/0

Source: OECD Health Statistics, 2017, www.oecd.org/health/health-statistics.htm: 215, consulted 11th July 2019.

Table 7.4 Long-term healthcare expenditure by mode of provision, 2015 (%)

	Inpatient	*Home-based*	*Other*
Netherlands	86	11	3
Sweden	64	31	5
France	77	23	0
UK	55	44	1
Italy	51	18	31

Note: 'Other' includes day cases and outpatient long-term care.

Source: OECD Health Statistics, 2017, www.oecd.org/health/health-statistics.htm: 215, consulted 11th July 2019.

Table 7.5 Annual growth rate in expenditure on long-term care by government and compulsory insurance schemes, 2005–15 (%)

Netherlands	2.9
Germany	3.3
France	3.3
Spain	4
Sweden	2
USA	1.8

Source: OECD Health Statistics, 2017, www.oecd.org/health/health-statistics.htm: 215, consulted 11th July 2019.

(although here the UK is almost at the French level). However, one should note that in France a much larger amount of this expenditure is classified as 'social' rather than 'health' care than in the UK or even Sweden. Perhaps paradoxically, however, a final key point concerns the medicalization of long-term care in France. In contrast to the UK and Sweden, where as much as 44% and 31% respectively of healthcare for the old is now administered in the home, in France this figure is still as low as 23%. In other words, despite a general shift in the Western world back towards caring for the elderly sick in their homes or within those of their families, the general expectation and practice in France is that this will still take place in a hospital or specialized nursing home.

Experts disagree over the causes of change or continuity in where the elderly are cared for, both in general and when they are ill. For some, the shifts observed result positively from the taking on board of research into what old people want and what is best for their health and well-being. This point of view is defended in particular by supporters of reforms, notably Dominique Libault (2019), President of the *Haut Conseil du Financement de la protection sociale* and the lead author of a report to the Minister for Health and Social Affairs published in March 2019. Amongst many other propositions, this report gave further impetus for policy instruments designed both to encourage care for 'the dependent' in their own homes, but also an 'improvement' in the standard of nursing homes. In short, seen from this angle, the public problem of 'dependency' is not simply a financial challenge. Instead, it must be framed more globally, then respond with a series of measures that include better regulation of collective homes for the elderly and, more generally, a national plan to create jobs in the care sector.

For other experts in this domain, however, changes in patterns of care, and in particular the reduction in hospital and long-term care beds, result quite simply from governmental cost-cutting and the introduction of neo-liberal policy recipes into the health and social service sectors (Capuano, 2018). Moreover, from a similar angle, research has shown that in many instances, the transfer of decision-making authority to the level of the *département* has not meant that the elderly who live locally are given the chance to participate more in defining priorities and shaping policy implementation (Pouchadon and Martin, 2018). On the contrary, at least in the Gironde *département* that surrounds Bordeaux, a utilitarian logic of financing predominates, i.e. one of help to the dependent purely as a service to be delivered.

In order to explain the societal structures that set parameters upon the way policy for the elderly is made in France, it is, of course, vital to look more closely at the actors involved. For the state, the Ministry of Solidarity and Health is obviously a key player. However, given the importance of social insurance for the actual funding of healthcare, it is as important to take into account representatives of the *Caisse nationale d'assurance vieillesse* (*CNAV*), together with those of complementary 'mutualist' insurance, notably *La Mutualité française*. Moreover, in the case of care in the home, as we have seen, the *Conseils départementaux*, widely recognized as being under-financed and insufficiently equipped in terms of expertise (Lafore, 2013), also need to be taken into account. Over the last three decades, actors from the Ministry of Solidarity and Health have been put under pressure, notably by the French Ministry of Finance, the European Commission and the European Central Bank, to reduce expenditure. This, in turn, has reduced the budgets of both state and local authority providers. Consequently, social and complementary insurance funds have had to fund the costs of care for the retired, thereby often putting the organizations concerned in great difficulty, as we shall see more clearly below. Not surprisingly, the overall outcome has been slow growth in publicly funded care for the old on the one hand and, on the other, no step-level change in the way the public problem of the elderly has been defined, instrumented and legitimated.

Moreover, in contrast to other countries, and in particular the US, in France it is important not to accord great importance to interest groups who claim to represent the elderly, i.e. to specialized collective actors whom one might think would provide a precious ally for others also seeking to increase public involvement in care for the dependent segment of this population. Although smaller organizations had existed beforehand, it was not until 2000 that the *Confédération française des retraités* (CFR) was founded. According to Viriot-Durandal (2003), this organization emerged as part of a concerted attempt to avoid splits between ex-public and private sector workers, as well as to consolidate the specialization of expertise on issues concerning the elderly. Indeed, given their high and ever-increasing number, potentially the elderly could constitute a powerful pressure group. However, as Caradec (2015) underlines, the old are not homogenous and never have been. Indeed, as Achim Goerres has highlighted in the cases of the UK and Germany, there is little evidence that 'seniors' have a common social or political identity (2009: 152). Instead, their values, beliefs and mobilizations are structured by socio-economic, class and educational variables that are general to the populations of the polities they live in. Indeed, in France this dispersion of interest representation for the old also reflects itself in the way trade unions tend to act over issues related to the elderly. Although each has its section for the retired and is involved in setting some relevant social policies at the national scale, already weakened by other causes (see chapter 3), each union is reluctant to create an inter-generational split by differentiating between its retired and working members when developing and defending their respective priorities and points of view (Viriot-Durandal, 2003: 323).

In summary, in terms of institutions and power relations, care for the old in France has certainly experienced high continuity over the past few decades. Nevertheless, increasingly it is being sent back to individuals and their families to fund and organize. More precisely, as Capuano underlines (2018: chapter 7), France is not like Italy or Spain where the family, and thus private incomes, are responsible for virtually everything that a 'dependent' old person requires. Nevertheless, in France much of such care is not covered by the state or the social security system, as it is in countries such as Sweden. Some actors from within and without the public bodies mentioned above have certainly attempted to increase public intervention in this issue area, but, for the moment at least, their political work has met with very limited success.

Staying alive: the best medical care in the world for the old?

Of course, the old are not necessarily ill. Indeed, in many instances, particularly after retiring and before the age of 75, they are often in good health. Nevertheless, statistically their demand for medical care is higher than for the rest of the adult population, a level of need that obviously tends to rise as the ageing process advances. Indeed, if it costs 2,000 euros a year in France to care for the health of a 50-year-old, this figure rises to 8,000 euros for an 80-year-old. Moreover, the health costs of the last year of an average life account for no fewer than 8% of their total cost (Bérard, 2016). In 2019, the aggregate cost of long-term care for the old in France constituted 1.9% of its GDP (as compared to 0.5% for the US, 1.2% for the UK and 3.2% for Sweden[3]). As chapter 1 began to describe and explain, France's health and care system has expanded massively since the 1940s and today provides a range of services to both the population as a whole and the elderly in particular. Indeed, as opinion surveys consistently show, although the French are often disgruntled with their lot, they clearly want to stay alive, notably by preserving a system of healthcare widely considered to be amongst the most comprehensive and most easily accessed in the world (a survey conducted in 2018 concluded that 84% of its respondents trusted the health service, a figure up from 80% ten years previously: Zmerli, 2019: 273). But just how has this level of care been maintained? Who has accomplished this political work, why and with what resources?

As Bruno Palier underlines (2017: 4), on the surface, most struggles have been about saving money. More fundamentally, however, they have been driven by attempts to make healthcare in France fit with overarching economic policies and, thus, a more cost-conscious approach to the relationship between the economic, the social and the state which is legitimized using the language of New Public Management. Indeed, as Juven *et al.* show (2019: 7), reductions in hospital beds have consistently, and disingenuously, been legitimized in France not using the rhetoric of cost savings, but in the name of 'better organization' and 'efficiency'.

Taking a slightly different view which highlights that the percentage of public expenditure as part of total health expenditure in France in 2014 was only 77% as compared to the UK's 84%, Brunn and Hassenteufel (2021) depict the overall process of institutional reproduction as one characterized not by 'retrenchment, but by the increase of social contributions to health insurance funds'. However, as they then underline, even 'by the mid-1980s, increasing contributions proved an economic dead-end, so attempts were then made to limit the growth of health insurance expenditure and to reduce the health insurance funds' deficit'. Indeed, as of 1992 the goal of slowing increases in spending on health has become a governmental priority. Breaks with the past have accordingly been attempted, in particular by introducing new principles (such as 'universality' and 'performance'), new organizations (such as medicines' agencies) and a range of new policy instruments drawn from theories of New Public Management and, indeed, neo-liberal ideology.

One particular method deployed has been to prioritize the policy concept of 'universalism'. This has been used as a rhetorical tool with which to legitimize attempts to plaster over the gaps left by a health system initially paid for essentially by social insurance contributions and segmented profession-linked 'funds'.[4] Consequently, those who had consistently been in work throughout their lives therefore benefited the most, leaving those who had instead had atypical careers (e.g. artists), or experienced long periods of unemployment, exposed to having to pay for their healthcare 'from their pockets' (Palier, 2014: 92). Successive reforms in the name of 'universal' coverage have sought to attenuate these differences in access to healthcare, with some limited success. More importantly still, however, universalism has also been used to shift some of the funding of healthcare away from social insurance and towards resources from income tax. In this respect, the introduction of the *Contribution sociale généralisé* (CSG) in 1990 constitutes a sharp break with previous practice. Currently set at between 6% and 9% of gross salaries but also pensions, the CSG now pays for roughly 40% of national government spending upon healthcare. In budgetary terms, the upshot of these reforms has been that already by 2014 nearly 5% of health expenditure was financed directly by the government from taxes, 74% by compulsory health insurance, 12.5% by voluntary health insurance and 6.4% by out-of-pocket payments by patients (DREES, 2018).

These changes in financing have affected the elderly both as regards what they pay in to the health system, as well as how the health services they can call upon are actually funded and run. Here much recent research has highlighted what it concludes are the deleterious effects of the introduction of a variety of instruments ostensibly to improve 'the performance' of healthcare (Juven *et al.*, 2019). Resulting, for example, in shorter hospital stays, such critics see this policy change as being all about moving from a purely budgetary logic to one based on financial regulation, i.e. reasoning in terms of the costs of each act and changing accounting procedures accordingly. Specifically, this translated in 2003 into 'billing for each medical act (*la tarification à l'acte*: T2A). This has entailed recoding patients, enrolling doctors into this way of thinking, then managing hospitals as a consequence. Moreover, to get their reforms through, the reformers have often strategically, and sometimes disingenuously, used studies that showed that French hospital care was more expensive compared to that of European neighbours (Juven, 2016: 13). Meanwhile, successive attempts have also been made to reduce the cost to the public purse of medicines through intensifying their assessment and evaluation (Benoît, 2020).

Notwithstanding these policy and organizational changes, together with their numerous effects for patients, medical personnel and taxpayers alike, in terms of actual healthcare outcomes, France is nonetheless still widely recognized as doing rather well. According to the OECD, in 2014 France had 6.2 hospital beds per 1,000 inhabitants, compared to an OECD average of 4.7 per 1,000 inhabitants.[5] Indeed, as Genieys and Hassenteufel show (2015), it is important to realize that reform of healthcare in a neo-liberal direction would almost certainly have been more pronounced had not a 'programmatic elite' within the Ministry of Health managed to fight off sustained demands for cuts in services emanating from the Ministry of Finance. Specifically, until at least the late 2000s, this elite succeeded in protecting existing levels of healthcare due to its positional resources (within the *Directorate de la sécurité sociale*), using the rhetoric of 'a sustainable social security system', their self-image as 'the new custodians of the state' (Genieys, 2010), and even by passing a law in 2004 which enhanced their role as regards that of the social partners. Nevertheless, as Brunn and Hassenteufel have underlined more recently, over the past decade 'differences in access' to health services have been on the rise and correlate to socio-economic disparities. To illustrate this claim they underline that 'In 2010, 16.5% of the population reported having forgone healthcare in the last twelve months for financial reasons, as against 14% in 2006' and that 'forgoing care increases inversely with income: those in the poorest quintile forgo three times more care than those in the richest quintile' (Brunn and Hassenteufel, 2021). Given that many in this quintile are elderly, one can reasonably consider that this deterioration of care has affected them particularly strongly.

Moreover, as many authors also highlight, another more frequently politicized issue is the intensification of 'territorial disparities' regarding healthcare. Dramatized by local politicians in particular using the term 'medical deserts', the latter generally signifies a lack of doctors in rural areas, disadvantaged suburbs and, since the *gilets jaunes* protests, many peri-urban areas. Until the COVID-19 crisis, this phenomenon was considered to be less about general practitioners and more about a perceived lack of specialist doctors, hospitals and even pharmacies – all of which, of course, tends to impact even more strongly upon the old than on younger sections of the population. That crisis, however, has shown starkly that certain regions (notably in the west) and the more wealthy neighbourhoods of cities possess much higher levels of healthcare supply than other parts of the country.

So who has resisted the initiatives for change outlined above and how have they so far managed to attenuate many of their effects on healthcare in general, and that of the elderly in particular? Unsurprisingly, such resistance has been most visibly led by actors situated on the left whom one would expect to defend all social policies, and those regarding health in particular. These include trade unionists, left-wing political parties and newspapers. But in France support for reproducing the status quo stems also from powerful actors, generally but not always situated on the political right, who act within the health system itself: doctors, pharmaceutical producers and patient pressure groups. As Palier highlights (2017), what these actors have in common is a commitment to defending 'liberty': the liberty of doctors to operate outside the public sector, of pharmaceutical producers to 'innovate' and of patients to choose the medical practitioners of their choice. The upshot of political work by such actors is that many hospital and other health services have been maintained, meaning in particular that there are rarely long waiting lists for treatment in France, unlike in countries such as the UK. However, the medium- to long-term cumulative effect of the successful defence of *'libérale'* medicine is also a health system which is intrinsically inflationist and extremely difficult to regulate politically.

So the jury is clearly out on what this has all meant for keeping the old alive and well in France. Bruno Palier concludes that in all health systems a relationship is worked out between four often contradictory goals: equal access to care, its quality, financial viability and the freedom of the actors who operate the system. In the French case, however, debates and the need to prioritize between these four dimensions are frequently blurred. Indeed, according to Palier, this in particular means that 'liberty and comfort is chosen to the detriment of equality' (2017: 120). This finding pertains as much to health and long-term care for the elderly as a whole as it does to the health system for all the population. Indeed, the category of the 'individual', together with the 'liberty' and material comfort they are often said to crave, has repeatedly been used in the health sector not so much to change its societal structures, as to maintain them in place. Nevertheless, the cumulative effect of this reproduction, as well as the emphasis upon individuals, has actually been to reduce the standards of, and access to, healthcare for all of France's inhabitants.

Funding the retired whilst trying to reform 'the unreformable'

In 2015, at 10,746.66 euros per inhabitant per year, France featured the highest level of social protection expenses amongst OECD countries. Corresponding in total to 34% of GDP, no fewer than 40% of this figure concerns pensions. Indeed, as Hassenteufel and Palier underline, when one adds 'the half of national expenditure on sickness that is benefiting people aged over 60, and the benefits for the frail elderly, more than two thirds of social expenditure is devoted to people aged over 60 … Like in other Bismarckian systems, there is a structural tendency towards a more senior orientation, at the expense of spending on younger people' (Hassenteufel and Palier, 2019). When restricting this outcome to pensions alone, it is therefore first important to grasp the societal structures that brought this situation about, before then proceeding to analyse the political work that has been carried out to change or reproduce it.

In terms of institutions, once again the legacy of policy developed just after the Second World War is highly important. At that point in time, the first genuine national pension scheme was devised on a flat-rate basis. Moreover, just as many who had begun paying into the scheme after the war began to approach retirement, in 1971–72 a substantial increase in pension rates, together with a system of earnings-related contributions that supplemented the standard state pension, were enacted. Both these developments meant that by as early as 1979 the average French pension was set at 80% of final salaries – an outcome that at the time was greeted as a major policy success (Palier, 2014: 15–20). However, this calibration of pension instruments was also structurally inflationist in the sense that because they were based upon social insurance rather than tax, and were thus directly earnings-related, when the system as a whole began to come under financial pressure in the 1980s, politically it has proved easier to increase contributions than it has to cut the benefits themselves (Palier, 2000: 120). Indeed, in the 1980s much of this financial pressure stemmed on the one hand from unemployment rising (causing contributions to social insurance to fall) and, on the other, from an increasing number of retired people beginning to claim their pensions. Moreover, and confusedly, initially the state reacted to rising unemployment by lavishly funding early retirement schemes (to the tune of 700,000 retirements in 1983 alone!), thereby exacerbating contradictions within the pension system as a whole.

In terms of social distribution, the consequences of the above have been dramatic. Indeed, Louis Chauvel (2014) has gone so far as to claim that it generated a 'spoiled generation' of workers born between 1920 and 1955, one able to retire on a generous full pension during the period 1980 and 2015. By contrast, the problem for those born since 1955, is that:

- many have experienced long periods in unemployment and have therefore paid less into their respective pension funds;
- those who have studied for longer periods have also paid in less, meaning that, except for those at the very top, the effort needed to acquire a qualification has not been compensated for by high salaries;

- for large swathes of the population, their pay has stagnated in relative terms, and thus their social insurance contributions too;
- meanwhile the cost of housing has gone up considerably.

All this has added up to what Chauvel calls a 'generational fracture' at the heart of French society, one which has in turn engendered a 'spiralling' accumulation of advantages for the old and the older, whilst retrograding the young and making their economic futures much darker (2016: 178). Indeed, through protecting the institutions which lie at the heart of the French pension system, powerful actors within the most influential trade unions have been at the forefront of resisting its change. Meanwhile, representatives of business have criticized the budgetary deficit of the national pension system and pushed for more French workers to join private, voluntary contribution schemes (but only 10% have done so). However, they have singularly avoided working politically towards a reform of the system as a whole.

Instead, led by successive governments, and as with health policies, since the early 1990s attempts at major reform of the French pensions system have been begun, with varying degrees of actual institutional impact. First, changes were introduced for employees in the private sector. Shortly thereafter, however, much greater resistance was encountered in the public sector, and this to such an extent that the government of the day was virtually brought to a standstill by it. Ever since, successive governments have almost invariably been tetanized by the perceived 'dangers' of reforming pensions, a framing of 'the problem' which, not surprisingly, has contributed strongly to the relatively low levels of institutional change that have been adopted over the last quarter-century. Indeed, as I seek to highlight below, it is this very perception of 'political danger' that needs to be placed at the heart of analysis.

Retrospectively, however, for reformers things began rather well: in 1993, for all private sector employees, the right-wing government of the day, with the agreement of two major moderate trade unions (*CFDT* and *CGC*), managed to adopt a reform that contained two significant changes: 1) the indexation of benefits would no longer be based on earnings but on inflation rates; and 2) the qualifying period for a full pension was extended from 37.5 to 40 years. More specifically, the period over which the reference salary was calculated was moved from the best ten years of pay to the best twenty-five. In short, private sector employees were encouraged to contribute more by working longer in exchange for higher pensions. In so doing, for the first time since the 1970s, they were actively discouraged from retiring early and thus paying less into the pension system as a whole.

Given the size of the French public sector, however, this initial reform left a large swathe of the population untouched. At least in the eyes of the right-wing government then in power, by preventing them from controlling the rise in public sector pensions, this not only perpetuated a financial problem, it also deepened a public-private divide – one which, moreover, made many of their own electors particularly disgruntled. For all these reasons, and following Jacques Chirac's first election as president, in 1995 Prime Minister Alain Juppé himself led the charge by introducing a bill to Parliament which would, in effect, bring about the same reforms of public sector pensions as the private sector had just undergone. Moreover, this bill sought to consolidate a private pension option within the French system. This time, however, resistance to reform was ferocious and sustained. The substance of what was proposed, of course, largely explains this opposition: depicting it as radically new and 'dangerous', opponents were quick to caricature and dramatize the *plan Juppé* as the beginning of an inexorable move towards 'a minimal welfare state', and thus the destruction of the post-1945 '*acquis social*'. Just as importantly, however, the plans for reform were prepared in secret by Juppé and his close advisers, then presented in one lump not only to 'the social partners' but even to the rest of the government. Not surprisingly, the *CGT* and the *FO* immediately came out strongly against the plan, organizing mass demonstrations and strikes, in particular by rail workers, which brought much of the country to a standstill. But the lack of consultation also alienated the *CFDT*, a union which had ended up supporting the 1993 reforms (Palier, 2000). In short, despite a huge parliamentary majority, Juppé and his plan failed in its attempt to reframe social protection policy general, and pensions in particular, as being in need of considerable change. Indeed, not only were the policy instruments proposed strongly contested, the very discourse used to legitimize change was critiqued and denigrated.

An immediate consequence of the politicized failure of the 'Juppé reforms' was that no further modifications of the pension system were attempted by the succeeding *Parti Socialiste* government led by Lionel Jospin. Specifically, although of course closer to the unions and the *CFDT* in particular, this government chose not to take the risk of alienating its supporters by attempting what its right-wing opponents had failed to achieve. Instead, and controversially, it concentrated much of its efforts upon reducing the working week to thirty-five hours as a means of not only lightening the burden of work for each employee, but also creating more jobs for those out of work (and thus increasing contributions to national pension funds).

However, the *UMP* government which subsequently came to power in 2002 under Prime Minister Raffarin sought again to align the public system with the private one and, moreover, to expand the length of contribution of all French workers. Indeed, ever since then, French employment policy has, amongst its other goals, sought more actively to increase contributions to pension funds, thereby contributing to what many see as the paradox of now wanting the old to work longer at a time of high youth unemployment

(Palier 2014: 114). Again strong resistance was mounted to the Raffarin plan and was particularly successful for workers who had already worked for forty years before the age of 60. Nevertheless, following changes of president and of government all dominated by the right, pressure from the EU to reduce France's budget deficit, together with the fallout from the international economic crisis of 2007–08, in 2010 a new reform plan was adopted which featured increases in the minimum statutory retirement age from 60 to 62 years, in the minimum age to receive a full pension without any penalty from 65 to 67 years, and in the minimum contribution period to 41.5 years. Moreover, a commitment was made to harmonize contribution rates between public-sector and private-sector statutory schemes within ten years.

In short, fifteen years after Juppé's failure, significant reform of the pension system thereby came to be institutionalized in a set of policy instruments, all wedded to a definition of the public problem and legitimizing rhetoric which considers that 'France simply could not go on as before'. Crucially, governments, employers and some trade unions participated in these reforms. Indeed, according to specialists of this question:

> The introduction of new measures at the margins facilitated their acceptance by the major defenders of the core system, either because they did not feel concerned by them, because they were targeted at those least able to protest, or because they believed that these new measures would help them to defend the very nature of social insurance ... However, the French experience shows that the growth of initially marginal new measures can lead to a systemic change for the welfare state, progressively moving away from its Bismarckian bases by becoming more universal, more tax-financed and more state-governed. (Hassenteufel and Palier, 2019)

Symbolically, in July 2012, the newly elected *PS* government attenuated these reforms a little by allowing people who started working before the age of 20 to retire at 60, then by creating a 'hard working conditions account' for relevant occupations. Nevertheless, as a whole the 2010 reform has remained in place. Indeed, it has been the starting point from which, in the form of a report entitled *Pour un système universel de retraite*,[6] in July 2019 the Macron presidency launched a new set of policy proposals. These include:

- the phasing out of special 'regimes' for certain professions in favour of a 'universal' system that applies to all and ends any private-public distinction in contribution rates;
- whilst maintaining the minimum age at which one can access one's pension at 62, the creation of a 'point of equlibrium' (*âge d'équilibre*) at which each individual can access their full entitlement;
- a system of points so as to better take into account increased job mobility throughout each career.

Between the publishing of this report and the beginning of the COVID-19 pandemic in March 2020, the government sought to define in detail and promote this reform. Resistance has thus far been very strong both in the form of demonstrations and actors making counter-proposals. Certain unions (notably the *CGT* and *FO*) have simply rejected the proposals outright, whilst the *CFDT* has left the door open in the hopes they can be attenuated. In the wake of the upheavals caused by the virus, it is no longer clear how much the government will stick to its guns on this issue. For the moment at least, there appears to be growing public awareness that in France today, there are not just three generations involved, but four: the young, the working, the early retired (seniors) and the very old. Consequently, for some actors a vague discourse about 'refounding a pact' between the generations[7] appears to have some resonance. This is so in part because a comparable 'pact' is often presented as being at the origins of the French welfare state in 1945 (a description of what happened which in itself is a myth, given that it was a compromise more than a pact). However, it is too early to say whether this discourse is a key or a marginal aspect of the debate now opened, or to predict its impact upon proceedings.

More generally, looking back at what is now thirty years of attempts to reform France's pension institutions, it is important to note that a number of changes in policy instrumentation have actually taken root. The age of retirement has been pushed back a little and certain aspects of pensions are no longer taboo, such as the 'sanctuarization' of their content for public sector workers or even the possibility of privately funded pensions. Nevertheless, at least to date, continuity has strongly tended to trump change. Indeed, as highly charged symbols of what France is reputed to have achieved during *les trente glorieuses* in terms of social protection, pensions continue to be totems of not only the nation's welfare state, but of the state's very legitimacy.

Passing on

One can have good long-term care, 'the best health sector in the world' and generous pensions, but one day even people in France pass on. This said, singularities remain to be understood in the way that death is handled in this country, as well as how the dead pass on material resources to the living.

Death in France

Whereas in the nineteenth century the population barely increased and life expectancy was around 60 years, since then there has been steady

Table 7.6 Numbers of annual deaths in France, 2008–18

	Number of deaths	*Deaths per 100,000 inhabitants*
2018	614,000	9.2
2017	606,274	9.1
2016	593,865	8.9
2015	593,680	8.9
2014	559,293	8.4
2013	569,236	8.7
2012	569,868	8.7
2011	545,057	8.4
2010	551,218	8.5
2009	548,541	8.5
2008	542,575	8.5

Source: INSEE, www.insee.fr/fr/statistiques/2383440#tableau-Donnes, consulted 11th July 2019.

demographic growth, and life expectancy has risen to around 85. Nevertheless, as Table 7.6 shows, in recent years the number of annual deaths has risen progressively from 8.5 per 100,000 inhabitants to 9.5 – figures which mean that about 1% of the population die annually.

Death, of course, means a lot of things, but at the most prosaic level it implies disposing of bodies, an activity which until very recently equated in France almost exclusively with burials. This can be explained in general terms around the historical importance of the Catholic Church in this country and its opposition to cremation until 1963. Indeed, if each year 36% of corpses are now cremated in this country (as compared to 77% in the UK), this figure was as low as 10% in 1944. Even today there are only around 150 crematoriums in the whole of France, a figure that also hides considerable territorial disparities.

More interestingly in terms of the effects of societal structures, like many other sectors discussed in this book, that of funerals has experienced considerably upheaval and even some significant change since the 1980s. Here analysis benefits from original and painstaking sociological research conducted by Pascale Trompette and published in book form in 2008. Her analysis shows first how and why until the 1980s, interdependencies and compromises between the church, the state, municipalities and a limited set of private companies generated a market situation characterized by monopolies or the abuse of dominant positions. More precisely, this situation reflected a concession made by Napoleon in 1804 that enabled the church to reposition itself at the centre of funeral arrangements in virtually all non-urban areas, whilst over the nineteenth century a system of urban monopolies was allowed to emerge and institutionalize. Trompette highlights how the Third Republic contributed to the 'industry-like' structuration of funeral arrangements through imposing compromises between liberals and defenders of municipal monopolies. Indeed, it was the growth of one company from its base around Paris – *les Pompes funèbres généraux* (PFG) – which gradually extended the supply of such services into rural areas, a shift linked to the medicalization of the end of life and, more generally, change in 'the symbolic construction of the relationship to death and the dead' which increasingly took the latter out of private homes and into funeral parlours. In a word, all this generated a new 'public problem' to which the state and local authorities sought to respond (Trompette, 2008: 67).

Dominated by local monopolies, the institutions, policy instruments and power relations that had developed over preceding decades were largely allowed to roll on until the 1970s. By this time 65% of funeral activity had become private, in the sense that funeral departments of local authorities themselves had progressively lost their levels of market share. Moreover, by this time PFG accounted for no less than 80% of the private market and 50% of the market as a whole. Competition between operators became more aggressive, generating numerous dramatic incidents that were frequently related in the media. More significantly still, by the early 1980s a 'collective actor' emerged proposing the liberalization of the sector and seeking to centre public debate upon the negative effects of its domination by 'monopolies'. Led in part by Michel Leclerc, a member of a powerful family best known for its chain of supermarkets, the promoters of reform first deliberately contravened the law in order to contest local market domination. They then engaged in judicial action in order to justify and legalize their actions. This mobilization eventually led to initial legislation opening up the sector in 1986, then in 1993 a more fundamental law that explicitly 'liberalized it' (Trompette, 2008: chapter 4).

Since then easily identifiable barriers to new entry have virtually disappeared and funeral insurance has come to play a much stronger role (Boissin and Trompette, 2017). Yet one should note that even today the *PFG*, reinforced by becoming part of a larger group and using its 700 agencies, still accounts for 25% of market share. Meanwhile, in some cities, firms backed by the state and local authorities continue to monopolize supply. More precisely, if the French funeral sector comprises around 3,500 firms of which 95% are now private, three-quarters of them have only ten workers or fewer and 60% have five or fewer. In short, as in so many other sectors and industries in this country, dualization predominates. Specifically, despite the relatively high prices it generates for the bereaved (*c.* 3,500 euros a funeral), this dual productive system reflects a set of economic power relations which representatives of the state and local authorities clearly help reproduce on a regular, if not daily, basis.

Passing wealth on: inheritance institutions and social reproduction

Early in chapter 1, I cited a Bob Dylan song that featured the line 'getting born'. Curiously, it is Dylan who will almost have the last word here with the title of another of his classics: 'Death is not the end' (1988). Although this composer did not mean it quite this way, death is also not the end because most of us leave behind not only memories, but also at least some material goods. Indeed, the institutions and power relations that structure inheritance in any country deserve a great deal of attention because, as Thomas Piketty underlines, 'the past tends to devour the future: wealth originating in the past automatically grows more rapidly, even without labour, than wealth stemming from work ... This tends to give lasting, disproportionate importance to inequalities created in the past, and therefore to inheritance' (2014: 378). Moreover, as Piketty shows subsequently, when economic growth slows, this phenomenon is exacerbated. Indeed, 'slower growth explains the accelerated ageing of wealth and the rebound of inherited wealth that have occurred since the 1980s' (2014: 400). Despite this importance of inheritance as a societal structure, to date it has given rise to relatively little political work in France, nor indeed to much genuine research. The best this section can therefore do at this stage is to describe the development of French inheritance laws using the analyses that do exist, then return to Piketty to examine some of their socio-economic impacts.

As the one sociologist specialized in this subject in France, Anne Gotman, underlines, inheritance in all countries is both about goods and bonds (2017). Indeed, as the drama generally associated with a death unfolds and the question *who inherits what?* is raised in both concrete and emotive terms, relationships within a family face a new test. It is precisely to regulate behaviour and outcomes during such moments that inheritance institutions have been developed. In the French case, it is crucial to grasp that today's rules, norms and expectations in this regard stem largely from a key aspect of the 1789 Revolution: the decisive move made to break with 'a privilege' bestowed by the *ancien régime* upon fathers to pass on their worldly goods to whom they wished. In considering that this custom-enshrined rule too often resulted in paternal despotism, active participants in post-revolutionary France introduced legislation which, instead, redirected the estate of the deceased to all their children. Enshrined in the *Code civil* in 1804, this problem definition and policy instrument had at least two structural effects. First, unlike in Germany, it gave little legal protection to the surviving spouse of the deceased. This meant that until rectifying legislation introduced as late as 2001, widowed mothers were often dependant upon the goodwill of their children to avoid being effectively disinherited. Second, automatically dividing up property amongst all one's children has frequently led either to the fragmentation of estates, or to the inability of all descendants to decide about what to do with a property. Consequently, much of France is not only full of empty not-for-sale houses, it is also affected by inheritances that frequently reignite intra-family tension rather than providing catalysts for emotional 'closure'. Indeed, French literature abounds with tales of brothers and sisters falling out over whether to sell the family house or not – this recurrent trait being exacerbated by the fact that in France only 5% of the dead leave behind a will, as compared to around a third in the UK.

Notwithstanding all the above, the passing down of property has risen recently in France from 50% of deaths in 1984 to 65% in 2000 (Gotman, 2006: 17). This, of course, reflects rising property ownership in general (see chapters 1 and 4), and of 'small inheritances' in particular. Indeed, although in 2000 only 13% of properties were acquired solely through inheritance, no fewer than one-quarter of second homes were handed down in this way. Moreover, this socio-economic practice is of considerable importance to the state. According to Gotman, the latter raises 3% of its budget from inheritance taxes which, again revealingly, are imposed upon each inheritor rather than upon the estate as a whole before it is divided up (as occurs in the US, for example).

This data on the relationship between inheritance, the nation and the state can be deepened by returning to Piketty's major study of the relationship between wealth and capitalism (2014). In the French case he shows the relationship between trends in the annual value of inheritance and gifts as a percentage of national income, and inequalities between the revenues of individuals and families. Specifically, there was 'a spectacular decrease in the flow of inheritances between 1910 and 1950' from 24% of national income to under 4%. This shift was caused by a crisis experienced by the aristocracy, then latterly a period of economic growth during which the middle classes accumulated their own wealth to a large extent. However, this period was 'followed by a steady rebound thereafter, with an acceleration in the 1980s' (to 13.5% in 2010 (2014: 425)). Piketty rightly emphasizes that the latter trend 'reflects deep changes in the perception as well as the reality of inheritance' and the very 'structure of inequality' in France. Consequently, for those born in the 1970s and 1980s 'inheritance is playing a larger part in their lives, careers, and individual and family choices than it did with the baby boomers' (2014: 380–381).

However, what Piketty's data also highlights is that because people are living longer, those who inherit in France today do so at a much later stage of their lives than hitherto. Whereas in 1960, the average age at which one inherited was as low as 40, today it is just over 50. Moreover, by 2040 this figure is predicted to rise as high as 55. Although this trend obviously affects each family very differently, when aggregated it has already had significant effects upon when people are able to buy property, together with the types of mortgages they commit themselves to. Moreover, this shift knocks onto the practices of banks and national patterns of credit as a whole. Indeed, as Piketty also underlines, the more inheritance occurs later in life, the more gifts prior to death take on individual and societal importance. According to his figures, such gifts now account for about half of inheritance flows in France (2014: 392), thereby strongly contributing to what he calls the rise of a 'patrimonial middle class' and a 'society of *petits rentiers*' (418). Indeed, all of the above feeds into the deepening of materialism that has been encountered on numerous occasions in earlier chapters of this book. Piketty himself even concludes that this shift presents a danger for the 'meritocatic hope' attached to democracy in this country (422).

Without necessarily buying into the totality of this conclusion, Piketty's data certainly generates important insights into the workings of the French economy and its societal structures as regards inheritance. More generally, his ground-breaking research clearly now deserves to be followed up by studies in political science and sociology targeted upon the political work which has not only reproduced these institutions and power relations for decades, but which today continues to consolidate the myth that these societal structures are 'unreformable'.

Conclusion

By focusing upon the elderly and the end of life, this chapter has shown once again the depth of the structures that have shaped socio-economic practices in France, recently and usually for much longer. Be it as regards long-term care of the old, health services for this part of the population, pensions, funerals or inheritance laws, some change to these institutions and power relations has certainly been wrought since the 1980s. In a word, they were always 'reformable' and have been modified to some extent in recent years. Moreover, whilst working politically towards such change, its advocates have frequently evoked 'globalization' or 'the liberty of the individual' as motives for transforming French practices, or even explicitly drawn upon neo-liberal policy recipes in order to develop their respective propositions. Nevertheless, judged in terms of shifts in institutions and power relations, the overall outcome points more to continuity than it does to deep mutation. Put differently, those growing old in today's France certainly do so differently from their predecessors in the period 1960 to 1990, but this level of difference has been attenuated by reproduction of the institutions and power relations that have continued to structure their societal conditions. Indeed, for the moment at least, opponents of change have succeeded in continuing to breathe resonance into the problem definitions and legitimizing discourse which largely brought about these societal structures in the first place. Part of their 'political equipment' has definitely begun to show signs of wear and tear. But until now these resources and methods have largely 'done the job' of resisting structural change. It remains to be seen whether the COVID-19 crisis will be seized upon either to further shore up this dimension of French social protection, or to revamp it.

Notes

1 At the time of writing (18th May 2020), government statistics relate that COVID-19 has contributed to the deaths of 28,239 people in France. This figure equates to 42 deaths per 100,000 inhabitants, as compared to 52 in the UK, 59 in Spain and 10 in Germany. www.data.gouv.fr/fr/reuses/statistiques-et-evolution-du-coronavirus-covid-19-en-france-pays-departement-region-et-dans-le-monde-cartographie-graphiques-et-courbes-devolution/.

2 Importantly, the ratio of the old living in nursing homes differs considerably between parts of France (more live at home in the north-east, Massif Central and south than the west) and between those who once occupied working-class or blue-collar jobs (the former being more likely to be looked after at home) (Brunel and Carrère, 2019). Moreover, another explanation of such differences lies in the actual availability of places in homes for the elderly. This is higher in the west of France than elsewhere, for example. In 2016, nationally 44% of these 8,000 homes (with 600,000 places in total) were public, 31% were private but run on a not-for-profit basis and 25% were purely private. The health system pays for the medical care received, whilst the state's social services pay for basic services and private sources (i.e. the person and/or their family) fund 'rent' and food.

3 www.oecd.org/health/health-statistics.htm, consulted 15th March 2020.

4 One should recall that in the mid-1940s the *Union nationale* government attempted to make coverage the same for all, but this was opposed by interest groups linked to sectorized insurance funds. Indeed, more of such funds were subsequently created for employees working in agriculture (1961), then the self-employed (1966) (Palier, 2005).

5 www.oecd.org/health/health-statistics.htm, consulted 15th March 2020.

6 *Pour un système universel de retraite. Préconisations de Jean-Paul Delevoye, haut-commissaire à la réforme des retraites*, 18th July 2019. https://reforme-retraite.gouv.fr/actualites/actualites-du-haut-commissaire/article/pour-un-systeme-universel-de-retraite-preconisations-de-jean-paul-delevoye-haut, consulted 15th March 2020.

7 For example, see the article published in *Le Monde* by the sociologist Anne-Marie Guillemard: 'Refonder le pacte entre les générations' (7th–8th July 2019). www.lemonde.fr/idees/article/2019/04/26/anne-marie-guillemard-la-construction-d-un-pacte-intergenerationnel-equilibre-devrait-etre-au-c-ur-de-la-grande-reforme-des-retraites_5455131_3232.html, consulted 9th July 2019. See also her book on the challenges of an ageing population (2010).

Conclusion: French-made today v. yesterday

The France of when this book was written obviously differs in many respects from the country which its author arrived in just over thirty years previously. More fundamentally, a number of economic, social and political shifts that have occurred since the 1980s in virtually all Western liberal democracies have clearly also impacted heavily upon France and the French. Nevertheless, as the preceding pages have sought to highlight, one can only take the measure of such change, then begin to explain it, by closely examining well-defined segments of what constitutes France and, above all, the societal structures that have shaped them. For this reason, in what follows I will first briefly recall what has happened to the institutions and power relations which, from the cradle to the grave, have heavily shaped life in France over the last four decades. On the basis of this assessment, I then proceed to offer some explanations of what has changed and what has not. More precisely, the second section of this conclusion will not only revisit the three themes flagged at the outset of the book as possible causes of change or stasis: neo-liberalization, globalization and social mobility. It will also address more generally what one recurrent aspect of French societal structures – the state – has become. Finally, because the content of this book has drawn so heavily upon the contribution of social science to knowledge about not only France but also other comparable countries, this conclusion will close with a short reflection upon the approach and concepts adopted throughout this book, together with how they could now be refined in order to study and understand societal phenomena even better.

Throughout, a certain change of tone as regards the preceding chapters will become apparent. In part, this stems from these pages necessarily being a synthesis of what has come before. More fundamentally, however, the often critical and sometimes tough conclusions I draw reflect the deep-seated political problems that currently beset France and the French. As I stated right at the outset of this book, France is a country which has many qualities, one where I generally feel comfortable and for which I have considerable affection. At the same time, along with the social science drawn on throughout my analysis, I clearly consider that it is also marked by a range of structural characteristics which, today at least, are deeply problematic.

Strong continuity and infrequent but revealing change

So what societal structures in France have changed since the 1980s and which of them have essentially been reproduced? In order to be relatively brief here, this section adopts a typology of levels of change, then refers back to the preceding chapters for detailed justification of why here I have placed my findings on a continuum from 'no' to 'deep change'. To do so, Peter Hall's well-known definition of 'orders' of change (1993: 278) will be embraced. Specifically, his typology will help distinguish between institutions and power relations which have undergone either no significant mutations or:

- first-order change, concerning the precise settings of policy instruments;
- second-order change to both the range of policy instruments adopted and implemented, together with their settings;
- third-order change, which includes not only all the above, but also entails a transformation in overarching goals, and even 'the paradigm' within which the institution or power relation is located.

As regards facets of French societal structures that have experienced virtually no change over the last decades, a first set concerns infancy and childhood. As chapter 1 demonstrates, from the continued power of doctors as regards birthing and paediatrics, to the ongoing prevalence of untrained child-minding and smacking, together with the deep continuity that has marked *maternelle* and primary schooling, very little has changed over the last four decades. Instead, the strength of medicalization, adult-centred education, the power of teachers and a reluctance to even seriously entertain the results and recommendations of social science research have all essentially been maintained as they were in the 1980s, if not before.

Indeed, this high degree of conservatism has also marked two other key parts of the French education field. On the one hand, the *collège* continues to be a 'make-or-break' fulcrum of the educational system. Between the ages of 11 and 15/16, and thus as children turn into teenagers, they are either applauded to the skies in the case of the happy few, or repeatedly told that their best is simply not good enough. Indeed, it is at this stage that an approach to meritocracy that leaves little place for either equality or differences in the time over which teenagers mature and learn begins to have lasting effects upon both individuals and the system as a whole. Indeed, the impact of the institutions and power relations at the root of this approach to 'middle' schooling can be seen most clearly when one realizes that it is mirrored almost perfectly by what happens during higher education. Here, through the system of *grandes écoles*, together with the *prépa* schools which both feed and feed off them, an elite that had already largely been rewarded during its years in *collège* continues to be encouraged by the institutions and power relations that structure education in France as a whole. Indeed, *grande école* pupils are even nourished, materially and generously, by the state itself, without this provoking any sustained societal challenge.

As will be seen below, meritocracy *à la française* has many other deep effects upon aspects of French life way beyond the sphere of education. Within the world of French business, for example, as chapter 3 underlined, management–employee relations are also deeply affected by hierarchies that stem from those with decisional power almost always being the persons in a company with the highest diplomas. Little has changed in this regard over the past four decades, neither have experience and practical knowledge been upgraded as criteria for the legitimacy to be a decision-maker. More generally still, except in some exceptional cases, there is scant evidence that workplaces in France have become less rigid. This refers not only to how standard working procedures are imposed, but also over who gets to negotiate their setting in the first place.

A final example of a French societal structure that has undergone virtually no change since the 1980s concerns inheritance. Although in 2001 a law was introduced that gave greater leverage to surviving spouses, institutions in this issue area continue to be dominated by the automatic sharing amongst all the deceased's children of all the material goods they leave behind – a practice that dates back to Napoleon I. One could argue, of course, that the 2001 law actually constitutes a first-order change because it changes the formal justification of French rules and norms of succession. Moreover, there is no denying that this change in the law has made the practice of transferring property different from what it was hitherto, thereby improving the lot of many women in particular. Indeed, and much more generally, a certain amount of change, particularly in formal law, has been introduced which has ameliorated the position of women in French society. These changes range from rules and norms over equal pay, to the number of women who now have to be on any company's board, to the gender of the candidates political parties have to feature on their electoral lists. Each of these changes have their significance and have modified power relations to a certain extent. Nevertheless, in nearly all instances, it would be an exaggeration to claim that anything beyond first-order change has thus far been institutionalized. In the world of business, 'a glass ceiling' on both salaries and promotions clearly remains in place, just as in political parties the best positions on any electoral list remain dominated by men. More pervasively, as a succession of #MeToo scandals have revealed since 2017, and the content of French advertising confirms on a daily basis, deeply ingrained sexism continues to predominate in most social milieux.

Higher secondary education is another wide issue area over which superficial commentary often considers that deep change has occurred, whereas actual modification of power relations and institutions for the moment remains slight. My finding here may seem curious given that a governmental commitment was made in the early 1980s to ensure that 80% of all students leave school with a *baccalauréat*, and that this goal has indeed been attained. As chapter 2 details, however, this seemingly positive result has largely been achieved through the transformation of most *lycées* into gigantic, impersonal organizations on the one hand, and a large increase in symbolically devalued and under-resourced *lycées professionnels* on the other. Whilst these changes have certainly enabled a much greater proportion of pupils to stay on at school than was the case until the mid-1980s, this does not mean that all those who would previously have left at 16 have been genuinely encouraged to develop appropriate skills and enhance their life chances. To translate the title of Stéphane Beaud's seminal book (2002) on this subject: '80% with the *bac*, but so what?' Ultimately, because the expansion of the *lycée* has not been thought of in more holistic terms which encompass a commitment to genuine social redistribution, and because the French education system as a whole is still guided by a Darwinian form of meritocracy, in reality change in higher secondary education has ultimately not surpassed that of the second order at the most.

Change at this level of mixtures of policy instruments is also what has transpired within the dimensions of French business devoted to production, marketing and sales. Be it within the defence sector, housing, cultural or funeral industries, as chapters 4, 5 and 7 have underlined, contrary to previous practice, actual monopolies have become rarities. Pushed by EU legislation and the European Commission's Directorate-General for Competition in particular, companies, including those still partly owned by the state, have been forced to open up markets to new entrants and avoid the cartels and collusive price-setting of yesteryear. This said, however, in many industries 'dominant positions' remain more than common, and abuse of their power often goes unchecked. Indeed, this trait is inseparable from the fact that the state not only continues to intervene heavily, and often directly, within the production of goods and services in France, it also constrains and orientates the way markets are segmented (e.g. *AOC* wines) and goods are marketed (e.g. by actively encouraging advertising campaigns financed and run by collective action bodies known as *interprofessions*). Certainly, as we will see again below, the state is much less active in the capitalization and financing of most industries than it was during the years 1945–84. However, at least as regards the structuring of production and markets, in many major industries neo-*dirigisme* is still very much alive (Ansaloni and Smith, 2018).

Perhaps less surprisingly, this renewed form of *dirigisme* is still omnipresent in both the cultural and sport industries, as well as throughout the broad policy domain of 'social protection'. In both the former, although considerably affected since the 1980s by the increased involvement of municipalities, *départements* and regions, the state continues to have the deepest influence. Specifically, if certain new policy instruments, such as funding mechanisms, have been introduced, the elitism of both cultural affairs and sport continues to be driven and maintained in place largely by representatives of the state. Similarly, although social insurance rather than income tax plays the most important role in French health and pensions policies, since the 1990s the 'social partners' (unions and employer associations) who once had more direct power over decision-making have seen their roles reduced by the increased involvement of state representatives. More precisely, armed with new legitimizing discourse around the term 'universalism', together with policy instruments partly inspired by New Public Management and thus neo-liberalism (see below), the latter have pushed through many reforms that have changed the hierarchy of many policy objectives and implementation systems. The way hospitals are run or the age at which one can retire on a full pension provide examples of this shift. Notwithstanding their effects, however, it is not possible to conclude that either the health service or the pensions system has undergone paradigmatic change since the 1980s. Instead, most of the key institutions and power relations have been kept in place. This has led to continuity in standards of service, but also inflation in their costs and high levels of dependence upon the public purse.

So has any deep, third-order change been introduced in France, and if so where? At least four of the issue areas covered in this book have experienced change belonging to this category. Although quite different in many ways, the first two – schooling and capitalization – have both entailed a devaluing of the public and a revaluing of the private. In the case of education, the deep change that has occurred is quite simply the number of students in secondary schools and places of higher education which are privately funded. In the case of the former, a key driver has been criticisms of the public education system, aided and abetted by the rolling on of a key decision taken in the early 1980s by the first Mitterrand government to continue the state's subsidizing of private schools. Similarly, despite the high cost of their fees, the growth of private higher education establishments, and of business schools in particular, has been legitimized on the one hand by their emphasis upon 'practical' internships and immediate employability. Whilst on the other, this trend has also been fuelled by the state's failure to protect and enhance public universities as places of fundamental learning which are also crucial for employment and the development of life chances.

Moreover, this sea change in favour of private education is ultimately linked to a wider revalorization of the generation of private capital and property ownership that has spread throughout France, as in most other countries, since the 1980s. Specifically, the relaunching of the French stock exchange in the mid-1980s, together with the privatization and liberalization of commercial banks, has encouraged both a shift towards the more 'impatient' financing of business and a rise in home ownership. The latter has been facilitated by the removal of statist controls upon mortgages and other forms of credit. More generally, as chapter 4 relates, stocks, shares and private equity have come to play a greater part in French capitalism, one that has become both 'financialized' and more fully integrated within international capital markets and flows. Moreover, foreign ownership of firms in France, and even of firms presented as French (e.g. Thales), has grown significantly since the 1980s.

Indeed, both the latter dimension of internationalization and financialization more generally have had deep effects upon a third set of French societal structures that concern capital–labour relations. Here paradigmatic change has notably taken the form of a steep rise in short-term employment contracts and thus of job precariousness. Accompanied by a reduction in the influence of the trade unions upon pay and conditions in many industries, further falls in union membership and greater legitimacy being accorded to employers, and their peak organization the *MEDEF* in particular, all this amounts to a change in the very goal of employment practices and policies to which, as we shall see below, the state has contributed directly.

Moreover, this involvement of the state is in turn linked to changes within political parties 'of government'. These parties constitute the fourth and final set of societal structures dealt with in this book that has undergone third-order change since the 1980s. As chapter 6 explains, both on the centre-left (the *PS*) and centre-right (the *RPR*, *UDF*, then the *UMP* and now *LR*), these parties that have been elected to govern France since 1981 have all been deeply delegitimized over the past decade. More precisely, at different times and often for different reasons, they have not only lost members and even the capacity for party activism, but have also squandered their traditional sources of electoral support. Confirmed and consolidated by the 2017 elections and the rise of Emmanuel Macron and his *La République En Marche* party, this seismic change in the French party system is still, of course, bedding in. But its effects on the parties listed above have already been dramatic.

In summary, much more could and should be said about which of France's societal structures have changed and to what extent. Consequently, this section and Table 8.1 that seeks to encapsulate it are more a means of synthesizing an assessment and inviting discussion than conclusive statements

Table 8.1 Degrees of change in French societal structures, 1980–2020

Reproduction	*First-order change*	*Second-order*	*Third-order*
Education	Education	Education	Education
Adult-centredness	Introduction of primary-level testing	Expansion of lycées	A rise in private collèges and lycées
Teacher power	Adult-centred education	More 'profession-centred' schooling	
	The role of *les grandes écoles*	More private higher education	
Capital–labour relations	Capital–labour relations	Capital–labour relations	Capital–labour relations
	Manager–employee relations	The role of women at work	Greater precariousness
	Inheritance laws	Pensions	Devaluing of trade unions
		Health Policy	Revaluing of the *MEDEF*
Business	Business	Business	Business
Company hierarchies	Women on company boards	State involvement in production and markets	More 'impatient capital' and foreign ownership
Activism	Activism	Activism	Activism
State involvement	Environmentalism	'Spontaneous' protesting	Decline in union and party memberships
		Policing methods	Collapse of *PS* and centre-right

about what has happened to these structures over the past four decades. Indeed, their principal role has been to set the scene for what is ultimately more important: analysis of why some of these structures have changed, whereas others have not.

The cause of change or stasis: political work

The overarching claim made in the introduction to this book is that all change or reproduction of societal structures (i.e. institutions and power relations) can be explained as a consequence of political work: struggles between specific sets of actors over the definition of public problems, instrumentation of policy responses and the legitimation of both these processes. This claim will now be re-examined in the light of the data presented in each chapter. More precisely, having first reformulated the three causal narratives of change advocated by others (neo-liberalization, globalization, *embourgeoised* social mobility) using both the concept of political work and the empirical evidence presented in previous chapters, this section will then directly tackle what France's state has become.

Neo-liberalization, globalization and embourgeoisement *revisited*

The cases of deep structural mutation I have just presented provide tests of whether neo-liberalism or globalization have been the causes of change in France since the 1980s. Put bluntly, the first question to be readdressed here is whether these phenomena have modified this country's societal structures? When the question is framed in this way, my overall answer is a resounding 'no': in none of the cases studied in this book have neo-liberal ideology or 'the threat of globalization' triumphed by engendering the replacement of institutions and power relations. However, when woven into political work in certain ways by actors equipped with the appropriate resources and repertoires, in certain cases both these reservoirs of diagnoses and prognoses have played a certain role in prompting change. More precisely, the argument developed below is that neo-liberalism and globalization have gained more purchase in domains of French life where individualization of social practices has taken greater hold and/or where a renaissance of materialism has occurred.

Importantly, however, neither of these two trends add up to the *embourgeoisement* of the French population as a whole (Laferté, 2018). Such a process has certainly occurred within certain sectors and parts of the middle class. But greater individualization and materialism within French society are more pervasive. Indeed, they are linked even more closely to revenue than to class itself, and thus to the social distinctions that money, rather than education or birthright, can now 'buy'.

Similarly, in the French case, no generalized spreading of 'authoritarian populism' (Norris and Inglehart, 2019) has occurred over the last four decades. This phenomenon has certainly participated in the rise of an extreme-right party led by the Le Pen family. Moreover, it also played a role in the *gilets jaunes* movement of 2018–19. However, for the moment at least, the social conservatism strand of this populism continues to enjoy only limited support. Apart from over immigration policy and policing (two domains unfortunately not covered in this book), such conservatism has not directly impacted upon France's societal structures. This said, the second major strand of such populism – mistrust of 'the establishment' – has had more effects, which will be further discussed below.

In the case of neo-liberalism, from as early as the 1970s this ideology began to provide new intellectual nourishment and rallying calls for liberals within both French business and the state who had largely been marginalized during the heyday of Keynesian *dirigisme*. As has been stressed repeatedly in the preceding chapters, economic liberalism has a long history in France and never disappeared, even when the country's largest firms were nationalized and its most senior politicians and civil servants promoted *planification*, protectionism and interventionism. In the face of the structural economic challenges that became highly visible between 1973 and 1983, these liberals (e.g. President Giscard d'Estaing, Raymond Barre) began to resurface, join forces and propose new ways of orientating the economy and thence French society. More precisely, the very problem of national economic performance was reframed. This was partly done by taking analyses of 'the crisis' and proposals for change 'off the shelf' that had been initiated by liberal, then developed by neo-liberal, theorists and advocates. In turn, the latter also impacted upon policy re-instrumentation as, behind the spearhead of the liberalization of capital, banks were reprivatized and new patterns of individualized consumption were encouraged to develop, notably of housing but also of innumerable consumer goods. As neo-liberal theories of economics always promote, this process entailed not only deregulation, but also strong intervention by the state in order to bring it about and run it. Indeed, once they had been reprogrammed in this direction through changes in its own personnel, parts of the French state, notably its Ministry of Finance, were well armed in terms of expertise, legitimacy and positions to bring about deep change. Accordingly, the tools originally developed for *dirigisme* have been made compatible with certain neo-liberal problem definitions in many instances. Moreover, as Benjamin Lemoine (2016) has shown so well, this shift within the heart of government in France was paralleled by another at the scale of the EU which entailed a great deal of collaboration between 'Bercy' and the European Commission's DG II (now DG ECFIN).

The liberalization of capital in turn created a resource for company directors to reorient the management of their respective firms by weakening the power of labour within them. More precisely, through delegitimizing collective bargaining arrangements and proposing instead more individualized methods of setting pay and envisaging career development, here neo-liberal policy recipes were used to slow wage inflation, reduce strikes and, ultimately, weaken the trade union movement. This said, in France this process has been mediated by the structural fragmentation of these unions and a sharp drop in their membership that began well before the penetration of company management by neo-liberal ideology. In this instance, that set of ideals and ideas was certainly used subsequently to consolidate change in the way capital–labour relations were framed and instrumented. However, this was not its initial and primary cause.

Similarly, the growth in private schools that has occurred within French higher and secondary education cannot be attributed to a supposedly all-consuming rise in neo-liberalism in this country. Private education has existed for decades if not centuries. Indeed, it continued to be supported directly (private *collèges* and *lycées*) and indirectly (*écoles de commerce*) by the state even during high *dirigisme*. What has changed since the 1980s is that these schools, and those created in their wake, have been legitimized as sanctuarized 'greenhouses' for the fostering of economic liberalism and individualized, materialist consumption. Indeed, this process has been worked for not only by the management of such schools themselves, but by a wide range of business leaders, teachers within even public technical colleges, together with parents all keen to segregate 'their' teenagers away from the public system. Indeed, as elsewhere, the political work at the origins of the rise in private education in France can only be fully grasped by analysing how and why it has also entailed the systematic denigration of state schools and universities. Meanwhile, already weakened by reductions in their respective budgets, representatives of the latter have often experienced great difficulty in proposing renewed definitions of their societal role and of their practices. In a word, they have rarely equipped themselves appropriately for promoting why they should be both better supported by the public purse and socially valued more highly.

Similarly, neo-liberalism has also only had indirect impacts upon the decline of French political parties which, from the 1980s to 2017, were known as those 'of government': the *PS* and the various guises successively taken on by the centre-right (the *RPR* and *UDF*, the *UMP* then *LR*). This conclusion may initially appear curious, since the latter explicitly embraced neo-liberalism as of 1986 and the former increasingly turned to its policy recipes during their periods in office. As chapter 6 highlights, this taking on of parts of the neo-liberal package has clearly alienated some militants who have left these parties either for the *Front National* (now the *RN*) or *La République En Marche*, or for *La France Insoumise* or *les Ecologistes*. But closer examination of the decline of these parties entails taking them seriously as organizations with their own histories, structures and processes. From this angle, one can see more clearly, for example, that the recent failure of the *UMP* then the *LR* has been directly linked to an inability of their leaderships to transform a loose coalition of competing parties into a single political 'machine'. Conversely, whereas the *PS* became such as machine in the 1980s and early 1990s, thereafter the political work that had been devoted to structuring and galvanizing its militants began to dissipate and, ultimately, fall into disuse. In short, neo-liberalism certainly did inspire some politicians in both the

PS and the centre-right parties. Moreover, its presence in these organizations came to envenom relationships between a considerable number of its militants. However, in itself it has not been a direct cause of the sharp drop in their respective memberships or organizational cohesion.

If neo-liberalism has so rarely been a direct cause of change in France's societal structures, what then of 'globalization'? This term alone is clearly not an ideology. Nevertheless, since the 1980s it has certainly been used as a rallying call for transforming how public problems are defined, policy instruments are set and power relations are critiqued or justified. Indeed, this book largely confirms that globalization has been used widely as a weapon in order to attain such ends. However, observing a correlation between evocations of this term and change in the structuring of a society does not mean that the former have had a causal impact. To return to the example of the sharp decline experienced in the membership of previously 'governmental' parties in recent years, there is much evidence to show that supporters of the *Front National* have used the term globalization in order to argue in favour of an end to immigration, protectionism and other measures framed in terms of *la préférence nationale*. Indeed, and not surprisingly, the COVID-19 crisis has reinforced this policy goal. Similarly, militants from *La France Insoumise* have led calls for a profound re-regulation of 'global capitalism', an end to free-trade agreements and renationalizing the banks. Whilst accepting the sincerity of these actors, it is nevertheless vital to recall that each of the parties they belong to participates in a national party system that is highly competitive and can only be understood relationally. Revealingly, however, in neither case has a fight against 'globalization' actually constituted the cornerstone around which the party's programme, and thus its differentiation from others, has been built. Instead, 'globalization' is a weapon from the armoury used within and by the party as part of its respective political work on a wide range of issues and power relationships.

For this same reason, 'globalization' has actually been used by a much wider range of actors to reproduce many key societal structures in France, ones that notably include the health service, pensions and cultural policies. As chapter 7 relates regarding health, over the past three decades governments have sought to introduce a number of reforms to not only make organizations such as hospitals 'more efficient', but also to reduce budgets. In this instance, however, favourable comparisons with other national health systems – and thus globalization as scaremongering – have frequently been used to justify the preservation of much of the status quo in order to shore up the quality attributed to the French health service as a whole. Specifically, framing a high standard of healthcare as being part of an 'untouchable' social *acquis* has participated fully in political work that has thus far been largely successful in preventing a dismantling of services in the name of aligning with so-called 'global' practices and norms. Indeed, in the case of health, individuation and the reduction of its services to units of consumption have thus far been strongly, and often successfully, resisted.

Similarly, pensions in France have largely been preserved using the same type of 'social *acquis*' rhetoric as for health. Here, however, increases in the minimum age at which one can receive a full pension have nevertheless been justified not only by shifts in demographics and the labour market, but also by 'the need' to decrease public spending and thus comply with criteria that stem from managing the euro. Both in terms of sources of policy recipes and through creating supposedly 'external' budgetary constraints, for pensions it is the EU and not 'the global' which has, alongside purely domestic impetuses, clearly played a role in causing change in both institutions and power relations (Hay, 2006).

The EU has also been an important site for political work regarding another aspect of French societal structures that have changed little in the past thirty years: those pertaining to culture. Heavily influenced by state-led cultural policies which began under de Gaulle in the early 1960s and were relaunched two decades later under President Mitterrand, the institutions and power relations that have shaped French music, cinema, theatre, dance and art so strongly have in part been reproduced because the EU has provided them with a derogation from the liberalization of trade and concomitant bans on public intervention in the relevant markets. Crucially French actors, 'in Paris' but also 'in Brussels', were key to negotiating this protection from a deregulated global. Specifically, it was multi-scale political work which defined the problem, then instrumented and legitimized it as 'cultural exceptionalism' in the early 1990s. In so doing, a generalized reduction of cultural markets to being purely sites of individualized consumption, and thus materialism, has been relatively successfully resisted.

To conclude as regards the effects of 'globalization' and neo-liberalism, as well as individuation and materialism, on French societal structures, my findings here are ultimately threefold. First, there are clearly domains of activity in France where none of these phenomena have had any significant impact (e.g. primary schooling, family policies and those for the elderly), and others where such influence has been significant but indirect (e.g. the liberalization of capital, the decline of trade unions). Secondly, in all cases of indirect impact, it has been mediated, and often attenuated, by pre-existing institutions (e.g. state involvement in the housing market) and shifts within key power relations (e.g. within the wine industry). Thirdly, impact appears to be greatest when the social practices it affects have already been destabilized by the increased individuation of behaviour (e.g. the growth of private schooling, the volatility of voting) and the renaissance of materialism (e.g. the importing and mass purchasing of cheap clothes made in Asia). Indeed,

Table 8.2 Testing transversal claims as variables to explain either deep or no structural change

	Neo-liberalization	Globalization	Individualization	Greater materialism
Cases of deep change				
More private education	yes	yes	yes	yes
Greater precariousness	yes	yes	yes	no
Weaker trade unions	yes	yes	yes	no
Stronger business peak body	yes	yes	yes	yes
More impatient capital	yes	yes	yes	yes
Collapse of the *PS* and centre-right	yes	no	yes	yes
Cases of no change				
Adult-centred education	no	no	yes	no
Teacher power	no	no	no	no
Doctor power	no	no	no	yes
Distant company management	yes	no	no	no
NGO activism	no	yes	yes	no

Note: yes = a significant effect upon this societal structure; no = no significant effect.

Table 8.2 seeks to encapsulate this point by examining these three variables systematically. For virtually all the cases of deep change, references to neo-liberalism and globalization have played a role, but this in large part because they have gone hand in hand with rises in individualization and materialism. It is difficult to ascertain for the moment if the latter are driving the former or vice versa. What is certain is that, when moving in concert, all these trends provide fertile ground for changing institutions and power relations. Conversely, in cases of no such change, one finds little trace of neo-liberalism, globalization, individualization or greater materialism having played a causal role. Particularly when summarized in this way, these findings remain tentative. However, when backed by the causal stories related in previous chapters, they become more robust. At the very least, they merit systematic testing in future research.

The flailing state

Within the political work discussed above, representatives of a wide variety of organizations and social groups have played roles that all merit careful analysis. However, because those of the state have been involved in virtually every issue area I have evoked, and as they are ostensibly the servants of the nation itself, here explanation of shifts within this part of French public authorities will be brought centre-stage. The argument made here is that since the 1980s, those who work for the French state consider first that they now operate within a web of budgetary and EU-imposed constraints. Consequently, many senior civil servants consider that today they can only act incrementally and through inducements rather than punishments, i.e. by using 'carrots' rather than 'sticks' (*l'Etat petit bras*: Ansaloni and Smith, 2017: 26). More profoundly still, and for reasons that are singular to the French polity (Le Galès, 2014; King and Le Galès, 2017), state officials and their ministers have also become underequipped ideologically and cognitively to engage assertively in the society that surrounds them and for the French people they claim 'to serve'.

The first trait of the contemporary French state that needs unpacking is its very ethos, i.e. what its representatives consider to be fair, just and 'the right thing to do'. On an everyday basis, these criteria are obviously affected by the values and priorities of the government in office. However, at least until now, the state in France has generally been quite autonomous from its ministers and president, and this in particular as regards the ethos of its officials and their conception of 'the general interest'. Indeed, armed with the latter term, from the Liberation until the 1980s, most state officials bought into the *dirigiste* model of interventionism and strong top-down steering of the economy and society more generally. Since then, however, the revaluation of liberals already working for the state, the availability of neo-liberal rhetoric and recipes, together with greater competition from local politicians and administrations, has sapped the coherence of what, for forty years of continuous growth, had been the state's guiding light. More specifically, in this country neo-liberalism has not simply replaced the value hierarchy which previously dominated the state, rather it has become part of its neo-*dirigiste* approach to governing. The overall result has thus been a hybrid which, in turn, has been difficult for its own officials to decipher, let alone the general public. In short, as recent controversies over labour law and pension reform highlight, the French state as a whole is like a ship without a compass. Indeed, this is one of the reasons why it has such difficulty in being convincing when it proposes 'new' public problem definitions, advocates revised policy instruments and communicates using novel registers of legitimation. Emmanuel Macron's emphasis upon 'being neither on the right or the left' in order to symbolize and justify his actions, provides a case in point.

Indeed, it is through its attempts to modify societal institutions using public policy that the contemporary French state reveals not only many of its key characteristics, but also its recurrent blind spots and their causes. Despite taking up the rhetoric of 'participation' and even the launching in 2019 of *un grand débat national* entailing a plethora of public meetings and other methods of consultation,[1] state officials continue to work essentially using a method developed in the 1950s and 1960s. This consists of synthesizing what they consider representatives of civil society want, debating their first drafts amongst themselves within confined interministerial and inter-*cabinet* settings, then expecting the prime minister and their cabinet, and sometimes that of the president, to produce the state's final position. During this overall process, the established hierarchy between ministries, together with the *grands corps* that determine who works within them, play a considerable role, thereby contributing to the early elimination of most proposals that differ greatly from the status quo. In addition, this is a process that leaves little room for genuine consultation, nor even for the involvement of expertise that is particularly pertinent to the subject at hand. Indeed, the controlling hand of the *grands corps* not only explains why the evaluation of public policy is so weakly institutionalized as part of French decision-making (Duran and Monnier, 1992; Fouquet, 2013), it also explains why social science research is so rarely listened to when diagnoses of policy challenges are made, and when proposals for 'new' policy instruments are developed. Revealingly, in contrast to many other Western states and indeed the European Commission, hardly any French state officials possess a doctorate, and those who do often find their chances of promotion to be thin because they lack the support of a *grand corps*.

Far from being simply harmless idiosyncrasies of the Fifth Republic, the training of state officials in France, together with the way they define public problems and set policy instruments, constantly impacts upon French government and the way it is now perceived by much of the population. From this perspective, the *gilets jaunes* mouvement of 2018–19 provides a case in point. Alerted to the relationship between high pollution levels and the prevalence in France of diesel-fuelled cars, the government sought to discourage both by simply raising the price of this fuel. What it failed to appreciate was that this price hike would have immediate and iniquitous impacts upon many people living and working in peri-urban and rural parts of the country, and in particular on those who were already having difficulty making ends meet. Moreover, most of these people already considered President Macron and his government to be particularly illegitimate. In short, rather than develop a more holistic approach to ecological transition which would have included not only a more ambitious mobility policy but a taking into account of social and 'environmental' inequalities, the state acted precipitously, in a top-down manner and with a total disregard for precisely which people were being made to change their modes of living and how they would go about doing so. Indeed, and more generally, the bumbling way adapting to climate change and environmental pollution has thus far been handled in France provides numerous insights into how most senior state officials continue to think and operate. Far from being capable of medium-term planning which sets clear priorities, anticipates knock-on effects of policy and justifies the trade-offs it inevitably entails, this state continues to flail around in a manner that has thus far failed to improve environmental outcomes. Moreover, in so doing it has alienated much of the population.

Another example of this flailing state concerns pension reforms. As chapter 7 has set out in detail, after more than twenty-five years of hesitations and incremental modifications, in July 2019 a proposal for an overhaul of the French system was discreetly published. Since then, wider consultation of 'the social partners' and other interest groups has slowly begun. What is remarkable, however, is the extent to which so many protagonists outside the state appear to have discovered the state's intentions so late in the day, as well as the lack of input from the wide range of experts on this subject. Despite what state officials seem to think, a range of academics in particular possess relevant knowledge and data about this subject in economics, sociology and political science.

A third and final dimension of the French state that will be briefly discussed here concerns the way it fits with the bureaucracies of the European Union. As I have had course to relate in many of this book's chapters, French officials have consistently been involved in the making of EU policies since the 1950s. Indeed, through developing close, long-term relations with their opposite numbers in the European Commission, 'France' has often been able to have considerable influence upon aspects of the consolidation of a European scale of governing. This notably includes monetary union, the scope of public intervention in markets and the Common Agricultural Policy (CAP). This said, the launching of a new reform of the latter in 2020 provides further evidence that although the French state is very well equipped to influence EU negotiations once they have begun in earnest (due to the relative efficiency of its interministerial co-ordination and the weighting of its vote in the Council), its capacity to envisage and structure policy change is much weaker. In the case of the CAP, because of the continued importance of farming and the agro-food industry in France, this weakness is particularly paradoxical. One might have expected that a country with this manifest 'national interest', together with its considerable research capacity on agricultural and rural affairs, would take the lead in initiating a far-sighted reform in this issue area. However, to the time of writing at least, there is virtually no evidence of the French state taking up such a stance. Instead, tetanized by the likelihood of protests from the most powerful farming union, the *Fédération nationale des syndicats d'exploitants agricoles (FNSEA)*, its officials already appear to have concentrated their political work upon defending as much of the existing CAP as possible (Ansaloni and Smith, 2021).

In summary, contrary to its own self-image and international reputation as a well-oiled machine run by 'brilliant' public servants, the contemporary French state possesses a number of structural characteristics which contribute strongly to the frequently sub-optimal outcomes of its internal and external actions. Indeed, its own institutions and power relations are themselves key societal structures which impact constantly upon those of France, its socio-economics and its polity as a whole.

The road to even greater analytical purchase

The introduction set out the theory and concepts used to plan and write this book, so I have no intention of repeating here what was explained and justified at that stage. What instead remains to be done is to briefly provide a view on what these analytical tools have enabled me to discover and present, together with how they might be sharpened then applied to new socio-economic and political phenomena.

First, by concentrating upon societal structures defined as institutions and the power relations within which they are embedded, I have sought to identify the deep, recurrent sets of rules, norms, expectations and patterns of domination which have been made in France and which, in turn, have made this country what it is today. Although many of these institutions and power relations are contested to varying degrees, for the most part they set clear parameters upon French social, economic and political behaviour. I therefore make no excuses for the structuralist dimension of my approach to understanding a country such as France. On the contrary, I simply cannot see much merit in endeavouring to analyse how any society is shaped, let alone to compare it with others, without first setting out its societal structures, then assessing the extent to which they have been modified or reproduced over time.

However, structuralism alone is desperately dry, descriptive and static. Indeed, this is precisely the reason why in this book institutions and power relations have not been left on their own to do the job of showing why they have taken the form they have, changed or remained essentially the same. Instead, constructivist epistemology and theory have provided the sources of nourishment with which I have sought to make the preceding chapters more about explanation than simply providing a set of 'photographs' of French structures. Specifically, constructivism has been drawn upon in two complementary ways.

First, by considering, as constructivists do, that there is no universal reality or rationality, this standpoint has led me to constantly underline that institutions and power relations do not simply impose themselves upon the human beings who inhabit any societal space. Rather, both these sets of structures are constantly being interpreted and reassessed by those inhabitants. What this means first is that the stabilized rules, norms and expectations that constitute institutions do not take their effects solely, or even chiefly, because of the threat of sanctions when they are transgressed. Instead, those institutions that remain in place do so because the persons they affect the most either believe in their legitimacy, or at least consider them to be sufficiently legitimate to be obeyed for the most part. The second consequence of envisaging institutions from a constructivist viewpoint is that their modification or even deep change must always be considered plausible (François, 2011). Theoretically, the key term here is 'contingency': as soon as one considers institutions to be contingent, analysis can focus, as it should do, upon who is seeking to change or maintain them, why and how (Hay, 2016).

Perhaps more unexpectedly, I also consider that power relations are fundamentally contingent. This may come as a surprise, because many colleagues in the social sciences would consider that analysis in terms of power relations leads one to buy so far into structuralism that the possibility of these relationships changing is virtually discounted. Jumping to that conclusion is, however, completely erroneous from the point of view of both theory and empirical research (Georgakakis, 2013; Mérand, 2015). Moreover, this caricature of the form of structuralism I practise is often a tactic used by proponents of other theories (notably the fundamentally interactionist 'Actor Network Theory' of Bruno Latour and Michel Callon) to discredit as 'determinist' any attempt to systematically describe the positions held by actors in a social space in terms of their relative powerfulness or powerlessness. On the contrary, the stance adopted and illustrated throughout this book has been to consider that it is only by carefully describing the power of each actor studied in relation to others that one can begin to understand both shifts in these relationships themselves, and how they are inextricably linked to the change or reproduction of institutions. In a word, institutions participate in the structuring of power relations, just as the latter are integral components of stabilized rules, norms and expectations.

From these theory-backed premises, the second way this book has drawn heavily upon constructivism is via the analytical framework it has proposed to study how and why institutions and power relations change or do not. Held together by the overarching concept of 'political work' (Smith, 2016, 2019), this framework has led each issue evoked in the French case to be systematically analysed using the overlapping concepts of problematization, instrumentation and legitimation. Specifically, by delving into the actors, relations and processes through which public problems have been defined, policy instruments have been set (or failed to be set) and the registers of legitimation all this has, successfully or unsuccessfully, entailed, I have sought to show, or at least indicate, why France's societal structures take the form they do today. From there, I have also analysed why this state of affairs either differs from how these institutions and power relations were shaped in the 1980s, or why they remain remarkably similar to how they looked three or four decades ago.

Of course, all the empirical examples developed in this book deserve even deeper and longer analyses than those which appear in the preceding pages. As many of the references I have drawn upon testify, there is a great deal to be said for analyses of societal structures and political work that are more exhaustive than those presented here. Indeed, in my own future research I intend to invest even more in the detailed data on actor 'capital' generated by field analysis. The aim here is to enrich and deepen analysis of how power relations link to institutions on the one hand, and to political work on the other. Similarly, once I have accumulated an equivalent amount of knowledge about societal structures and political work in the UK, and hopefully also Spain, I remain convinced that genuine comparative analysis will also enable me to both sharpen my findings and improve further upon the analytical tools I will use in order to generate them.

But for the moment allow me to very briefly return to the case of France and, specifically, what its presentation in this book has enabled me to do so far: plunge myself and the reader into an exploration into this fascinating and thought-provoking country. In so doing I have attempted to open a window upon its people, the lives they lead individually and collectively, what has caused them 'societally' and what, inescapably, will participate strongly in the directions they take over the years to come. As I write these closing lines, the COVID-19 crisis is still ongoing and will, of course, have a multitude of impacts upon France, just as it will throughout the world. Over the last few weeks, a plethora of academics, politicians and even business leaders have published numerous 'op eds' proclaiming that the time for deep change has now come. Many of the proposals made have been exciting and convincing on many levels. But, at least in France, in order for any of them to actually become reality, they will now have to take on through political work most of the societal structures described in the foregoing chapters. The contingency of many of these structures does appear to be particularly clear at this moment in time. So the stage is logically now set for a new act in French, and indeed global, history. Let's now see what scripts, costumes and props the actors give themselves in order to act upon it, then how this new story unfolds.

Note

1   https://granddebat.fr/, consulted 20th December 2019.

References

Abdelal, R., Blyth, M. and Parsons, C. (2010) *Constructing the International Economy*, Ithaca, NY: Cornell University Press.

Agrikoliansky, E. (2008) *Les partis politiques en France*, Paris: Armand Colin.

Allal, A., Catusse, M. and Emparador Badimon, M. (eds) (2018) *Quand l'industrie proteste? Fondements moraux des (in)soumissions ouvrières*, Rennes: Presses Universitaires de Rennes.

Allouch, A. (2017) *La société de concours: l'empire des classements scolaires*, Paris, Seuil.

Andolfatto, D. and Labbé, D. (2006) *Histoire des syndicats (1906–2006)*, Paris: Seuil.

Ansaloni, M. and Smith, A. (2017) 'Des marchés au service de l'Etat?', *Gouvernement et action publique*, 6(4): 9–28.

Ansaloni, M. and Smith, A. (2018) 'The neo-dirigiste production of French capitalism since 1980: The view from three major industries', *French Politics*, 16(2): 154–178.

Ansaloni, M. and Smith, A. (2021) *L'expropriation des agriculteurs. Régimes d'accumulation et champs sociaux*, Paris: Editions du Croquant.

Arnaud, L. (2018) *Agir par la culture. Acteurs, enjeux et mutations des mouvements culturels*, Toulouse: Editions de l'Attribut.

Astor, S. (2019) 'Célibataires et couples: des trajectoires de plus en plus diversifiés', in P. Bréchon, F. Gonthier and S. Astor (eds), *La France des valeurs: quarante ans d'évolutions*, Grenoble: Presses Universitaires de Grenoble, pp. 37–42.

Baccaro, L. and Howell, C. (2017) *Trajectories of Neo-liberal Transformation: European industrial relations since the 1970s*, Cambridge: Cambridge University Press.

Barthélemy, M. (2000) *Associations: un nouvel âge de la participation?*, Paris: Presses de Sciences Po.

Baud, C. and Chiapello, E. (2015) 'Comment les firmes se financiarisent: le role de la réglementation et des instruments de gestion. Le cas du crédit bancaire', *Revue française de sociologie*, 56(3): 439–468.

Beaud, S. (2002) *80% au Bac … et alors? Les enfants de la democratisation scolaire*, Paris: La Découverte.

Beaud, S. (2018) *La France des Belhoumis*, Paris: La Découverte.

Beaud, S. and Convert B. (2010) '30% de boursiers en grande école … et après?', *Actes de la recherche en sciences sociales*, 183: 4–13.

Beaud, S. and Mauger, G. (eds) (2017) *Une génération sacrifiée? Jeunes des classes populaires dans la France désindustrialisée*, Paris: Editions rue d'Ulm.

Benoît, C. (2020) *Réguler l'accès aux médicaments*, Grenoble: Presses Universitaires de Grenoble.

Bérard, A. (2016) 'L'évolution de la politique de santé face à l'enjeu du vieillisement de la population', *Vie sociale*, 15(3): 131–147.

Béraud-Sudreau, L. (2014) 'Un changement politisé dans la politique de défense: le cas des ventes d'armes', *Gouvernement et action publique*, 3(3): 79–103.

Bernard, P-Y. and Troger, V. (2015) 'Les lycéens et la réforme du Bac Pro en trois ans: nouveau contexte, nouveaux parcours?', *Formation emploi*, 131: 23–40.

Berny, N. (2019) *Défendre la cause de l'environnement. Une approche organisationnelle*, Rennes: Presses Universitaires de Rennes.

Bigi, M., Cousin, O., Meda, D., Sibaud, L. and Wieviorka, M. (2015) *Travailler au XXIe siècle. Des salaires en quête de reconnaissance*, Paris: Robert Laffont.

Bodin, R. and Orange, S. (2019) 'La gestion des risques scolaires. "Avec Parcoursup, je ne serais peut-être pas là"', *Sociologie*, 10(2): 217–224.

Boissin, O. and Trompette, P. (2017) 'L'assurance obsèques au sein du marché funéraire', *Revue française de gestion*, 262: 73–88.

Boltanski, L. and Esquerre, A. (2017) *L'enrichissement*, Paris: Presses Universitaires de France.

Bonet, L. and Négrier, E. (eds) (2008) *La fin des cultures nationales? Les politiques culturelles à l'épreuve de la diversité*, Paris: La Découverte.

Bonin, H. (1992) *Le Crédit agricole de la Gironde: la passion d'une région 1901–91*, Bordeaux: l'Horizon chimérique.

Bornstein, R. (2019) 'En immersion numérique avec "les gilets jaunes"', *Le Débat*, 204: 38–51.

Bouquillion, P. (2017) 'Les politiques publiques en direction des industries culturelles', in P. Poirrier (ed.), *Politique et politiques de la culture*, Paris: La Documentation française, pp. 169–190.

Bourdes, E., Dubois, C. and Meriaux, O. (2014) *L'industrie jardinière du territoire ou comment les entreprises s'engagent dans le développement des compétences*, Paris: Presses des Mines.

Bourdieu, P. (1980) *La distinction*, Paris: Seuil.

Bourdieu, P. (1989) *La noblesse d'Etat. Grands corps et esprit de corps*, Paris: Les Editions de Minuit.

Bourdieu, P. (1992) 'The logic of fields', in P. Bourdieu, *An Invitation to Reflexive Sociology*, Chicago: University of Chicago Press, pp. 94–114.

Bourdieu, P. (2000) *Les structures sociales de l'économie*, Paris: Seuil.

Bourdieu, P. and Passeron J-C. (1970) *La reproduction. Eléments pour une théorie du système d'enseignement*, Paris: Les Editions de Minuit.

Boy, D., Brugidou, M., Halpern, C. and Lascoumes, P. (eds) (2012) *Le Grenelle de l'environnement: acteurs, discours, effets*, Paris: Armand Colin.

Boyer, R. (2015) *Economie politique du capitalisme: théorie de la regulation et des crises*, Paris: La Découverte.

Bréchon, P., Gonthier, F. and Astor, S. (eds) (2019a) *La France des valeurs: quarante ans d'évolutions*, Grenoble: Presses Universitaires de Grenoble.

Bréchon, P., Gonthier, F. and Astor, S. (2019b) 'Conclusion', in P. Bréchon, F. Gonthier and S. Astor (eds), *La France des valeurs: quarante ans d'évolutions*, Grenoble: Presses Universitaires de Grenoble, pp. 363–371.

Brouard, S. (2011) 'Systematic institutional advantage of government in lawmaking', in B. Rasch and G. Tsebelis (eds), *The Role of Governments in Legislative Agenda-Setting*, Abingdon: Routledge, pp. 38–52.

Brunel, M. and Carrère, A. (2019) 'La perte d'autonomie des personnes âgées à domicile. Quelles disparités entre départements?', *Les dossiers de la DREES*, 34.

Brunn, M. and Hassenteufel, P. (2021) 'France: The changing balance between statism and corporatism', in E. Immergut (ed.), *Health Politics in Europe: A Handbook*, Oxford: Oxford University Press.

Brutel, S. and Levy, D. (2011) 'Le nouveau zonage en aires urbains de 2010', *Insée première*, 1374, October.

Buisson-Fenet, H. and Rey, O. (2016) 'Le lycée professionnel, relégué et pourtant avant-gardiste', in J-P. Kaplinsky (ed.), *Le lycée professionnel: relégué ou avant garde?*, Lyon: Presses de l'ENS de Lyon, pp. 7–10.

Bussmann, K., Erthal, C. and Shroth, A. (2012) 'Impact en Europe de l'intediction de châtiments corporels', *Déviance et société*, 36(1): 85–106.

Cagé, J. (2018) *Le prix de la démocratie*, Paris: Fayard.

Callède, J-P. (2000) *Les politiques sportives en France*, Paris: Economica.

Callède, J-P. (2002) 'Les politiques du sport en France', *L'Année sociologique*, 52(2): 437–457.

Capuano, C. (2018) *Que faire de nos vieux? Une histoire de la protection sociale de 1880 à nos jours*, Paris: Presses de Sciences Po.

Caradec, V. (2015) *Sociologie de la vieillesse et du vieillissement*, Paris: Armand Colin.

Carter, C. (2018) *The Politics of Aquaculture*, London: Routledge.

Carter C., Ramirez Perez, S. and Smith, A. (2014) 'Trade policy: All pervasive but to what end?', in A. Smith and B. Jullien (eds), *The EU's Government of Industries. Markets, Institutions and Politics*, Abingdon: Routledge, pp. 216–240.

Castel, R. (2009) *La montée des incertitudes: travail, protections, statut de l'individu*, Paris: Seuil.

CEREQ (2018) *20 ans d'insertion professionnelle des jeunes: entre permanences et évolutions*, Official report.

Charles, N. (2014) 'France: A low fee, low aid system challenged from the margins', in H. Ertl and C. Dupuy (eds), *Students, Markets and Social Justice: Higher Education Fee and Student Support Policies in Western Europe and Beyond*, Providence: Symposium Books, pp. 67–83.

Charles, N. (2015) *Enseignement supérieur et justice sociale: sociologie des experiences étudiantes en Europe*, Paris: La Documentation française.

Charvolin, F. (2003) *L'invention de l'environnement en France*, Paris: La Découverte.

Chauvel, L. (2014) *Le destin des générations. Structure sociale et cohort en France au XXe siècle*, 2nd ed., Paris: Presses Universitaires de France.

Chauvel, L. (2016) *La spirale du déclassement. Essai sur la société des illusions*, Paris: Seuil.

Chauvin, P-M. (2010) *Le marché des reputations. Une sociologie du monde des vins de Bordeaux*, Bordeaux: Editions Féret.

Christen, G. and Hamman, P. (2015) *Transition énergétique et inégalités environnementales*, Strasbourg: Presses Universitaires de Strasbourg.

Christen, G. and Hamman, P. (2017) 'La transition énergétique face aux inégalités écologiques urbaines', *Géographie, économie, société*, 19(2): 267–294.

Clift, B. (2002) 'Comparative capitalisms, ideational political economy and French post-*dirigiste* responses to the global financial crisis', *New Political Economy*, 17(5): 566–590.

Cohen, E. (1989) *L'Etat brancardier: politiques du déclin industriel 1974–84*, Paris: Calmann-Lévy.

Cohen, E. (1992) *Le colbertisme 'high tech'. Economie des telecom et du grand projet*, Paris, Hachette.

Cohen, E. and Buigues, P-A. (2014) *Le décrochage industriel*, Paris: Fayard.

Collectif d'enquête sur les gilets jaunes (2019) 'Enquêter in situ par questionnaire sur une mobilisation en cours', *Revue française de science politique*, 69(5–6): 869–892.

Collovald, A. (1999) *Jacques Chirac et le Gaullisme*, Paris: Belin.

Comby, J-B. (2015) *La question climatique: genèse et dépolitisation d'un problème public*, Paris: Raisons d'Agir.

Costa, O. (2013) 'Introduction: Parliamentary Representation in France', *Journal of Legislative Studies*, 19(2): 129–140.

Coulangeon, P. (2016) *Sociologie des pratiques culturelles*, Paris: La Découverte.

Coulangeon, P. and Lamel, Y. (2009) 'Les pratiques culturelles et sportives des Français: arbitrage, diversité et cumul', *Economie et statistique*, 423: 3–30.

Cousin, O. (2019) *Pourquoi la rentabilité économique tue le travail*, Bordeaux: Editions Le bord de l'eau.

Culpepper, P. (2003) *Creating Co-operation: How States Develop Human Capital in Europe*, Ithaca, NY: Cornell University Press.

Culpepper, P. (2006) 'Capitalism, co-ordination and economic change: The French political economy since 1985', in P. Culpepper, P. Hall and B. Palier (eds) (2006) *Changing France: The Politics that Markets Make*, Basingstoke: Palgrave, pp. 29–49.

Culpepper, P., Hall, P. and Palier, B. (eds) (2006) *Changing France: The Politics that Markets Make*, Basingstoke: Palgrave.

Darmon, M. (2013) *Classes préparatoires. La fabrique d'une jeunesse dominante*, Paris: La Découverte.

Delès, R. (2018) *Quand on n'a 'que' le diplôme … Les jeunes diplômés et l'insertion professionnelle*, Paris: Presses Universitaires de France.

Déloye, Y. (1994) *Ecole et citoyenneté. L'individualisme républicain de Jules Ferry à Vichy: controverses*, Paris: Presses de la Fondation nationale des sciences politiques.

Del Prete, D. (2011) 'Le rôle des collectivités territoriales en matière de sport', in S. Monchaud and P. Dantin (eds), *Le modèle sportif français*, Paris: Lavoisier, pp. 161–179.

Demazière, D. (1995) *La sociologie du chômage*, Paris: La Découverte.

Demazière, D. (2019) 'The boundaries of unemployment. Institutional rules and real-life experiences', in A. Serrano-Pascual and M. Jepsen (eds), *The Deconstruction of Unemployment as a Political Question: Employment as a Floating Signifier*, Basingstoke: Palgrave, pp. 233–245.

Demazière, D. (2020) 'The successful job search of the formerly unemployed: Paradoxically, a self-discipline', *Critical Policy Studies*, DOI: 10.1080/19460171.2020.1746372

Demazière, D. and Zune, M. (2016) 'L'emploi et le travail vus depuis le chômage: Enquête sur l'expérience des chômeurs', *Revue de l'IRES*, 89(2): 3–26.

Denord, F. (2007) *Le néolibéralisme à la française. Histoire d'une idéologie politique*, Paris: Agone.

Didry, C. (2016) *L'institution du travail*, Paris: La Dispute.

Dolez, B., Fretel, J. and Lefebvre, R. (eds) (2019) *L'entreprise Macron*, Grenoble: Presses Universitaires de Grenoble.

DREES (2018) *Les Comptes de la santé: données*, www.data.drees.sante.gouv.fr, consulted 23rd March 2018.

Dubar, C. (2010) *La Socialisation*, 4th ed., Paris: Armand Colin.

Dubet, F. (2014) 'Préface', in T. Berthet and J. Zaffran (eds), *Le décrochage scolaire: enjeux, acteurs et politiques de lutte contre la déscolarisation*, Rennes: Presses Universitaires de Rennes, pp. 9–17.

Dubet, F. (2016a) 'Pourquoi est-il si difficile de réformer?', in F. Dubet and P. Merle (eds) (2016) *Réformer le collège*, Paris: Presses Universitaires de France, pp. 17–29.

Dubet, F. (2016b) 'Conclusion générale', in F. Dubet and P. Merle (eds) (2016) *Réformer le collège*, Paris: Presses Universitaires de France, pp. 107–109.

Dubet, F. (2018) 'Durkheim et les questions scolaires: hier et aujourd'hui', in C. Cuiin et R. Hervouet (eds), *Durkheim aujourd'hui*, Paris: Presses Universitaires de France, pp. 48–66.

Dubet, F. (2019) 'La transformation des colères en politiques est-elle possible?', in Analyse Opinion Critique (ed.), *'Gilets jaunes': hypothèses sur un mouvement*, Paris: La Découverte, pp. 43–51.

Dubet, F. and Duru-Bellet, M. (2015) *10 propositions pour changer l'école*, Paris: Seuil.

Dubet, F., Duru-Bellet, M. and Vérétout, A. (2010) *Les sociétés et leur école. Emprise du diplôme et cohésion sociale*, Paris: Seuil.

Dubois, V. (1999) *La politique culturelle: genèse d'une catégorie d'intervention publique*, Paris: Belin.

Dubois, V. (2012) *Le politique, l'artiste et le gestionnaire: (re)configurations locales et (dé)politisation de la culture*, Paris: Editions du Croquant.

Dudouet, F-X. and Grémont, E. (2010) *Les grands patrons en France. Du capitalisme de l'État à la financiarisation*, Paris: Lignes de Repères.

Dumons, B. and Pollet, G. (1994) *L'Etat et les retraites: genèse d'une politique*, Paris: Belin.

Dupuis, X. (2017) 'Culture et management', in P. Poirrier (ed.) *Politique et politiques de la culture*, Paris: La Documentation française, pp. 52–55.

Duran, P. and Monnier, E. (1992) 'Le développement de l'évaluation en France. Necessités techniques et exigence politiques', *Revue française de science politique*, 42(2): 235–262.

Ebbinghaus, B. and Gronwald, M. (2011) 'The changing public–private pensions mix in Europe: From path dependence to path departure', in B. Ebbinghaus (ed.), *The Variety of Pensions Governance*, Oxford: Oxford University Press.

Elgie, R. and Griggs, S. (2000) *French Politics: Debates and Controversies*, London: Routledge.

Epstein, R. (2015) 'La gouvernance territoriale: une affaire d'Etat. La dimension de la construction de l'action collective dans les territoires', *L'Année sociologique*, 65(2): 457–484.

Eurofound (2015) *Third European Company Survey: Workplace Practices*, Luxembourg: Publications Office of the EU.

Eurofound (2017) *Sixth European Working Conditions Survey*, Luxembourg: Publications Office of the EU.

Faucher, F. (1999) *Les habits verts de la politique*, Paris: Presses de Sciences Po.

Faure, A. (1992) *Le village et la politique. Essai sur les maires ruraux en action*, Paris: L'Harmattan.

Faure, A. and Smith, A. (1994) 'L'évaluation, objet de savoir et de pouvoir: le cas des politiques publiques locales', *Sciences de la société*, 32: 101–111.

Faure, S. (2016) *Variétés de la decision. Le dilemme de la politique d'armement en Europe: le cas de la France 1945 à nos jours*, PhD Dissertation, Sciences Po Paris.

Faure, S., Joltreau, T. and Smith, A. (2019), 'The differentiated integration of defence companies in Europe. A sociology of (trans)national economic elites', *European Review of International Studies*, 6(2): 135–162.

Filleule, O. and Tartakowsky, D. (2013) *La manifestation*, Paris: Presses de Sciences Po.

Fleuriel, S. and Schotté, M. (2015) 'Des sportifs sans qualité? Genèse du modèle étatique de production de l'élite sportive française', *Sociologie du travail*, 57(3): 422–445.

Fligstein, N. (2001), *The Architecture of Markets*, Princeton, NJ: Princeton University Press.

Florida, R. (2002) *The Rise of the Creative Class. And how it's transforming work, leisure and everyday life*, New York: Basic Books.

Florida, R. (2005) *Cities and the Creative Class*, London: Routledge.

Foret, F. (2008) *Légitimer l'Europe. Pouvoir et symbolique à l'ère de la gouvernance*, Paris: Presses de Sciences Po.

Fouquet, A. (2013) 'L'évaluation des politiques publiques: etat(s) de l'art et controverses', *Revue française d'administration publique*, 148: 835–847.

France Stratégie (governmental think tank) (2018) *Un nouvel âge pour l'école maternelle?*, Report no. 66.

François, P. (2007) '"Le marché et le politique" : le rôle de l'action publique dans le développement du monde de la musique ancienne', *Revue française de science politique*, 57(5): 629–647.

François, P. (ed.) (2008) *La musique – une industrie, des pratiques*, Paris: La Documentation française.

François, P. (ed.) (2011) *Vie et mort des institutions marchandes*, Paris: Presses de Sciences Po.

Francou, Q., Panico, L. and Solaz, A. (2017) 'De la naissance à l'école maternelle: des parcours de mode d'accueil diversifés', *Revue française des affaires sociales*, 2: 123–147.

Frandji, D. and Morel, R. (2017) *La réforme des rythmes scolaires et les projects éducatifs territoriaux: première analyse des évaluations, bilans et autres expertises réalisées entre 2013 et 2017*, Report to the CNESCO.

Frétigny, R. (2015) *Financer la cité. La Caisse des dépôts et les politiques de développement urbain en France*, PhD dissertation, Sciences Po Lyon.

Frinault, T. (2009) *La dépendance: un nouveau défi pour l'action publique*, Rennes: Presses Universitaires de Rennes.

Frouillou, L., Pin, C. and Van Zanten, A. (2019) 'Le rôle des instruments dans la sélection des bacheliers dans l'enseignement supérieur', *Sociologie*, 10(2): 209–215.

Gaïti, B. (1998) *De Gaulle, prophète de la cinquième République*, Paris: Presses de Sciences Po.

Garnier, P. and Brougère, G. (2017) 'Des tout-petits "peu performants" en maternelle. Ambition et misère d'une scolarisation précoce', *Revue française des affaires sociales*, 2.

Genestier, P. (2019) 'Les Gilets jaunes: d'une question d'autonomie autant que d'automobile', *Le Débat*, 204: 16–34.

Genieys, W. (2010) *The New Custodians of the State: The Programmatic Elites in French Society*, New Brunswick: Transaction Books.

Genieys, W. and Hassenteufel, P. (2015) 'The shaping of new state elites: Healthcare policymaking in France since 1981', *Comparative Politics*, 47(3): 280–295.

Genieys, W. and Michel, L. (2006) 'Au-delà du complexe militaro-industriel: le rôle d'une élite sectorielle dans le programme du char Leclerc', *Revue française de sociologie*, 47(1): 117–142.

Georgakakis, D. (2013) 'Tensions within Eurocracy: A socio-morphological perspective', in D. Georgakakis and J. Rowell (eds), *The Field of Eurocracy*, Basingstoke: Palgrave, pp. 35–60.

Gershoff, E. and Grogan-Kaylor, A. (2016) 'Spanking and child outcomes: Old controversies and new meta-analyses', *Journal of Family Psychology*, 30(4): 453–469.

Gilbert, C. and Henry, E. (2012) 'La définition de problèmes publiques: entre discretion et publicité', *Revue française de sociologie*, 53(1): 35–59.

Giraud, B., Yon, K. and Béroud, S. (2018) *Sociologie politique du syndicalisme*, Paris: Armand Colin.

Giry, B. and Smith, A. (2019a) 'Supporting Atlas: Franco-British co-operation to service Europe's military airlifter', *European Review of International Studies*, 6(2): 115–134.

Giry, B. and Smith, A. (2019b) 'Defence capability in the UK since 2010: Explaining change in procurement practices', *British Politics*, https://doi.org/10.1057/ s41293–019–00125–4.

Goerres, A. (2009) *The Political Participation of Older People in Europe. The Greying of our Democracies*, Basingstoke: Palgrave.

Gotman, A. (2006) *L'héritage*, Paris: Presses Universitaires de France.

Gotman, A. (2017) 'Le pavillon, la famille et l'héritage: itinéraire d'une recherche', *SociologieS*, an online journal, https://journals.openedition.org/sociologies/5882, consulted 30th March 2019.

Gourges, G. and Yon, K. (2018) 'Le rapport salarial', in C. Hay and A. Smith (eds), *Dictionnaire d'économie politique*, Paris: Presses de Sciences Po, pp. 391–402.

Goyer, M. (2006) 'La transformation du gouvernement d'entreprise', in P. Culpepper, P. Hall and B. Palier, *La France en mutation 1980–2005*, Paris: Presses de Sciences Po, pp. 71–107.

Goyer, M. and Glatzer, M. (2016) 'Globalization: French ambivalence as a critical case', in R. Elgie, E. Grossman and A. Mazur (eds), *The Oxford Handbook of French Politics*, Oxford: Oxford University Press, pp. 151–173.

Goyer, M. and Valdivielso des Real, R. (2014) 'Protection of domestic bank ownership in France and Germany', *Review of International Political Economy*, 21(4): 790–819.

Gualmini, E. and Schmidt, V. (2013) 'State transformation in Italy and France: Technocratic versus political leadership on the road from non neo-liberalism to neo-liberalism', in Schmidt, V. and Thatcher, M. (eds), *Resilient Neoliberalism*, Oxford, Oxford University Press, pp. 346–373.

Guerra, T., Alexandre, C. and Gonthier, F. (2019) 'Populist attitudes among the French Yellow Vests', *Populism*, 2(2): 1–12.

Guillaume, S. and Pochic, S. (2009) 'La professionnaliation de l'activité syndicale: talon d'Achille de la politique de syndicalisation de la CFDT?, *Politix*, 85: 31–56.

Guillemard, A-M. (2010) *Les défis du vieillissement*, Paris: Armand Colin.

Gusfield, J. (1981) *The Culture of Public Problems. Drink-driving and the Symbolic Order*, Chicago: University of Chicago Press.

Hacker, J. (1998) 'The historical logic of national health insurance', *Studies in American Political Development*, 12: 57–130.

Haegel, F. (2012) *Les droites en fusion. Transformations de l'UMP*, Paris: Presses de Sciences Po.

Haegel, F. (2015) 'La primaire à l'UMP: genèse et effets', *Pouvoirs*, 154: 89–98.

Haegel, F. (2016) 'Parties and party systems: Making the French sociocultural approach matter', in R. Elgie, E. Grossman and A. Mazur (eds), *The Oxford Handbook of French Politics*, Oxford: Oxford University Press, pp. 373–393.

Hall, P. (1986) *Governing the Economy. The Politics of State Intervention in Britain and France*, Oxford: Oxford University Press.

Hall, P. (1993) 'Policy paradigms, social learning and the state: The case of economic policy in Britain', *Comparative Politics*, 25(3): 275–296.

Hall, P. and Lamont, M. (eds) (2009) *Successful Societies. How Institutions and Culture Affect Health*, Cambridge: Cambridge University Press.

Hall, P. and Soskice, D. (eds) (2001) *Varieties of capitalism. The institutional foundations of comparative advantages*, Oxford: Oxford University Press.

Hall, P. and Taylor, R. (2009) 'Health, social relations and public policy', in P. Hall and M. Lamont (eds) *Successful Societies. How Institutions and Culture Affect Health*, Cambridge: Cambridge University Press, pp. 82–103.

Halpern, C., Lascoumes, P. and Le Galès, P. (eds) (2014) *L'instrumentation de l'action publique*, Paris: Presses de Sciences Po.

Halpern, C. and Pollard, J. (2017) 'Les effets du Grenelle de l'environnement sur l'action publique. Analyse de deux secteurs: déchets et bâtiment', *Gouvernement et action publique*, 6(2): 107–130.

Hamman, P., Frank, C. and Mangold, M. (2014) 'Les trajectoires de conversion écologique face aux enjeux économiques et sociaux du "logement durable" en France', *Vertigo*, 14(2), https://journals.openedition.org/vertigo/15018, consulted 10th December 2018.

Hassenteufel, P. (1997) *Les médecins face à l'Etat. Une comparaison européenne*, Paris: Presses de Sciences Po.

Hassenteufel, P. (2016) 'Muddling through the crisis. The French welfare state under financial stress', in J. Kuhlmann and K. Schubert (eds), *Challenges to European Welfare Systems*, Springer, pp. 247–270.

Hassenteufel, P. and Palier, B. (2019), 'The recalibration of the French welfare state', in S. Blum, J. Kuhlmann and K. Schubert (eds), *Handbook of European Welfare States*, London: Routledge, chapter 12.

Hay, C. (2006) 'What's globalization got to do with it? Economic interdependence and the future of European welfare states', *Government and Opposition*, 41(1): 1–22.

Hay, C. (2016) 'Good in a crisis: The ontological institutionalism of social constructivism', *New Political Economy*, 21(6): 520–535.

Hazareesingh, S. (2016) *How the French Think*, London: Penguin.

Hoeffler, C. (2013) 'L'émergence d'une politique industrielle de défense libérale en Europe. Appréhender le changement de la politique d'armement par ses instruments', *Gouvernement et action publique*, 2(4): 641–665.

Hoeffler, C. and Mérand, F. (2015) 'Avions de combat. Pourquoi il n'y a pas eu d'européanisation?', *Politique européenne*, 48: 52–80.

Honta, M. (2010) *Gouverner le sport. Action publique et territoires*, Grenoble: Presses Universitaires de Grenoble.

Honta, M. and Illivi, F. (2017) 'L'accès de tous à la pratique sportive: l'Etat local en action', *Revue française d'administration publique*, 164: 873–886.

Honta, M. and Julhe, S. (2013) 'Les professions du secteur public saisis par la privatisation: le cas des conseillers techniques sportifs', *Gouvernement et action publique*, 2(1): 63–85.

Hugrée, C. (2017) 'Une photographie statistique des patronats en France (années 1990–années 2010', in M. Offerlé (ed.), *Patrons en France*, Paris: La Découverte, pp. 28–40.

Inglehart, R. (1971) 'The silent revolution in Europe. Intergenerational change in post-industrial societies', *American Political Science Review*, 65(4): 991–1017.

Inglehart, R. (1977) *The Silent Revolution: Changing Values and Political Styles among Western Publics*, Princeton: Princeton University Press.

Isin, E. (1998) 'Governing Toronto without government: Liberalism and neoliberalism', *Studies in Political Economy*, 56: 169–192.

Itçaina, X., Roger, A. and Smith, A. (2016) *Varietals of Capitalism. A Political Economy of the Changing Wine Industry*. Ithaca, NY: Cornell University Press.

Ivalidi, G. and Massoleni, O. (2019) 'Economic populism and producerism. European right-wing parties in a transatlantic perspective', *Populism*, 2(1): 1–28.

Jacques, B. (2007) *Sociologie de l'accouchement*, Paris: Presses Universitaires de France.

Joana, J. and Smith, A. (2006) 'Changing French military procurement policy: The state, "industry" and "Europe" in the case of the A400M', *West European Politics*, 29(1): 70–89.

Jobert, B. and Muller, P. (1987) *L'Etat en action*, Paris: Presses Universitaires de France.

Jobert, B. and Théret, B. (1994) 'France: la consécration républicaine du néolibéralisme', in B. Jobert (ed.), *Le tournant néolibéral en Europe. Idées et recettes dans les pratiques gouvernementales*, Paris: L'Harmattan, pp. 21–86.

Jullien, B. and Lung, Y. (2011) *L'industrie automobile. La croisée des chemins*, Paris: La Documentation française.

Jullien, B. and Smith, A. (eds) (2014) *The EU's Government of Industries*, London: Routledge.

Juven, P-A. (2016) *Une santé qui compte? Les coûts et tarifs les controverses de l'hôpital public*, Paris: Presses Universitaires de France.

Juven, P-A., Pierru, F. and Vincent, F. (2019) *La casse du siècle: à propos des réformes de l'hôpital public*, Paris: Raisons d'Agir.

Kaplan, S. (2001) *La fin des corporations*, Paris: Fayard.

King, D. and Le Galès, P. (eds) (2017) *Reconfiguring European States in Crisis*, Oxford: Oxford University Press.

Kitzmann, M. (2016) *Le role et le recours aux grands-parents dans la prise en charge des enfants en bas âge: entre pratiques, norms et inégalités*, Report published by the *Direction de la recherche, des études, de l'évaluation et des statistiques* (DREES) of the *Ministère des solidarités et de la santé*.

Kolopp, S. (2018) '"La main de l'étranger?" Les voies de l'international dans la réforme financière en France: le cas du "souci international" de la direction du Trésor', *Politix*, 124: 161–181.

Kuisel, R. (1984) *Le capitalisme et l'État en France. Modernisation et dirigisme au 20ème siècle*, Paris: Gallimard.

Laferté, G. (2018) *L'embourgeoisement: une enquête chez les céréaliers*, Paris: Raisons d'Agir.

Lafore, R. (2013) 'Où en est-on du "département-providence"?', *Informations sociales*, 179: 12–27.

Lafore, R. (2019) *L'individu contre le collectif. Qu'arrive t-il à nos institutions?*, Rennes: Presses de l'EHESP.

Lagneau-Ymonet, P. and Riva, A. (2015) *Histoire de la bourse*, Paris: La Découverte.

Lagroye, J. (1985) 'La légitimation', in M. Grawitz and J. Leca (eds), *Traité de science politique*, vol. 1, Paris: Presses Universitaires de France, pp. 395–467.

Lahire, B. (2000) *Culture écrite et inégalités scolaires: sociologie de l'échec scolaire à l'école primaire*, Lyon: Presses Universitaires de Lyon.

Lahire, B. (ed.) (2019) *Enfances de classe. De l'inégalité parmi les enfants*, Paris: Seuil.

Lardeux, L. (2019) 'Engagement associatif: une nouvelle participation citoyenne?', in P. Bréchon, F. Gonthier and S. Astor (eds), *La France des valeurs: quarante ans d'évolutions*, Grenoble: Presses Universitaires de Grenoble, pp. 74–79.

Larner, W. (2000) 'Neo-liberalism: Policy, ideology, governmentality', *Studies in Political Economy*, 63: 5–25.

Lascoumes, P. (1994) *L'éco-pouvoir. Environnement et politiques*, Paris: La Découverte.

Lascoumes, P. and Le Galès, P. (2007) 'Introduction: Understanding public policy through its instruments', *Governance*, 20(1): 1–21.

Lascoumes, P., Bonnaud, L., Le Bourhis, J-P. and Martinais, E. (2014) *Le développement durable: une nouvelle affaire d'Etat*, Paris: Presses Universitaires de France.

Laufer, J. (2014) *L'égalité professionnelle entre les femmes et les hommes*, Paris: La Découverte.

Lazarus, J. (2012) *L'épreuve de l'argent. Banques, banquiers, clients*, Paris: Calmann-Lévy.

Lefebvre, R. (2016) 'Les primaires à droite. Processus d'adoption et transformations du jeu partisan', in R. Lefebvre and E. Treille (eds), *Les primaires ouvertes en France*, Rennes: Presses Universitaires de Rennes, pp. 65–104.

Lefebvre, R. (2017) '"Dépassement" ou effacement du Parti socialiste', *Mouvements*, 89: 11–21.

Lefebvre, R. and Sawicki, F. (2006) *La société des socialistes. Le PS aujourd'hui*, Paris: Editions du Croquant.

Lefebvre, R. and Treille, E. (2016) 'Introduction: Vers une primarisation de la vie politique française?', in R. Lefebvre and E. Treille (eds), *Les primaires ouvertes en France*, Rennes: Presses Universitaires de Rennes, pp. 11–36.

Le Galès, P. (1993) *Politiques urbaines et développement local: une comparaison franco-britannique*, Paris: L'Harmattan.

Le Galès, P. (2014) 'Recomposition de l'Etat: changements d'échelles, norms extérieures, nouvelles organisations', in P. Le Galès and N. Vezinat (eds), *L'Etat recomposé*, Paris: Presses Universitaires de France.

Lemoine, B. (2016) *L'ordre de la dette. Enquête sur les infortunés de l'Etat et la prospérité du marché*, Paris: La Découverte.

Levy, J. (1999) *Tocqueville's Revenge. State, Society and Economy in Contemporary France*, Cambridge, MA: Harvard University Press.

Libault, D. (2019) *Concertation grand âge et dépendance*, Report to the Minister of Solidarity and Health, March, https://solidarites-sante.gouv.fr/actualites/presse/communiques-de-presse/article/remise-du-rapport-libault-sur-la-concertation-grand-age-et-autonomie, consulted 10th June 2019.

Macé, E. (2015) *L'après-patriarcat*, Paris: Seuil.

Maclean, M., Harvey, C. and Press, J. (2006) *Business Elites and Corporate Governance in France and the UK*, Basingstoke: Palgrave.

Maillard, F. (2015) 'Postface: Le baccalauréat professionnel 30 ans après sa création: de la marché forcée à la banalisation?', *Formation emploi*, 131: 169–187.

Mangenot, M. and Rowell, J. (2010) 'What Europe constructs: towards a sociological constructivism', in J. Rowell and M. Mangenot (eds), *A Political Sociology of the European Union. Reassessing Constructivism*, Manchester: Manchester University Press, pp. 1–22.

March, J. and Olsen, J. (1989) *Rediscovering Institutions*, Oxford: Oxford University Press.

Marchal, H. (2014) *Un sociologue au volant: le rapport de l'individu à sa voiture en milieu urbain*, Paris: L'Harmattan.

Martin, C. (2010) 'Les politiques de la famille', in O. Borraz and V. Giraudon (eds), Politiques publique 2. Changer la société, Paris: Presses de Sciences Po, pp. 31–55.

Martin, C. (ed.) (2013) *La dépendance des personnes âgées. Quelles politiques en Europe?* Rennes: Presses Universitaires de Rennes.

Martin, C. (2017) 'Gouverner la parentalité; gouverner par les parents', in C. Martin (ed.), *Accompagner les parents dans leur travail éducatif et de soin*, Paris: La Documentation française.

Martin, J-L. (1999) *La politique de l'éducation physique sous la cinquième République: l'élan gaullien*, Paris: Presses Universitaires de France.

Martin, P. (2014) *La dépendance des personnes âgées, un défi pour l'Etat social*, Bordeaux: Presses Universitaires de Bordeaux.

Maruani, M. (ed.) (2005) *Femmes, genre et sociétés*, Paris: La Découverte.

Mathiot, P. (2018) *Un nouveau baccalauréat pour construire le lycée des possibles*, Report to the Minister for Education, January.

Mathiot, P. and Sawicki, F. (1999a) 'Recrutement et reconversion des élites gouvernementales socialistes. Une étude des membres des cabinets ministériels (1981–93) – Première partie: caractéristiques sociales et filières de recrutement', *Revue française de science politique*, 49(1): 1–27.

Mathiot, P. and Sawicki, F. (1999b) 'Recrutement et reconversion des élites gouvernementales socialistes. Une étude des membres des cabinets ministériels (1981–93) – Séconde partie: stratégies de reconversion', *Revue française de science politique*, 49(1): 231–264.

Maurice, M., Sellier, F. and Silvestre, J-J. (1982) *Politique d'éducation et organisation industrielle en France et en Allemagne*, Paris: Presses Universitaires de France.

Mayer, N. (1999) *Ces français qui votent FN*, Paris: Flammarion.

Mayer, N. (2004) 'Le temps des manifestations', *Revue européenne des sciences sociales*, 42(129): 219–224.

Mayer, N. and Tiberj, V. (2016) 'How to study political culture without naming it', in R. Elgie, E. Grossman and A. Mazur (eds), *The Oxford Handbook of French Politics*, Oxford: Oxford University Press, pp. 329–348.

Méda, D. (2010) *Le travail. Une valeur en voie de disparition?* 2nd ed., Paris: Flammarion.

Méda, D. (2011) *Travail: la revolution necessaire*, Paris: Editions de l'Aube.

Méda, D. and Vendramin P. (2013) *Réinventer le travail*, Paris: Presses Universitaires de France.

Mérand, F. (2015) 'Champ', in G. Devin (ed.), *10 concepts sociologiques en relations internationales*, Paris: CNRS éditions.

Mérand, F. and Barrette, P. (2013) 'Military power in Europe', in N. Kauppi and M-R. Madsen (eds), *Transnational Power Elites*, London: Routledge.

Ministère de la culture (2018) *Atlas régional de la culture*, Paris: Ministère de la culture.

Mischi, J. (2007) 'Pour une histoire sociale du déclin du Parti Communiste', in F. Haegel (ed.), *Partis politiques et système partisan en France*, Paris: Presses de Sciences Po, pp. 69–101.

Mons, N. (2007) *Les nouvelles politiques éducatives*, Paris: Presses Universitaires de France.

Muller, P. (1984) *Le technocrate et le paysan*, Paris: L'Harmattan (republished in 2015).

Muller, P. (1989) *Airbus, l'ambition européenne: logique d'Etat, logique de marché*, Paris: L'Harmattan.

Musselin, C. (2001) *La longue marche des universités françaises*, Paris: Presses Universitaires de France.

Musselin, C. (2017) *La grande course des universités*, Paris: Presses de Sciences Po.

Négrier, E. (2005) *La question métropolitaine. Les politiques à l'épreuve du changement d'échelle*, Grenoble: Presses Universitaires de Grenoble.

Négrier, E. and Teillet, P. (2014) 'Le tournant instrumental des politiques culturelles', *Pôle Sud*, 41: 83–100.

Neveu, E. (2015) *Sociologie des mouvements sociaux*, 6th ed., Paris: La Découverte.

Nezosi, G. (1999) *La fin de l'homme de fer: syndicalisme et crise de la sidérurgie*, Paris: L'Harmattan.

Norris, P. and Inglehart, R. (2019) *Cultural Backlash. Trump, Brexit and Authoritarian Populism*, Cambridge: Cambridge University Press.

Nys, J-F. (2011) 'Le renouvellement des besoins et des objectifs en matière de sport', in S. Monchaud and P. Dantin (eds), *Le modèle sportif français*, Paris: Lavoisier, pp. 215–231.

Offer, A. (2018) 'Patient and impatient capital: Time horizons as market boundaries', *Oxford Economic and Social History Working Papers*, no. 165, University of Oxford, Department of Economics.

Offerlé, M. (2009) *Sociologie des organisations patronales*, Paris: La Découverte.

Offerlé, M. (2013) *Les patrons des patrons. Histoire du MEDEF*, Paris: Odile Jacob.

Offerlé, M. (2017) 'Prologue' pp. 5–8, 'Introduction générale' pp. 9–27, 'Conclusion' pp. 569–608, in M. Offerlé (ed.), *Patrons en France*, Paris: La Découverte.

Offerlé, M. (2018) *Les partis politiques*, 9th ed., Paris: Presses Universitaires de France.

Ollitrault, S. (2008) *Militer pour la planète: sociologie des écologistes*, Rennes: Presses Universitaires de Rennes.

Olsen, M. (1965) *Logic of Collective Action*, Cambridge, MA: Harvard University Press.

Orange, S. (2010) 'Le choix du BTS. Entre construction et encadrement des aspirations des bacheliers d'origine populaire', *Actes de la recherché en sciences sociales*, 183: 32–47.

Orange, S. (2011) 'Le BTS, genèse d'un seuil scolaire', in M. Millet and G. Moreau (eds), *La société des diplômés*, Paris: La Dispute, pp. 161–176.

Pailhé, A. and Solaz, A. (eds) (2009) *Entre famille et travail, des arrangements de couple aux pratiques des employeurs*, Paris: La Découverte.

Palheta, U. (2012) *La domination scolaire: sociologie de l'enseignement professionnel et de son public*, Paris: Presses Universitaires de France.

Palier, B. (2000) '"Defrosting" the French welfare state', *West European Politics*, 23(2): 113–136.

Palier, B. (2005) *Gouverner la sécurité sociale. Les réformes du système français de protection sociale depuis 1945*, Paris: Presses Universitaires de France.

Palier, B. (2010), 'The Dualizations of the French Welfare System', in B. Palier (ed.) *A Long Goodbye to Bismarck? The Politics of Welfare Reforms in Continental Europe*, Amsterdam: Amsterdam University Press, pp. 73–100.

Palier, B. (2014) *La réforme des retraites*, 5th ed., Paris: Presses Universitaires de France.

Palier, B. (2017) *La réforme des systèmes de santé*, 8th ed., Paris: Presses Universitaires de France.

Palier, B. (2018) 'Stratégie de croissance et protection sociale', in C. Hay and A. Smith (eds), *Dictionnaire de l'économie politique*, Paris: Presses de Sciences Po, pp. 440–452.

Parsons, C. (2015) 'Before eclecticism: Competing alternatives in constructivist research', *International Theory*, 7(3): 501–538.

Patriat, C. (2017) 'Le ministère de la culture dans la spirale des réformes', in P. Poirrier (ed.), *Politique et politiques de la culture*, Paris: La Documentation française, pp. 25–37.

Paugam, S. (2013) *Les formes élémentaires de la pauvrété*, 3rd ed., Paris: PUF.

Paugam, S. (2019) 'Face au mépris social, la revanche des invisibles', in Analyse Opinion Critique (ed.), *'Gilets jaunes': Hypothèses sur un mouvement*, Paris: La Découverte, pp. 37–42.

Paxton, R. (2001) *Vichy France. Old Guard and New Order 1940–44*, 2nd ed., New York: Columbia University Press.

Penissat, E. and Rowell, J. (2015) 'The creation of a European socio-economic classification: Limits of expert-driven statistical integration', *Journal of European Integration*, 37(2): 281–297.

Peugny, C. (2013) *Le destin au berceau. Inégalités et reproduction sociale*, Paris: Seuil.

Philippon, T. (2007) *Le capitalisme d'héritiers. La crise française du travail*, Paris: Seuil.

Piketty, T. (2014) *Capital in the Twenty-First Century*, Paris: University of Harvard Press.

Pinçon, M. and Pinçon-Charlot, M. (2016) *Sociologie de la bourgeoisie*, Paris: La Découverte.

Pinson, G., and Morel Journel, C. (2017) 'Neoliberalization is not enough. French urban development corporations and the limits of neoliberalization theories', in G. Pinson and C. Morel Journel (eds), *Debating the Neo-liberal City*, London: Routledge.

Piotet, F. (2009) 'La CGT, une anarchie (plus ou moins) organisée?', *Politix*, 85: 9–30.

Poirrier, P. (2016) *Les politiques de la culture en France*, Paris: La Documentation française.

Poirrier, P. (ed.) (2017) *Politique et politiques de la culture*, Paris: La Documentation française.

Pollard, J. (2018) *L'Etat, le promoteur et le maire. La fabrication des politiques du logement*, Paris: Presses de Sciences Po.

Polo, J-F. (2003) 'La politique cinématographique de Jack Lang. De la réhabilitation des industries culturelles à la proclamation de l'exception culturelle', *Politix*, 61: 123–149.

Pouchadon, M-L. and Martin, P. (2018) 'Politiques de vieillesse, politiques d'autonomie: quelles dynamiques territoriales et dynamiques?', *Retraite et société*, 79: 83–103.

Pudal, B. (2009) *Un monde défait. Les communistes français de 1956 à nos jours*, Paris: Editions du Croquant.

Quijoux, M. (2018) *Adieu au patronat. Lutte et gestion ouvrières dans une usine reprise en cooperative*, Paris: Editions du Croquant.

Rémond, R. (1982) *Les droites en France*, Paris: Auber.

Rochefort, D. and Cobb, R. (1994), *The Politics of Problem Definition*, Lawrence, KS: University Press of Kansas.

Roger, A. (2010a) 'De la vigne à la rue. La difficile mobilisation des viticulteurs dans le département de l'Aude', *Sociologie du travail*, 52(1): 21–39.

Roger, A. (2010b) 'Scholarly constructs and the legitimization of European policies. The circulation of knowledge on wine and the vine', *Revue française de science politique*, 60(2): 1–22.

Roy, O. (2004) *Globalized Islam: The Search for a New Ummah*, New York: Columbia University Press.

Saez, G. (2012) 'Le tournant métropolitain des politiques culturelles', in G. Saez and J-P. Saez (eds), *Les nouveaux enjeux des politiques culturelles*, Paris: La Découverte, pp. 23–71.

Safi, M. (2013) *Les inégalités ethno-raciales*, Paris: La Découverte.

Sauger, N. (2009) 'The French party system: Fifty years of change', in A. Appelton, S. Brouard and A. Mazur (eds), *The French Fifth Republic at Fifty*, Basingstoke: Palgrave, pp. 79–98.

Sawicki, F. (1999) *Les réseaux du Parti Socialiste. Sociologie d'un milieu partisan*, Paris: Belin.

Sawicki, F. (2012a) 'Pour une sociologie des problématisations politiques de l'école', *Politix*, 98: 7–33.

Sawicki, F. (2012b) 'La résistible politisation du football. Le cas de l'affaire du grand stade de Lille-Métropôle', *Sciences sociales et sport*, 5(1): 193–241.

Sawicki, F. (2016) 'Toujours plus grand, toujours plus cher! Les collectivités territoriales et "leurs" stade de football', *Métropolitiques*, online open edition journal, www.metropolitiques.eu/toujours-plus-grand-toujours-plus.html.

Sawicki, F. (2017) 'L'épreuve du pouvoir est-elle vouée à être fatale au Parti socialiste? Retour sur le quinquennat de François Hollande', *Pouvoirs*, 163: 27–41.

Sawicki, F. and Siméant, J. (2009) 'Décoloisonner la sociologie de l'engagement militant. Note critique sur quelques tendances récentes des travaux français', *Sociologie du travail*, 51(1): 97–125.

Schmidt, V. (2003) 'French capitalism transformed, yet still a third variety of capitalism', *Economy and Society*, 32(4): 526–554.

Schmidt, V. and Thatcher, M. (eds) (2013) *Resilient Liberalism in Europe's Political Economy*, Oxford: Oxford University Press.

Scott, J-C. (1976) *The Moral Economy of the Peasant: Rebellion and Subsistence in Southeast Asia*, Princeton, NJ: Yale University Press.

Scott, J. W. (2007) *The Politics of the Veil*, Princeton, NJ: Princeton University Press.

Segalen, M. (2005) *Sociologie de la famille*, Paris: Armand Colin.

Segas, S. (2018) 'Le stade ultime du néolibéralisme? De l'économie politique des stades à la sociologie critique des équipements de spectacle sportif', *Métropoles*, anniversary issue: 1–20.

Seiler, D. (2011) *Partis et familles politiques en Europe*, Bruxelles: Editions de l'Université de Bruxelles.

Singly, F. de (2000) *Libres ensemble. L'individualisme dans la vie commune*, Paris: Nathan.

Singly, F. de (2017) *Sociologie de la famille contemporaine*, 6th ed., Paris: Armand Colin.

Smith, A. (2002) *La passion du sport. Le football, le rugby et les appartenances en Europe*, Rennes: Presses Universitaires de Rennes.

Smith, A. (2016) *The Politics of Economic Activity*, Oxford: Oxford University Press.

Smith, A. (2019) 'Travail politique et changement institutionnel: une grille d'analyse', *Sociologie du Travail*, 61(1).

Smith, A., De Maillard, J. and Costa, O. (2007) *Vin et politique: Bordeaux, la France, la mondialisation*, Paris: Presses de Sciences Po.

Sorokin, P. (1927) *Social Mobility*, New York: Harper.

Stanziani, A. (2005) *Histoire de la qualité alimentaire XIX-XXe siècle*, Paris: Seuil.

Steinmo, S., Thelen, K. and Longstreth F. (eds) (1992) *Structuring Politics: Historical Institutionalism in Comparative Analysis*, Cambridge: Cambridge University Press.

Surel, Y. (1997) *L'Etat et le livre: les politiques publiques du livre en France*, Paris: L'Harmattan.

Terra Nova (2016) 'Le capital patient: un horizon pour la France et pour l'Europe', note published 12th May 2016.

Thelen, K. (2014) *Varieties of Liberalization and the New Politics of Social Solidarity*, Cambridge: Cambridge University Press.

Théry, I. (1998) *Couple, filiation et parenté aujourd'hui*, Paris: La Documentation française.

Thoenig, J-C. (1987) *L'ère des technocrates*, Paris: L'Harmattan.

Thompson, E. P. (1968) *The Making of the English Working Class*, London: Penguin Books.

Tiberj, V. (2017) *Les citoyens qui viennent*, Paris: Presses Universitaires de France.

Tilly, C. (1976) *From Mobilization to Revolution*, Reading: Addison-Wesley.

Topalov, C. (1987) *Le logement en France. Histoire d'une marchandise impossible*, Paris: Presses de la Fondation Nationale des Sciences Politiques.

Torrès, O. (2005) *La guerre des vins: l'affaire Mondavi*, Paris: Dunod.

Trompette, P. (2008) *Le marché des défunts*, Paris: Presses de Sciences Po.

Urfalino, P. (1990) *Quatre voix pour un opéra*, Paris: Metaillé.

Urfalino, P. (1996) *L'invention de la politique culturelle*, Paris: La Documentation française.

Van de Velde, C. (2008) *Devenir adulte: sociologie compare de la jeunesse en Europe*, Paris: Presses Universitaires de France.

Van Zanten, A. (2006) 'La construction des politiques d'éducation. De la centralisation à la délégation au local', in P. Culpepper, P. Hall and B. Palier (eds), *La France en mutation 1980–2005*, Paris: Presses de Sciences Po, pp. 229–262.

Van Zanten, A. (2009) *Choisir son école. Stratégies parentales et médiations locales*, Paris: Presses Universitaires de France.

Verdier, E. (2016) 'L'enseignement professionnel à la française à la croisée des chemins', in J-P. Kaplinsky (ed.), *Le lycée professionnel: relégué ou avant garde?*, Lyon: Presses de l'ENS de Lyon, pp. 13–26.

Vergnies, J-F. (2015) 'Du Bac pro … aux Bac pros', *Formation emploi*, 131: 1–2.

Vincent, G. (1980) *L'école primaire française. Etude sociologique*, Lyon: Presses Universitaires de Lyon.

Viriot-Durandal, J-P. (2003) *Le pouvoir gris. Sociologie des groupes de pression de retraités*, Paris: Presses Universitaires de France.

Wacquant, L. (2012) 'Three steps to a historical anthropology of actually existing neoliberalism', *Social Anthropology*, 1: 66–79.

Weber, E. (1976) *Peasants into Frenchmen: The Modernization of Rural France 1870–2014*, Stanford, CA: Stanford University Press.

Wylie, L. (1957) *A Village in the Vaucluse*, Cambridge, MA: Harvard University Press.

Yon, K. (2009) 'Quand le syndicalisme s'éprouve hors du lieu de travail. La production du sens confédéral à Force ouvrière', *Politix*, 85: 57–79.

Zmerli, S. (2019) 'Toutes les institutions ne sont pas discréditées!', in P. Bréchon, F. Gonthier and S. Astor (eds), *La France des valeurs: quarante ans d'évolutions*, Grenoble: Presses Universitaires de Grenoble, pp. 273–279.

Zysman, J. (1983) *Governments, Markets and Growth. Financial Systems and the Politics of Industrial Change*, Ithaca, NY: Cornell University Press.

Index

EU authorised representative for GPSR:
Easy Access System Europe, Mustamäe tee 50,
10621 Tallinn, Estonia
gpsr.requests@easproject.com